AQA German
Teacher's Book

GCSE

Roy Dexter
Jean-Claude Gilles
David Riddell
Sue Smart
Marcus Waltl

Nelson Thornes

Text © Roy Dexter, Jean-Claude Gilles, David Riddell, Sue Smart and Marcus Waltl 2009
Original illustrations © Nelson Thornes Ltd 2009

The right of Roy Dexter, Jean-Claude Gilles, David Riddell, Sue Smart and Marcus Waltl to be identified as authors of this work has been asserted by them in accordance with the Copyright, Designs and Patents Act 1988.

All rights reserved. No part of this publication may be reproduced or transmitted in any form or by any means, electronic or mechanical, including photocopy, recording or any information storage and retrieval system, without permission in writing from the publisher or under licence from the Copyright Licensing Agency Limited, of Saffron House, 6–10 Kirby Street, London, EC1N 8TS.

Any person who commits any unauthorised act in relation to this publication may be liable to criminal prosecution and civil claims for damages.

Published in 2009 by:
Nelson Thornes Ltd
Delta Place
27 Bath Road
CHELTENHAM
GL53 7TH
United Kingdom

11 12 13 / 10 9 8 7 6 5 4 3 2

A catalogue record for this book is available from the British Library

ISBN 978 1 4085 0429 1

Cover photograph by Alamy/Hayden Richard Verry

Page make-up by GreenGate Publishing, Tonbridge, Kent

Printed by Multivista Global Ltd

Photographs courtesy of:
Fotolia.com
iStockphoto.com, p93, p129
Nelson Thornes, p15

Contents

Introduction	4
Course components	4
AQA GCSE German Student Book and kerboodle!	4
Controlled Assessment	4
Teacher's Book	4
Practice for Assessment: Listening and reading	4
Schemes of Work	6
Teaching Notes	10
Key Stage 3 Revision: Numbers 1 – 20, ages and days of the week; Weather and seasons; Telling the time; Months and birthdays; Classroom equipment and colours; Numbers and dates; Parts of the body and useful words	10
Context 1 – Lifestyle	35
Overview and kerboodle! resources	17
Key Stage 3 Revision: Food and drink; Ailments and solutions; Family members and pets	17
Topic 1 — Health	18
Topic 2 — Relationships and choices	27
Context 2 – Leisure	40
Overview and kerboodle! resources	42
Key Stage 3 Revision: Revision: Sport and leisure; Clothes; Transport; Places in town	42
Topic 1 — Free time and the media	43
Topic 2 — Holidays	54
Context 3 – Home and Environment	65
Overview and kerboodle! resources	67
Key Stage 3 Revision: Rooms in the house; Items of furniture; House types and locations; Daily routine; Helping at home	67
Topic 1 — Home and local area	69
Topic 2 — Environment	80
Context 4 – Work and Education	89
Overview and kerboodle! resources	91
Key Stage 3 Revision: School subjects; Places in school; Jobs and workplaces	91
Topic 1 — School / college and future plans	92
Topic 2 — Current and future jobs	101
Controlled Assessment	113
Controlled Assessment FAQs	116

Introduction

Welcome to the new AQA GCSE course material for German. The Nelson Thornes approach that you have chosen will allow your students to maximize their potential, leading to improved exam performance.

Written by a team of AQA Examiners, experienced teachers and writers of Key Stage 4 materials, this is the only GCSE German course to have been officially endorsed by AQA. The content is tailored precisely to the learning objectives of the specification so that it directly meets the needs of learners preparing for the AQA German GCSE assessment.

The course provides an accessible, engaging and integrated learning package through its unique blend of print-based and online *kerboodle!* resources.

Course components:

- A fully blended print and electronic resource provides:
- A Student Book for classroom-based teaching and homework.
- A corresponding Teacher's Book.
- Extensive online electronic support through *kerboodle!* including:
  - interactive reading, listening, grammar and video-based activities (with feedback)
  - differentiated support and extension activities and worksheets for all four skills areas
  - assessment preparation and practice
  - audio and video resources
- Audio CDs.

AQA GCSE German Student Book and *kerboodle!*

The Student Book is arranged in a sequence approved by AQA which matches precisely the structure of the GCSE specification.

- The Student Book begins with a section dedicated to Key Stage 3 revision to get students up to speed before beginning the GCSE specification.
- The content is then split into four sections, one for each Context of the specification.
- Each Context is split into two Topics – each beginning with further Key Stage 3 revision material.
- The Topics are divided into sub-topics which fit the Purposes of the specification.

At the beginning of each Context you will find the sub-topics, grammar and communication strategies listed, so you can see precisely how the content you are teaching matches the GCSE specifications, and be sure you are covering everything your students need to know for their exams.

The features in the Student Book include:

Lernziele – listed at the start of each teaching spread, reflecting the requirements of the new GCSE.

Reading icon – students can listen to the reading texts in the book on *kerboodle!* or on the CD, so they can hear the language spoken by native speakers as they read it. To complement the reading activities in the Student Book, interactive reading activities are also available on *kerboodle!*, along with Extension Reading worksheets (and answers) to stretch abler candidates.

Listening icon – audio material for listening (and audio for reading activities) is online and also on CD. To complement the listening activities in the Student Book, interactive listening activities are available on *kerboodle!* along with Extension Listening worksheets (and answers) to stretch abler candidates.

Video icon – videos can be found online to support the Student Book video-based activities; further interactive activities exploiting the video are also available on *kerboodle!*

Speaking icon – speaking activities in the Student Book are supported and developed by worksheets on *kerboodle!*

Further practice in Speaking skills is available through the Nelson Thornes Audio Role Play and Audio Record Tools, also available on *kerboodle!*

- Working with the audio role plays students can listen to a conversation between two native speakers, and they then have the opportunity to replace one speaker so they can record their own responses and play them back.
- The Audio Record Tool offers the opportunity for students to record free conversation, by themselves or in groups.

Writing icon – writing activities in the Student Book are supported and developed by worksheets on *kerboodle!*

Language structure boxes – show students how to construct key sentences designed to help carry out the Speaking and Writing tasks.

Strategie – outlines different strategies students can employ to help effective communication. The strategy box includes the icon of the skill it supports: Listening, Reading; Speaking or Writing.

Strategy icon – when this appears next to an activity, students should use the strategy box on that page to help them complete the task.

Tipp – provides handy hints which students can use to help with language learning.

Grammatik – provides a summary of the main grammar point practised on the spread. Further grammar points are also referenced here, and students should go to the pages listed to find activities to practise these.

G Grammar icon – identifies activities designed to help students practise the grammar point are identified by the Grammatik icon **G**. You will also find interactive grammar practice on *kerboodle!*

V Vocabulary – this indicates a vocabulary learning activity. The essential vocabulary used within each Topic is listed on Vocabulary pages. Here students can learn key words for each Topic. They can also go to *kerboodle!* to hear how the words should sound. Some words are in light grey. This is to indicate that students do not need to learn them for Listening and Reading exams, but they may find them useful for Speaking and Writing Controlled Assessments.

Audio files of the German vowel sounds, patterns of letters and the German alphabet are also available on *kerboodle!* to aid pronunciation.

AQA Examiner's tip – these provide hints from AQA examiners to help students with their study and prepare for their exams.

Teste dich! – a summary quiz at the end of each Context tests key language and grammar learnt in that Context. This is also available as a multiple choice quiz, with feedback, on *Kerboodle!*

Wusstest du schon? – an anecdotal insight into facts/figures relating to the Context.

Controlled Assessment

Our course books provide sample Controlled Assessment tasks in both Speaking and Writing for each of the four Contexts in the new specification: Lifestyle; Leisure; Home & Environment; Work & Education. Also provided are cross-Context Controlled Assessment task types that cover the entire topic range of the AQA GCSE.

Each of these tasks is accompanied by detailed guidance notes in the form of Examiner's Tips to take students through the process of developing a suitable response, outlining what points they could address in their answers, and key points to take into consideration.

Please note that the Controlled Assessment tasks in the student book are designed as a teaching resource and not as an assessment tool. They include levels of support and guidance which are not permissible in tasks used for assessment purposes.

These tasks cannot, therefore, be submitted to AQA. For any tasks which you adapt from the tasks in the student book or which you devise for your students, the level of guidance and support must comply with the guidelines in the specification and in AQA's Controlled Assessment Handbook.

Students can go to *kerboodle!* to review sample answers for each of the tasks. These are provided as 'On Your Marks' activities where students can analyse the sample answers to see what they think is good about each response, or how they think it could be improved. Students can compare their analysis with the Examiner's Observations.

Teacher's Book

The Teacher's Book follows the same order of presentation as the Student Book, with four main sections – one for each Context of the specification. The Teacher's Book provides guidance notes on how to work with each of the activities in the Student Book and presents these in the same order as they appear in the Student Book, except for Controlled Assessment which is a separate section at the back of this book (please see notes below).

In addition, the Teacher's Book provides:

- Starter and Plenary activity ideas for each teaching spread of the Student Book.
- The transcripts for all listening and video activities from the Student Book.
- Answers for all activities on the Student Book pages.
- Schemes of work (also available on Kerboodle).
- Cross-reference tables to show at a glance the electronic materials available on *Kerboodle!* for each spread of the student book.

The Teacher's Book contains a section dedicated to Controlled Assessment for the new GCSE specification.

This provides a brief overview of the purpose of Controlled Assessment, with guidance on how to work with the Controlled Assessment tasks provided in this course in the classroom for practice opportunity. The Topic and Context coverage we have incorporated to these tasks is also outlined here.

Detailed notes on Task Setting, Task Taking and Task Marking are then presented for each of Speaking and Writing Controlled Assessment. For Speaking Controlled Assessment, Task Marking is related back to the GCSE Assessment Criteria to provide further guidance on implementing this to your students' submitted work.

The final section lists Frequently Asked Questions and their answers, which are likely to arise from students encountering Controlled Assessment for the first time.

Practice for Assessment: Listening and reading

We have provided a set of Practice Assessment question worksheets in *kerboodle!* These are written in the style of the AQA exam to provide practice of the type of questions candidates will encounter in the Listening and Reading papers.

For each of the four Contexts of the specification, there are both Foundation and Higher Practice Assessment questions for Listening and for Reading skills.

All audio and transcripts for the Listening Practice Assessment questions are located on *kerboodle!*

All audio files for the reading texts and listening activities that feature in the Student Book are available free of charge on CD upon purchase of a *kerboodle!* user license.

AQA GCSE German — Schemes of Work

Key Stage 3 Revision (Student Book pages 9–14)

Numbers 1 to 20; Ages; Days of the week; Weather and seasons; Telling the time; Months and birthdays; Classroom equipment; Colours; Numbers and dates; Parts of the body; Useful words.

Context 1 – Lifestyle

Key Stage 3 Revision (Student Book pages 16–17)

Food and drink; Ailments and solutions; Family members and pets.

Specification Topic: Health

Specification Purpose: Healthy and unhealthy lifestyles and their consequences

Teaching spread	Student Book pages	Main grammar point	Subsidiary grammar point	Communication strategy
1.1 Gesund essen, gesund leben!	18–19	Using the present tense	Using the indefinite article with the accusative	Keeping conversations going
1.2 Ich bin in Form!	20–21	Using inversion	Using adverbs of frequency	Recognising and using near-cognates
1.3 Rauchen ist doch ungesund!	22–23	Using the modal verbs *wollen, können, sollen*	Forming negative phrases using *nicht* and *kein*	Using context to predict meanings
1.4 Alkohol und Drogen brauchen wir nicht! *(includes video)*	24–25	Using the modal verbs *dürfen, müssen, mögen*	Using *man*	Understanding word order better (*weil* with modal verbs)

Further support: Reading and listening (Student Book pages 26–27), Grammar (Student Book pages 28–29), Vocabulary (Student Book pages 30–31)

Specification Topic: Relationships and choices

Specification Purpose: Relationship with family and friends; Future plans regarding: marriage/partnership; Social issues and equality

Teaching spread	Student Book pages	Main grammar point	Subsidiary grammar point	Communication strategy
1.5 Familie und Freunde – zu Hause	32–33	Using the present tense of *haben* and *sein*	Using *ihr*	Identifying common patterns between German and English
1.6 Familie und Freunde – Beziehungen	34–35	Using possessive adjectives	Using adjectives after nouns with quantifiers / intensifiers	Using your knowledge of grammatical categories to work out meanings
1.7 Zukunftspläne – Heiraten, ja oder nein?	36–37	Using the present tense to talk about the future	Using adverbial phrases of time	Asking for help when unsure
1.8 Gleichheit für Männer und Frauen?	38–39	Understanding nouns and gender	Using the word 'it'	Matching German and English phrases
1.9 Ethnische Probleme	40–41	Using coordinating conjunctions	Using adverbs of place	Speaking and writing creatively
1.10 Armut	42–43	Using subordinating conjunctions	Using *um … zu …*	Identifying compound nouns

Further support: Reading and listening (Student Book pages 44–45), Grammar (Student Book pages 46–47), Vocabulary (Student Book pages 48–49)

Controlled Assessment – Speaking (Student Book pages 50–51)	Meine Familie: heute und in der Zukunft
Controlled Assessment – Writing (Student Book pages 52–53)	Ich will gesund leben

# Schemes of Work

Context 2 – Leisure

Key Stage 3 Revision (Student Book pages 55–56)
Sports and leisure; Clothes; Transport; Places in town.

Specification Topic: Free time and the media
Specification Purpose: Free time activities; Shopping, money, fashion and trends; Advantages and disadvantages of new technology

Teaching spread	Student Book pages	Main grammar point	Subsidiary grammar point	Communication strategy
2.1 Was hast du gestern gemacht?	58–59	Using the perfect tense with *haben*	Using separable verbs with the perfect tense	Reusing questions to give answers
2.2 Ich bin in die Stadt gegangen	60–61	Using the perfect tense with *sein*	Using the perfect tense with irregular past participles	Understanding question words in German
2.3 Wir bekommen nicht genug Taschengeld!	62–63	Using the perfect tense with *haben* and *sein*	Recognising the imperfect tenses of *haben* and *sein*	Checking auxiliary verbs
2.4 Wir waren im Einkaufszentrum	64–65	Using the imperfect tense	Revising modal verbs (present tense)	Paraphrasing
2.5 Ich lebe im Internet	66–67	Using different tenses (past and present)	Distinguishing between *wann*, *wenn* and *als*	Using notes when making a presentation

Further support: Reading and listening (Student Book pages 68–69), Grammar (Student Book pages 70–71), Vocabulary (Student Book pages 72–73)

Specification Topic: Holidays
Specification Purpose: Plans, preferences, experiences; What to see and getting around

Teaching spread	Student Book pages	Main grammar point	Subsidiary grammar point	Communication strategy
2.6 Ich möchte mal nach …	74–75	Using correct word order (time – manner – place)	Using the imperfect subjunctive of *mögen*	Recognising information presented in different ways
2.7 Urlaubspläne	76–77	Using the future tense with *werden*	Using *um … zu…, ohne … zu …* and *anstatt … zu …*	Applying grammar rules in new situations
2.8 Berlin ist cool!	78–79	Using different tenses (past, present and future)	Using adjectives after *etwas, nichts, viel, wenig* and *alles*	Tackling longer reading texts
2.9 Auf Achse (includes video)	80–81	Asking questions using interrogatives	Revising using the nominative and accusative cases	Making vocab lists

Further support: Reading and listening (Student Book pages 82–83), Grammar (Student Book pages 84–85), Vocabulary (Student Book pages 86–87)

Controlled Assessment – Speaking (Student Book pages 88–89)   Einkaufen ist toll!

Controlled Assessment – Writing (Student Book pages 90–91)   Meine Ferien

Context 3 – Home and Environment

Key Stage 3 Revision (Student Book pages 94–95; 96–97)
Rooms in the house; Items of furniture; House types and locations; Daily routine; Helping at home.

Specification Topic: Home and local area

Specification Purpose: Special occasions celebrated in the home; Home, town, neighbourhood and region, where it is and what it is like

Teaching spread	Student Book pages	Main grammar point	Subsidiary grammar point	Communication strategy
3.1 Feier mit uns!	98–99	Using prepositions taking the accusative case	Using reflexive verbs	Completing gap-fill exercises
3.2 Bei mir, bei dir	100–101	Using prepositions taking the dative case	Making comparisons (comparative adjectives and *nicht so … wie …*)	Using knowledge of social and cultural differences to work out meaning
3.3 Meine Gegend, deine Gegend	102–103	Using *in* with the dative or accusative	Using superlative adjectives	Using grammar to work out meaning
3.4 Kommen Sie nach Baden-Württemberg!	104–105	Using adjective endings after the definite article	Using adjective endings after the indefinite article	Using knowledge from other topic areas

Further support: Reading and listening (Student Book pages 106–107), Grammar (Student Book pages 108–109), Vocabulary (Student Book pages 110–111)

Specification Topic: Environment

Specification Purpose: Current problems facing the planet; Being environmentally friendly within the home and local area

Teaching spread	Student Book pages	Main grammar point	Subsidiary grammar point	Communication strategy
3.5 Umweltfreundlich oder umweltfeindlich?	112–113	Using qualifiers	Using prepositions taking the genitive case	Making what you say and write more expressive
3.6 Unsere Welt, unsere Umwelt	114–115	Using the imperative	Using the correct articles and cases (revision)	Giving a presentation
3.7 Global denken, lokal handeln *(includes video)*	116–117	Using verbs with *zu*	Using the future tense with *werden* (revision)	Dealing with new vocabulary

Further support: Reading and listening (Student Book pages 118–119), Grammar (Student Book pages 120–121), Vocabulary (Student Book pages 122–123)

Controlled Assessment – Writing (Student Book pages 124–125) Mein Wohnort

Controlled Assessment – Speaking (Student Book pages 126–127) Umweltsumfrage

Schemes of Work

Context 4 – Work and Education

Key Stage 3 Revision (Student Book pages 130–131)
School subjects; Places in school; Jobs and workplaces.

Specification Topic: School / college and future plans
Specification Purpose: What school / college is like; Pressures and problems

Teaching spread	Student Book pages	Main grammar point	Subsidiary grammar point	Communication strategy
4.1 Wie ist deine Schule?	132–133	Saying where you do things	Identifying and using subordinate clauses	Giving impressive answers to questions
4.2 Das Schulwesen anderswo	134–135	Using the imperfect tense of modals	Using different ways to denote possession	Revising vocabulary
4.3 Schulstress	136–137	Saying what you could or ought to do	Identifying (and using) the pluperfect tense	Matching people to information
4.4 Eine bessere Schule	138–139	Saying what you would do	Identifying (and using) the imperfect subjunctive of *haben*, *sein* and *geben*	Knowing which tense to use

Further support: Reading and listening (Student Book pages 140–141), Grammar (Student Book pages 142–143), Vocabulary (Student Book pages 144–145)

Specification Topic: Current and future jobs
Specification Purpose: Looking for and getting a job; Advantages and disadvantages of different jobs

Teaching spread	Student Book pages	Main grammar point	Subsidiary grammar point	Communication strategy
4.5 Nebenjobs und Arbeitspraktikum	146–147	Remembering when not to use the indefinite article	Identifying other instances when the indefinite article is not used	Planning a piece of writing
4.6 Ich suche einen Job *(includes video)*	148–149	Revising how to say 'when' (revision)	Using *seit* with the present tense	Using previously learned material
4.7 Am Arbeitsplatz	150–151	Using dative pronouns	Choosing the correct form of address (revision)	Taking notes effectively when listening
4.8 Was mache ich nach meinem Schulabschluss?	152–153	Talking about the future (revision)	Varying how you talk about future plans	Varying your language
4.9 Jobs und Berufe	154–155	Revising interrogatives	Identifying and using the conditional mood (revision)	Finding out information

Further support: Reading and listening (Student Book pages 156–157), Grammar (Student Book pages 158–159), Vocabulary (Student Book pages 160–161)

Controlled Assessment – Speaking (Student Book pages 162–163)	Geld verdienen
Controlled Assessment – Writing (Student Book pages 164–165)	Das britische Schulwesen
Cross-Context Controlled Assessment – Speaking (Student Book page 170)	Mein Geburtstag
Cross-Context Controlled Assessment – Writing (Student Book page 171)	Kommen Sie nach … !

Revision

Numbers 1–20, ages and days of the week

kerboodle! • Audio files for core reading texts

1a 📖 🎧 Read the texts above and answer the following questions in English.

A reading activity to revise numbers, giving ages and simple family vocabulary. Students can complete the activity for homework or give responses orally in class. The final question requires a small amount of lateral thinking!

The reading text is also available online as an audio file.

Answers:

a 9	b Monika	c 17	d Gabi
e 16	f Jan	g 19	

1b 💬 Work in pairs. One person makes a statement based on the texts above and the other identifies who it is. Then swap roles.

A speaking activity to practise giving ages. Students refer to the texts used in activity 1a to make up their answers. More able students can make general statements relating to family members, while less confident learners can stick to selecting different people and saying how old they are. This activity also revises using present tense forms of *sein*.

The reading text is also available online as an audio file.

Possible answers:

Ich bin neunzehn Jahre alt.
Du bist Brigitte. Ich habe keine Brüder.
Du bist Jan …

2a 📖 🎧 Read Lena's plans for what she will do when she is on holiday. Then put the sentences into the order she will do them (her holiday starts on a Monday).

A reading activity to practise days of the week. Students put the sentences into the correct order. They do not need to understand all of the information at this stage and can use the second *Vokabeln* box to help them.

The reading text is also available online as an audio file.

Answers:

e, c, a, g, f, d, b

2b 📖 🎧 Now write down in English what Lena is going to do each day. If you are unsure of some of the activities, look them up in the glossary

A reading activity to test comprehension of the sentences in activity 2a and revise activity vocabulary. Students can look up answers and write them down for homework or in class.

Another way of using the text may be to elicit answers orally regarding different activities and days e.g. *Was macht Lena am Montag? Wann geht Lena kegeln?* etc.

Answers:

Monday – swimming
Tuesday – football
Wednesday – buying souvenirs
Thursday – sightseeing tour of the town
Friday – bowling
Saturday – boat trip
Sunday – tennis

2c ✏️ 💬 Using Lena's sentences as a model, write down what you do each day. Then work with a partner. One person asks the other what he or she does on a particular day. Then swap roles.

A speaking activity to revise days of the week and activities. Refer students to the *Grammatik* box to ensure they use the correct form for saying what they are doing on a particular day, also pointing out the use of inversion after *Am Montag* etc. Students may also wish to say what they do regularly on specific days. If so, make sure they understand the difference between *Am Montag* and *montags* etc.

Possible answers:

Was machst du am Sonntag?
Am Sonntag gehe ich reiten. Was machst du am Donnerstag?
Am Donnerstag spiele ich Tennis.

> **Grammatik**
> This panel explains days of the week: how to say 'on Monday' and 'on Mondays' etc. in German. Make sure students understand the distinction between the two forms and remind them that unless the word appears at the start of a sentence, they do not use a capital letter for *montags*, *samstags* etc. With very able students, you may wish to explain that in the case of *Am Montag*, *Montag* is a noun, which explains why it is capitalised, while *montags*, as an adverb, is not.

Revision

Weather and seasons

kerboodle! • Audio files for core reading texts

1a 📖 🎧 Read the weather forecast below and compare it to the map. Correct the mistakes in the forecast.

A reading activity to revise understanding of weather vocabulary. With less able students, you may wish to introduce this task by checking they understand what each of the symbols on the map means, referring to the *Vokabeln* box below it. Students can write down their corrected weather report as homework. Alternatively (or in addition), more confident students may wish to read out the corrected report line by line.

The map also offers an opportunity for discussion of different locations in Germany and what students may know about them (check students know the English versions of *München*, *Köln* and *Nürnberg*).

The reading text is also available online as an audio file.

Answers:

Heute **regnet** es in Berlin meistens (OR Heute schneit es in **Stuttgart und Frankfurt am Main** meistens). Im Norden in Hamburg **friert** es mit Temperaturen bei 0 Grad Celsius. In Köln im Westen von Deutschland ist es sehr **windig** und in Dresden an der Elbe ist es ziemlich **neblig**. Und in Nürnberg ist es den ganzen Tag **kalt**.

1b Complete the following sentences, checking against the map to get the correct weather reading.

A writing activity practising weather vocabulary and using inversion. Refer students to the *Vokabeln* and *Grammatik* boxes before they get started.

As a follow-on activity, students can work in pairs to ask and answer questions about the weather in their area e.g. *Wie ist das Wetter in Manchester? In Manchester ist es sonnig* etc. Students could also write weather reports, combining revision of weather with revising days of the week e.g. *Am Montag regnet es. Am Dienstag ist es ...* etc.

Answers:

a In München ist es wolkig.
b In Stuttgart schneit es.
c In Hannover donnert und blitzt es.
d In Frankfurt am Main schneit es.
e In Bremen ist es sonnig.

> This panel explains inversion: that the verb in a German sentence is the second idea (though not necessarily the second word), and must be moved to that slot if something other than the subject comes first. They will need to do this in activity 1b – you could complete the first sentence together to help them. The panel also refers students to page 21 for further practice of inversion.
>
> *Grammatik*

2a Which season is it? Match up the sentences with the pictures.

A reading activity. Students match the pictures of the four seasons to the correct German phrase. Then practise pronouncing the four words for seasons – demonstrating the change involved with an umlaut on 'u', and the fact that the first letters of *Winter* and *Sommer* are said differently from the English equivalents.

The reading text is also available online as an audio file.

Answers:

a 3   b 1   c 4   d 2

2b What is the weather like during the different seasons? One person asks questions and the other answers. Then swap roles. Try to add some qualifiers (*sehr, ziemlich* etc.) if you can.

Pairwork, asking and answering questions about the weather in each season. Encourage students to extend their answers by adding qualifiers – you could provide suggestions for these if necessary.

Possible answers:

Wie ist das Wetter im Herbst?
Im Herbst ist es meistens kalt. Wie ist das Wetter im Frühling?
Im Frühling ist es ziemlich warm, aber oft regnet es.

Page 11

Revision

Telling the time, months and birthdays

kerboodle! • Audio files for core reading texts

1a Put the sentences below into the correct order, then note down each time in figures.

A reading activity to practise understanding the German 12-hour clock. You may wish to reinforce this with less confident students by using a clock to display and practise some times in German, and in particular to remind them that *halb* means 'half to' rather than 'half past'.

The reading text is also available online as an audio file.

Answers:

a, e, d, c, b
a 7:30 (am)
b 6:00–7:00 (pm)
c 2:15 (pm)
d 1:00 (pm)
e 10:30–10:50 (am)

1b Write down the correct times in words for each of these clocks using the German 12-hour clock.

A writing activity to practise active production of German 12-hour clock times. With less confident students, you could go through these eliciting verbal answers with the whole class, before they write them, and perhaps do some additional practice of German numbers 1–60 before looking at the *Grammatik* panel relating to the 24-hour clock.

Answers:

a Es ist zehn nach zwei.
b Es ist Viertel nach drei.
c Es ist halb fünf.
d Es ist Viertel vor sechs.
e Es ist fünf vor elf.

> This panel explains how to say the time using the 24-hour clock in German. Point out that it isn't necessary to write the numbers down as words (i.e. they needn't worry about spelling them), just to be able to say them. Practise some example times with the class. Then students could work in pairs, writing a hidden list of 24-hour times in figures which they must say in German to their partner, who listens and writes the correct time down, again in figures, for checking.
>
> *Grammatik*

2a 📖 🎧 Match up the dates on the calendars with the birthdays.

A reading activity to practise understanding dates of birthdays. Refer students to the *Vokabeln* panel which shows the months in German.

The reading text is also available online as an audio file.

Answers:

a 3   b 4   c 5   d 1   e 2

2b 💬 Interview at least eight people in your class, asking them when their birthdays are. Each person has to answer using a full sentence.

A speaking activity to practise saying when your birthday is. Students could write down the dates they are told, to practise understanding the dates of other people's birthdays. Before starting, refer students to the *Grammatik* panel and to the *Vokabeln* panel. Demonstrate with volunteers so that all students hear examples of correct full sentences.

Possible answers:

Wann hast du Geburtstag?
Ich habe am ersten Juni Geburtstag.
Am ersten Juni …. Und du, wann hast du Geburtstag?
Ich habe am achten Mai Geburtstag …

> This panel explains to students how to construct a full sentence to say when their birthday is in German, which they need to do for speaking activity 2b.
> The panel refers students to pages 187–188 to find out more about ordinal numbers. You may wish to revise these before students do activity 2b.
>
> *Grammatik*

Page 12

Revision

Classroom equipment and colours

kerboodle! • Audio files for core reading texts

1a 📖 🎧 Read the description of Elke's bag, pictured above. Rewrite the text correcting the five errors.

A reading activity to practise understanding words for classroom equipment and colours. Refer students to the *Vokabeln* panels. Elicit the fact that in the text the colour words sometimes have endings on them – more able pupils should be able to explain or notice that this happens when the colour is before the noun it describes. Refer to the *Grammatik* panel about adjectives.

The reading text is also available online as an audio file.

Answers:

Elke geht zusammen mit Paul in die Schule. Sie hat eine **braune** Schultasche. In ihrer Tasche hat sie ein **rotes** Etui und zwei Hefte. Ein Heft ist rot und das zweite Heft ist **gelb**. Ihre Sportschuhe sind **grau**. Sie hat auch ein Lineal, einen blauen Kuli und einen **schwarzen** Bleistift.

1b ✏️ 💬 Use a dictionary to find the German for ten items you associate with a particular colour. Write the words down and swap lists. Write down an appropriate colour next to each word on your partner's list, then check that you both agree.

A writing and speaking activity to practise colours. Refer students to the *Vokabeln* panel for the colour words and ask for any others they know. Clarify the fact that in these dialogues, the colour comes after the noun it describes, so no adjective ending is required.

Possible answers:

Der Schokoriegel ist braun, oder?
Nein, der Schokoriegel ist weiß. Ist die Kuh schwarz und weiß?
Ja, die Kuh ist schwarz und weiß …

> This panel explains that adjectives in German take an ending (a spelling change) if they are placed before the noun they describe. Ask students to find examples of this in the text for activity 1. Explain that they will learn more about how to do this later in the course.
>
> *Grammatik*

2a 📖 🎧 Read Paul's text, then copy and complete the sentences.

A reading activity to practise understanding words for classroom equipment in more complex sentences. Refer students to the *Vokabeln* panel. Ask for translations of the final sentences to check comprehension.

The reading text is also available online as an audio file.

Answers:

a Paul hat viele Sachen in seiner <u>Schultasche</u>.
b In jeder Stunde schreibt er Aufgaben in sein <u>Heft</u>.
c Wenn er schreiben will, kann er einen <u>Kuli</u> / <u>Bleistift</u> oder einen <u>Bleistift</u> / <u>Kuli</u> in der Tasche finden.
d Am <u>Montag</u> ist seine Tasche immer voll, weil er seine <u>Sportsachen</u> braucht.

2b ✏️ 💬 Use a dictionary to find the German words for 10 other things in your classroom or schoolbag. Compare your lists in pairs.

A writing and speaking activity to practise extended vocabulary for classroom equipment, and using a dictionary. Encourage creativity if students don't have enough items in their bag to describe! They should then compare their list with a partner's list. Refer to the *Grammatik* panel about gender. More confident students should write down the genders of the nouns they look up, and be encouraged to use the correct form of *einen/ eine/ein* when comparing lists with a partner.

Possible answers:

Hast du ein Pult?
Ja, ich habe ein Pult. Hast du einen Bleistiftspitzer?
Nein, den habe ich nicht …

Revision **13**

This panel explains that all nouns in German have a gender, and shows how these are normally indicated in a dictionary. Students can practise identifying these when looking up new words for activity 2b. You may wish to show the class nominative and accusative forms of the definite and indefinite article for each gender. The panel refers students to page 174 for more information.

Page 13

Revision
Numbers and dates

kerboodle! • Audio files for core reading texts

1a 📖 🎧 Read the description of a city in Germany. For each of the following statements write T (True) or F (False)

A reading activity to practise understanding numbers, including those in the hundreds and thousands. Refer to the *Vokabeln* panel which gives examples of these. Before this or the next activity, you may wish to practise these numbers further with a quick quiz or game of lotto (limited to a certain range of numbers). Alternatively, use a numbers race: write a selection of high numbers as figures on the board twice – on the left and right hand sides. Divide the class into two teams. A member from each stands in front of their team's side of the board with a board marker, and they race to circle the number you say in German and win a point for their team. Wipe off the numbers already used, and select different team members for each go (you could number them and call out numbers to select randomly).

The reading text is also available online as an audio file.

Answers:

a T	b F	c F	d T
e T	f F	g F	h T

1b ✏️ Work out the answer to these sums in German and write the answer in words.

A writing activity to practise understanding and using German numbers. Refer to the *Vokabeln* list. Students could then work in pairs, making up similar sums for their partner to do – partners could either read or listen to these, then work out the answer and write it down in German.

Answers:

a siebenundzwanzig   b dreißig
c zweiundfünfzig   d vierundachtzig

2a 📖 🎧 Three famous people are saying when they were born. Match up the year of birth with the name of the person.

A reading activity to practise understanding dates and years in German. Refer to the *Grammatik* panel.

The reading text is also available online as an audio file.

Answers:

a 1976   b 1961   c 1973

This panel on dates explains how to say a particular year in German, and points out that there are two ways of saying when you were born. Practise with the class, using a range of years as examples, and ask students to say when they were born (firstly just the year, then also with their birth date). They will practise this further in activity 2b.

2b 💬 Work in pairs. One person names a famous person and the other gives his or her date of birth.

A speaking activity to practise saying dates of birth in German. Make it clear that students should say the name of the month where a number is given. Refer to the *Vokabeln* and *Grammatik* panels.

Possible answers:

Du bist Daniel Brühl. Wann bist du geboren?
Ich bin am sechzehnten Juni neunzehnhundertachtundsiebzig geboren. Du bist Britney Spears. Wann bist du geboren?
Ich bin am zweiten Dezember neunzehnhunderteinundachtzig geboren. Du bist ...

Page 14

Revision
Parts of the body, useful words

kerboodle! • Audio files for core reading texts

1a 📖 🎧 Read the text and answer the following questions in English.

A reading activity involving comprehension of German words for parts of the body, and associated compound nouns. Refer to the *Vokabeln* panel. Remind students that every noun in German is written with a capital letter, and has a gender (shown in the vocabulary list as *der/die/das*).

The reading text is also available online as an audio file.

Answers:

a a
b Richard has blue eyes; he has a goatee beard; Marion has long fingernails; she's wearing a bracelet.
c lipstick
d 7 – Kinnbart, Fingernagel, Armband, Handtasche, Lippenstift, Fußball, Schulterstand

This panel explains that the gender of compound nouns in German is the same as the gender of the second (or final) noun. Demonstrate with some examples. Students will practise this in activity 1b, and could also work out the genders of the compound nouns from the text in activity 1a.

1b ✎ Match up the following words to make compound nouns which include a part of the body.

A writing activity to practise building compound nouns, which could also be used to practise working out their genders. Ask students also to give the gender of each word they create by looking it up to check. Refer to the *Grammatik* panel.

Possible answers:

Handharmonika, Handschuh, Fußbad, Ohrring, Schulterblatt, Mundharmonika

2a 📖 🎧 Read the following text then fill in the gaps in the sentences, using the words from the box.

A reading activity which includes useful general words (e.g. *also, auch, immer, noch*). Refer to the second *Vokabeln* panel. You may wish to translate the text with the class to make sure the meanings of the useful words are clear. Point out that *also* is a false friend, not meaning the same as in English. Also point out the difference in meaning between *schon* and *schön*.

The reading text is also available online as an audio file.

Answers:

a Lothar steht <u>immer</u> um 6 Uhr auf.
b Lothar muss Hockey spielen <u>aber</u> Handball ist besser.
c Lothar findet <u>nichts</u> gut in der Schule.
d Lothar fährt nach Japan <u>und</u> will <u>also</u> Japanisch lernen.

2b ✎ Now write five sentences, each including one of the words from the vocab box on the right.

A writing activity to give students practice of the useful general words in the *Vokabeln* panel. Ask for volunteers to read out one or two of their sentences, so that all students hear several additional examples of their use.

1 Lifestyle

Health
Healthy and unhealthy lifestyles and their consequences

KS3 Revision:
Food and drink, ailments and solutions; Family members and pets

Online materials
- Audio files for core reading texts

1.1 Gesund essen, gesund leben!
- Using the present tense
- Keeping conversations going

- Audio file for core reading text
- Audio file and transcript for listening activity 3
- Reading activity: *Essen und trinken*
- Grammar activity: Using the present tense
- Writing worksheet
- Foundation reading worksheet
- Extension reading worksheet

1.2 Ich bin in Form!
- Using inversion
- Recognising and using near-cognates

- Audio file for core reading text
- Audio file and transcript for listening activity 3
- Listening activity and transcript: *Ich lebe gesund!*
- Grammar activity: Using inversion
- Writing worksheet
- Extension listening worksheet
- Audio file and transcript for extension listening worksheet (same as for activity 3)

1.3 Rauchen ist doch ungesund!
- Using the modal verbs *wollen, können, sollen*
- Using context to predict meanings

- Audio file for core reading text
- Audio file and transcript for listening activity 4
- Reading activity: *Warum rauchen Jugendliche?*
- Grammar activity: Using the modal verbs *wollen, können, sollen*
- Speaking worksheet
- Extension reading worksheet

1.4 Alkohol und Drogen brauchen wir nicht!
- Using the modal verbs *dürfen, müssen, mögen*
- Understanding word order better

- Audio file for core reading text
- Video and transcript for listening activity 3
- Grammar activity: Using the modal verbs *dürfen, müssen, mögen*
- Writing worksheet
- Foundation listening worksheet
- Extension listening worksheet
- Audio file and transcript for foundation and extension listening worksheets

Reading and listening

- Audio file for core reading text
- Audio file and transcript for listening activity 2

Grammar

Health
- Using the indefinite article and the accusative case
- Using adverbs of frequency
- Forming negative phrases using '*nicht*' and '*kein*'
- Using '*man*'

Vocabulary

Health
- MP3 files for each vocabulary list

Relationships and choices

Relationships with family and friends

1.5 Familie und Freunde – zu Hause ■ Using the present tense of *haben* and *sein* ■ Identifying common patterns between German and English	• Audio file for core reading text • Audio file and transcript for listening activity 3 • Listening activity and transcript: *Gibt es Probleme zu Hause?* • Grammar activity: Using the present tense of *haben* and *sein* • Writing worksheet • Foundation listening worksheet • Extension reading worksheet • Audio file and transcript for foundation listening worksheet
1.6 Familie und Freunde – Beziehungen ■ Using possessive adjectives ■ Using your knowledge of grammatical categories	• Audio file for core reading text • Audio file and transcript for listening activity 3 • Reading activity: *Wie verstehst du dich mit deiner Familie und deinen Freunden?* • Grammar activity: Using possessive adjectives • Speaking worksheet • Extension listening worksheet • Audio file and transcript for extension listening worksheet (same as for activity 3)

Future plans regarding: marriage / partnership

1.7 Zukunftspläne – Heiraten, ja oder nein? ■ Using the present tense to talk about the future ■ Asking for help when unsure	• Audio file for core reading text • Audio file and transcript for listening activity 3 • Listening activity and transcript: *Heiraten ist wichtig, oder?* • Grammar activity: Using the present tense to talk about the future • Writing worksheet • Extension reading worksheet

Social issues and equality

1.8 Gleichheit für Männer und Frauen? ■ Understanding nouns and gender ■ Matching German and English phrases	• Audio file for core reading text • Audio file and transcript for listening activity 3 • Reading activity: *Das ist keine Stelle für dich, oder?* • Grammar activity: Understanding nouns and gender • Writing worksheet • Extension listening worksheet • Audio file and transcript for extension listening worksheet (same as for activity 3)
1.9 Ethnische Probleme ■ Using coordinating conjunctions ■ Speaking and writing creatively	• Audio file for core reading text • Audio file and transcript for listening activity 3 • Listening activity and transcript: *Hier wollen wir keinen Rassismus!* • Grammar activity: Using coordinating conjunctions • Speaking worksheet • Extension reading worksheet
1.10 Armut ■ Using subordinating conjunctions ■ Identifying compound nouns	• Audio file for core reading text • Audio file and transcript for listening activity 3 • Reading activity: *Ist Geld wichtig, um glücklich zu sein?* • Grammar activity: Using subordinating conjunctions • Writing worksheet • Extension listening worksheet • Audio file and transcript for extension listening worksheet (same as for activity 3) • Foundation reading worksheet

Reading and listening

• Audio file for core reading text
• Audio files and transcripts for listening activity 2

Grammar

Relationships and choices

- Using *ihr*
- Using the word 'it'
- Adverbs of place
- Using *um ... zu ...*
- Adjectives after nouns; Quantifiers / intensifiers
- Adverbial phrases of time

Vocabulary

Relationships and choices	• MP3 files for each vocabulary list

Summative assessment

Lifestyle	• Interactive multiple-choice quiz

The opening page for Context 1, Lifestyle provides a quick-reference overview of how the teaching spreads, grammar and strategies within this Context in the Student Book map to the Topics and Purposes of Context 1 in the GCSE specification. Also included here is an overview of the online resources available for each of these spreads in the Student Book.

Context 1 Lifestyle 17

Page 16

Revision
Health

Food and drink, ailments and solutions

• Audio files for core reading texts

1a Read Jürgen's descriptions of his food preferences, then order a three-course meal with drinks for him.

A reading activity to practise food and drink vocabulary. Students read Jürgen's text then choose the menu items he would prefer. You may wish to go through the menu first with the class to check understanding of the food vocabulary. Students can write down their answers as homework or present them orally. Encourage them to give their answers using full sentences starting with *Ich möchte* …

The reading text is also available online as an audio file.

Answers:

Starter – Fleischsalat
Main course – Wurst mit Pommes
Dessert – Erdbeertorte
Drink – Wein

1b Work in pairs. Take it in turns to make an order, based on the preferences given below (then order something you would really like!).

A speaking activity to practise food and drink vocabulary and making orders. Students work in pairs to create dialogues based on the preferences given, then go on to make up their own. The restaurant role plays can be performed in front of the rest of the class.

The reading text is also available online as an audio file.

Possible answers:

a *Was möchten Sie?*
   Ich möchte Tomatensuppe, Wurst mit Pommes und Schokoladenkuchen mit Sahne.
   Und zu trinken?
   Kaffee, bitte.
b *Was möchten Sie?*
   Ich möchte Fleischsalat und Hähnchen mit Kartoffeln.
   Und zu trinken?
   Limonade, bitte.

2a Read the following conversation in a doctor's surgery then answer the questions in English.

A reading activity to revise ailments and remedies. With the help of the second *Vokabeln* box, students answer questions on the doctor's surgery dialogue. You may also wish to invite them to read it out in pairs. Ask more able students to identify where command forms are being used.

The reading text is also available online as an audio file.

Answers:

a She has a headache.
b Three times a day.
c After eating.
d She should stay in bed for four to five days.

> Refer students to the *Grammatik* box to remind them about the imperative form, which they will need to use in activity 2b. This form is covered in more detail later in the course in the Home and Environment context (see Student Book page 115).

Grammatik

2b Work in pairs, using the doctor and Trude's dialogue as a model. One partner says what is wrong based on the images and the other gives advice, choosing from the statements given. Then swap roles.

A speaking activity to revise language relating to ailments and remedies, and to practise using imperative forms. Once students have gone through the examples given in the book, see if they can recall more ways of describing complaints e.g. … *tut weh, Ich habe mir … gebrochen* etc.

Sample answers:

Ich habe Ohrenschmerzen.
Nimm diese Tropfen.

Ich habe Bauchschmerzen.
Nehmen Sie dieses Medikament und bleiben Sie im Bett.

Page 17

Revision
Relationships and choices

Family members and pets

• Audio files for core reading texts

1a Read the text then for each of the following statements, write T (true) or F (false).

A reading activity revising vocabulary for describing family members. Students could also draw Robert's family tree based on the information he gives. This may be a useful activity to complete in advance of answering the true / false questions.

You may also wish to draw attention to the use of possessive adjectives in this text.

The reading text is also available online as an audio file.

Answers:

a T   b F   c F   d T   e T   f F

1b Using Robert's text as a model, write several sentences on your own family. Then swap with a partner and draw each other's family trees.

A writing activity practising describing families, with a student-created reading comprehension to follow on.

Check students' texts for accuracy before they swap with a partner.

The descriptions and family trees could later be used in a starter activity. The family trees are laid out on a desk. Students each receive a description and have to find the corresponding family tree as soon as possible (with larger classes this could get quite unruly!).

2a 📖 🎧 **Read the two texts below then answer the questions.**

A reading activity to revise vocabulary for pets. The texts can also be used as a model for students to write about their own pets.

The reading texts are also available online as an audio file.

Answers:

a Bärbel
b Karl
c Neither Bärbel nor Karl have a horse
d Bärbel
e Karl

> Refer students to the *Grammatik* box to remind them about the use of indefinite and negative articles. Invite them to identify these in Karl and Bärbel's texts. They will need to use these in activity 2b.
> These grammar points are looked at in greater detail, with accompanying activities, in the first grammar practice spread on pages 28–29.

2b 💬 **Work in pairs. One person asks the other the following questions about pets. Then swap roles. (If you don't have any pets, why not talk about a pet you would like?)**

A speaking activity to practise talking about pets. Refer students to the *Vokabeln* box for help. Here, *es* is used for the singular but you may wish to encourage students to use more exact forms based on the gender of the noun (and not the sex of the individual pet!).

Sample answers:

Hast du ein Haustier?
Ja, ich habe einen Hund.
Wie heißt er?
Er heißt Charlie.
Wie alt ist er?
Er ist fünf Jahre alt.
Wie ist er?
Er ist wirklich süß.

Hast du ein Haustier?
Ja, ich habe zwei Katzen.
Wie heißen sie?
Sie heißen Castor und Pollux.
Wie alt sind sie?
Sie sind beide drei Jahre alt.
Wie sind sie?
Castor ist niedlich, aber Pollux ist ziemlich böse.

Pages 18–19

1.1 Gesund essen, gesund leben!

Healthy and unhealthy lifestyles and their consequences

Subject	Talking about different diets
G 1	Using the present tense
G 2	Saying 'I eat a / an ...'
💬	Keeping conversations going

kerboodle!
- Audio file for core reading text
- Audio file and transcript for listening activity 3
- Reading activity: *Essen und trinken*
- Grammar activity: Using the present tense
- Writing worksheet
- Foundation reading worksheet
- Extension reading worksheet

Starter activity

Students work in pairs or individually to produce two lists of vocabulary they can remember for food items, within a time limit: 10 which they think are healthy, and 10 which are unhealthy. Adjust the number required to suit your students and the time available. Weaker students could look for examples in the Reading text. Then elicit examples and discuss.

Gesund leben online Forum

A reading text about the eating habits of Klaus and his family. The text is in the present tense, and includes examples of the verb *essen* used with an accusative article (*einen/keinen* etc).

The reading text is also available online as an audio file.

1 📖 🎧 **Who is talking in each sentence?**
Students read the text and decide who is talking in each of the eight sentences given.

Answers:

a Jochen (brother)   b Hans (uncle)
c Monika (sister)   d Monika
e Klaus   f Sabine (mother)
g Klaus   h Monika

> This panel explains how to find the stem of a regular verb before adding present tense endings, and changes to the stem for irregular verbs. With weaker students, clarify their understanding of what the present tense is by using simple examples in English. If necessary, revise with students the meanings of the pronouns *ich, du, er/sie/es* etc, and look up the correct endings for each in the Grammar section. Practise finding the stem and applying the correct endings with several regular verbs. The reading and listening materials in activities 1 and 3 provide examples of present tense verb forms.
> This *Grammatik* panel also refers students to p.28 for information on saying 'I eat a / an ...' using the accusative indefinite article.

Context 1 Lifestyle 19

2a **G** Add the correct endings to the stem to complete the table for the regular verb *spielen*. Look at the endings Klaus uses in his text or refer to page 180 if you get stuck.

A grammar activity to practise present tense verb forms of regular verbs, as explained in the *Grammatik* panel. Students add the correct present tense endings to the parts of the regular verb *spielen*.

Answers:

ich spiele
du spielst
er/sie/es spielt
wir spielen
ihr spielt
sie spielen
Sie spielen

2b **G** Now do the same for the irregular verbs *essen* and *laufen*.

A grammar activity to practise present tense verb forms of irregular verbs, as explained in the *Grammatik* panel. Students write out the present tense forms of the irregular verbs *essen* and *laufen*. Remind them to refer to the *Grammatik* panel and the reading text.

Answers:

ich esse	ich laufe
du isst	du läufst
er/sie/es isst	er/sie/es läuft
wir essen	wir laufen
ihr esst	ihr lauft
sie essen	sie laufen
Sie essen	Sie laufen

Tipp

Use this box to assist pupils before doing the listening activity. After reading it with students, you could illustrate the technique of listening for even one or two familiar food words as clues by playing a small part of the listening extract 'blind' to the class, without looking at the grid, and asking them to signal as soon as they have understood a food word. Then elicit the words understood, and whether the speaker is likely to be a healthy eater. After completing the listening activity, students will be able to confirm if their guess was correct. Point out that this is a useful technique for the listening exam.

3 🎧 *Transcript:*

a *Maria, was isst du gern zum Frühstück?*
 Ich esse Schinken, Bratwurst und zwei Spiegeleier. Hmm. Lecker!
b *Was isst du in der Pause, Christoph?*
 Ich esse nur einen Apfel in der Pause. Das ist so langweilig.
c *Silke, hast du ein Lieblingsessen?*
 Salat esse ich nicht – das schmeckt mir einfach nicht. Ich esse lieber Pommes frites mit Mayo. Klasse!
d *Was isst du zu Mittag, Jürgen?*
 Zu Mittag esse ich gern Pizza und danach einen Schokoriegel. Das finde ich toll!

e *Und du, Daniela. Was isst du gern abends?*
 Ich esse jeden Abend Gemüse. Ich esse Gemüse sehr gern, aber keinen Blumenkohl oder Spinat. Das finde ich furchtbar – igitt!
f *Was isst du gern zum Frühstück, Heiko?*
 Ich esse morgens Haferflocken mit Milch und Obst. Ich finde das köstlich.

3 🎧 Listen to some young people talking about their diet. What do they eat? Is it healthy or not? Do they enjoy it? Copy and complete the table.

This audio extract consists of six young people being asked questions about their eating habits. Their replies include opinions about what they eat. The questions and answers illustrate present tense verb forms.

Students listen to the extract and fill in a copy of the grid to show their comprehension of the responses and opinions. Refer them to the accompanying *Tipp* before listening (see above).

Answers:

		What is eaten?	Healthy	Unhealthy	☺	☹
a	Maria	Ham, sausage, two fried eggs		✓	✓	
b	Christoph	Apple	✓			✓
c	Silke	Chips with mayonnaise		✓	✓	
d	Jürgen	Pizza, chocolate bar		✓	✓	
e	Daniela	Vegetables	✓		✓	
f	Heiko	Rolled oats with milk and fruit	✓		✓	

Strategie

Discuss the strategies for keeping conversations going, with the class, before they do the speaking activity. Demonstrate how they might apply these during the task to think of an alternative if they don't know the food or drink item they want to say. After completion of the task, ask for any examples of their use of this.

4a 💬 🍴 Work with a partner to conduct interviews on healthy eating. One partner asks the questions and the other answers. Then swap roles.

Students use the questions given to conduct interviews. You could support weaker students by demonstrating interviews using these questions and the answer structures given in activity 4b, and by eliciting or providing additional vocabulary for food and drink items they might use. More confident students should be able to supplement the language given with ideas of their own. Before starting, refer students to the *Strategie* panel, and remind them to focus on using correct verb endings. If time allows, they could conduct interviews with several partners, or a survey.

4b Now describe what your partner eats and drinks.

Students use the answer structures given to report on what they have found out about their partner. This practises third person present tense verb endings.

Plenary activity

Recap language used in the speaking task to decide whether the class are healthy or unhealthy breakfast eaters. For example, ask students who think they eat a healthy breakfast to raise their hands, ask a volunteer to count them, and do spot checks of these by asking some what they eat and drink (additional third person verification could come from others who interviewed them). Do the same for those who eat an unhealthy or no breakfast and announce the final tally.

Pages 20–21

1.2 Ich bin in Form!

Healthy and unhealthy lifestyles and their consequences

Subject	Understanding what prevents wellbeing
G 1	Using inversion
G 2	Using adverbs of frequency
	Recognising and using near-cognates

kerboodle!
- Audio file for core reading text
- Audio file and transcript for listening activity 3
- Listening activity and transcript: *Ich lebe gesund!*
- Grammar activity: Using inversion
- Writing worksheet
- Extension listening worksheet
- Audio file and transcript for extension listening worksheet

Starter activity

Display a list of infinitives of familiar verbs relating to the activities which follow, for example: *spielen, essen, rauchen, treiben, schlafen, trinken, schwimmen, sich entspannen*. Students use their knowledge of present tense forms to write or say a sentence using each. Weaker students may need to look up meanings first, and may limit themselves to using *ich*. More confident students could use a different pronoun and verb ending in each one.

Das Gesundheitsquiz!

This reading text presents key vocabulary for factors relating to wellbeing in the form of multiple-choice quiz questions about students' own habits, and illustrates both normal word order and inversion, and some near-cognates.

The reading text is also available online as an audio file.

Strategie

To practise the strategy of recognising and using near-cognates, ask students to find examples of near-cognates in the quiz. Point out that pronunciation of words which look similar to English will usually be different in German, and practise saying some examples (e.g. *Alkohol, Zigaretten, Portionen, Hamburger, Stress*).

1 Answer these multiple-choice questions by choosing an appropriate answer. Work out how many points you have scored to see how healthy you are.

Students could work through the quiz questions alone or with a partner, and should then calculate their total. You may wish to discuss the different outcomes with the class. Refer to the *Strategie* panel (see above).

Grammatik

This panel on using inversion explains why word order must sometimes be changed in German sentences, so that the verb remains as second idea. Discuss the examples given with the class, and make sure it is understood that 'second idea' is not always 'second word' – refer to the *Tipp*. You might wish to say that showing ability to do this could increase their marks in the Writing and Speaking units (range and accuracy of language).
This *Grammatik* panel also refers students to p.28 for information on how to use adverbs of frequency.

2 G Re-write the following sentences starting each with the underlined word or phrase.

This activity practises inversion, as explained in the *Grammatik* panel.

Students rearrange the sentences, putting the underlined word or phrase first, and adjusting word order accordingly so that the verb remains the second idea. Before starting the activity, discuss the *Grammatik* panel with the class.

Answers:

a Am Wochenende spiele ich Tennis.
b Einmal pro Woche essen wir Fastfood.
c Jeden Tag sieht mein Bruder vier Stunden fern.
d Dreimal pro Woche schwimmt meine Freundin im Hallenbad.
e Manchmal ist Stress ein Problem für mich.
f Leider haben meine Eltern nicht genug körperliche Bewegung.
g Am Samstag gehen mein Onkel und ich windsurfen.

Tipp

This box illustrates the fact that the first idea of a German sentence might consist of a phrase of several words, meaning that the verb as second idea is not always the second word. If needed, provide or elicit further examples to illustrate this.

Context 1 Lifestyle 21

3 🎧 *Transcript:*

a *Katharina, bist du gesund?*
Ja, ich bin gesund und so will ich bleiben. Jeden Morgen gehe ich gern schwimmen.

b *Isst du gesund, Leon?*
Nein, leider nicht. Jetzt bin ich zu dick, weil ich zu viele Hamburger und Pommes esse.

c *Steffi, hast du Stress in deinem Leben?*
Ich habe keinen Stress. Ich gehe jeden Tag mit meinem Hund spazieren.

d *Isst du gern Pommes, Sebastian?*
Nein, überhaupt nicht. Ich esse sehr gesund und das heißt: kein Fastfood für mich.

e *Treibst du Sport, Yvonne?*
Zwei- oder dreimal pro Woche gehe ich mit meinen Freundinnen Schlittschuh laufen. Das macht Spaß und hält auch fit!

f *Johann, du bist gesund, nicht wahr?*
Nein, ich bin nicht so gesund. Ich treffe meine Freunde fast jeden Abend und wir sitzen herum und trinken zusammen Bier.

g *Bist du sportlich, Paula?*
Ich treibe viel Sport, zum Beispiel Basketball, Fußball und Judo. Deshalb schlafe ich sieben bis acht Stunden pro Nacht.

h *Willst du rauchen, Markus?*
Meine Gesundheit ist mir wichtig – ich werde nie rauchen, weil es so schrecklich ist.

3 🎧 Listen to these young people talking about their lifestyles. Choose the appropriate picture for each.

This audio extract consists of eight young people being asked questions about health-related aspects of their lifestyle. Their replies include examples of inversion, adverbs of frequency and some near-cognates.

Students listen to the audio extract and decide which of the pictures given illustrates each person. They could then listen again for extra detail, for examples of near-cognates, or for examples of inversion.

Answers:

a Katharina = 2
b Leon = 5
c Steffi = 8
d Sebastian = 6
e Yvonne = 4
f Johann = 1
g Paula = 7
h Markus = 3

Extra detail: Paula plays basketball, football and judo, which is why she sleeps so well.

4 💬 ✏️ Interview your partner to find out how he or she keeps healthy, noting down the responses. Use the questions on the clipboard.

Students use the questions given to conduct interviews. You could support weaker students by demonstrating interviews using these questions with simpler answer forms. Refer to the *Grammatik* and *Tipp* panels. More confident students should be able to supplement the language given with ideas of their own (using inversion where possible) and could make up additional questions. If time allows, they could conduct interviews with several partners and report back on or write up their findings.

Plenary activity

Each student prepares three short statements about health-related aspects of his/her lifestyle. These could be simple sentences, or more complex ones using inversion. One statement should be untrue. Pairs of students listen to each other's three statements and guess which is the false one. Individuals could then read theirs out for the whole class to guess.

Pages 22–23

1.3 Rauchen ist doch ungesund!

Healthy and unhealthy lifestyles and their consequences

Subject	Talking about smoking
Ⓖ 1	Using the modal verbs *wollen, können, sollen*
Ⓖ 2	Forming the negative with *nicht* and *kein*
🔊	Using context to predict meanings

kerboodle!
• Audio file for core reading text
• Audio file and transcript for listening activity 4
• Reading activity: *Warum rauchen Jugendliche?*
• Grammar activity: Using the modal verbs *wollen, können, sollen*
• Speaking worksheet
• Extension reading worksheet

1 Ⓥ Match the following German and English words:

List the compound nouns from activity 1 (*Raucherhusten, Außenseiter*), and a couple of additional relevant examples (e.g. *Lungenkrebs, Großmutter* from the text in activity 2), on the board. Encourage the class to explain how these are 'built' – i.e. from which component words, and how this can help with deducing meanings. Can they think of any other examples of German compound nouns they already know?

Answers:

a 2   b 4   c 3   d 5   e 1

Core reading text

Four teenagers explain why they do or do not smoke and express their opinions about smoking. The text includes the modal verbs *wollen, können* and *sollen*, the negative with *nicht*, and sentences with *weil*.

The reading text is also available online as an audio file.

📖 After discussing with students the strategy of using context to predict meanings, elicit or provide other examples of new/difficult words from the text and invite the class to predict meanings based on context (e.g. *gefährlich, blöd, Raucherhusten*), then to look them up and check.

Strategie

2 📖 🎧 🌐 Match the following sentence beginnings and endings so that they make sense. Then decide who might make each statement – Kirsten, Stefan, Jörg or Hannah? (It could be more than one person!)

Students read the text. As there are a number of new vocabulary items, refer them to the *Strategie* panel. They then match sentence halves to create five statements about smoking, and decide which of the young people in the text might make each statement.

Answers:

a Meiner Meinung nach soll man nie rauchen. – Kirsten, Jörg
b Ich fühle mich wirklich cool, wenn ich rauche. – Stefan
c Ich habe nur einmal eine Zigarette probiert. – Kirsten
d Ich kann nicht aufhören, weil ich süchtig bin. – Stefan
e Ich will kein Außenseiter sein, also rauche ich mit meinen Freunden. – Stefan

> **Grammatik**
> This panel introduces the present tense forms of three modal verbs *wollen*, *können*, and *sollen*, and explains how these are used with an infinitive. Students could also search for sentences which include a modal verb in the text in activity 2, or make up simple smoking-related sentences of their own, using a modal verb and vocabulary from the text.
> The panel also suggests that students revise how to form the negative with *nicht* and *kein*, referring them to p.29.

3 🄖 Translate the following sentences into English.

This activity involves comprehension of the modal verbs *wollen*, *können* and *sollen*.

Before they translate the sentences, refer students to the *Grammatik* panel. You may need to check that students remember the meaning of *ihr* (use of *ihr* will be covered in the Grammar practice on p.46).

Answers:

a I ought to give up smoking now.
b We can't stop.
c My friend / boyfriend doesn't want to try (smoking) a cigarette / cigarettes because it's unhealthy.
d Do you want to get a smoker's cough?
e He can't give up because he's addicted.
f You should smoke in the garden and not in the house.

> **Tipp**
> Using *ich sollte*. Provide, then elicit from volunteers, example sentences to clarify the 'really should but might not' element of using *ich sollte*.

4 🎧 *Transcript:*

Wir sprechen heute über das Rauchen in Deutschland. Also, wie viele Leute rauchen?

25 Prozent aller Erwachsenen in Deutschland rauchen regelmäßig, 35 Prozent der Männer und 22 Prozent der Frauen rauchen. Unter jungen Leuten rauchen mehr Mädchen als Jungen.

Was passiert, wenn man raucht?

Tabak ist eine Droge, die süchtig macht. Raucher brauchen den Nikotin-Kick immer wieder aufs Neue. Es verursacht große Probleme mit der Gesundheit, meistens Herzprobleme und Lungenkrebs.

Ist es leicht, mit dem Rauchen aufzuhören?

Viele Leute wollen aufhören zu rauchen, finden es aber schwer. Es gibt aber Hilfe, zum Beispiel Pflaster, Kaugummis und Sprays. Wenn man nicht raucht, schmeckt das Essen besser. Man kann auch besser atmen und das Risiko für die Gesundheit ist geringer.

Wo kann man in Deutschland rauchen?

Im Moment ist Rauchen in allen Flugzeugen, Bussen, Schiffen und öffentlichen Gebäuden verboten, aber noch nicht in allen Gaststätten und Restaurants.

4 🎧 Read the statements below and check that you understand them. Then listen to the radio interview about smoking in Germany and decide whether the statements are true (T) or false (F).

This audio extract consists of questions and factual answers about smoking in Germany. These include smoking-related vocabulary and examples of modal verbs.

Students read the statements given, then listen to the audio extract and decide whether each is true or false.

Answers:

a T
b F
c F (heart and lungs are most badly affected)
d F
e T
f F
g F

5 💬 ✏️ Prepare a presentation in German for or against smoking. Try to give reasons.

Encourage students to make use of the available sources of relevant phrases and vocabulary (the text in activity 2 and the audio extract in activity 4), and to add to the range of their language by including modal verbs and sentences with *weil*. Refer them back to the *Grammatik* panel and both *Tipps*. These presentations could be illustrated, recorded, or form the basis of a piece of written work.

> **Tipp**
> Using *weil*. Ask students to find sentences with *weil* in the text for activity 2, and to identify the verb at the end of these. Illustrate formation of such sentences with a few simple examples related to smoking.

Plenary activity

Ask volunteers to give their presentation from activity 5 in front of the class and ask for simple and supportive verbal feedback in German from the audience – supply some useful phrases for this.

Context 1 Lifestyle 23

Pages 24–25

1.4 Alkohol und Drogen brauchen wir nicht!

Healthy and unhealthy lifestyles and their consequences

Subject	Talking about alcohol and drugs
G 1	Using the modal verbs *dürfen, müssen, mögen*
G 2	Using *man*
🎧	Understanding word order better

kerboodle!
- Audio file for core reading text
- Video and transcript for listening activity 3
- Grammar activity: Using the modal verbs *dürfen, müssen, mögen*
- Writing worksheet
- Foundation listening worksheet
- Extension listening worksheet
- Audio file and transcript for foundation and listening worksheets

Starter activity

To give students practice in understanding percentages (revision of numbers to 100), read out a list of five percentage figures in German (or sentences including percentages), to be written down, then repeated back to you in German.

Alkohol, Drogen und die Schweizer Jugend

The stimulus material consists of a table giving the results of a survey looking at alcohol and drugs use among 15-year-olds in Switzerland. This is followed by the text of a discussion between two teenagers about the survey and their own habits. The discussion includes present tense examples of the modal verbs *dürfen, müssen* and *mögen*, and of *weil, dass* and *wenn* used with modal verbs.

The reading text is also available online as an audio file.

1 📖 🎧 Two teenagers are discussing the above survey about alcohol and cannabis use amongst young people in Switzerland.

Students read the survey data, read and/or listen to the discussion, and answer the comprehension questions using full German sentences.

Answers:

Suggestions only – wording may vary:
a 19% (der 15-jährigen Mädchen waren schon zweimal betrunken.)
b 34% der Jungen und 27% der Mädchen (haben Erfahrung mit Cannabis.)
c (Franz und seine Freunde treffen sich) hinter dem Bahnhof.
d Sie trinken und rauchen Cannabis.
e Er muss immer viel arbeiten und darf nie machen, was er will.
f Er wird bestimmt Probleme bekommen.
g Marion ist Sportlerin und muss ihre Gesundheit schützen.

Grammatik

This panel introduces the present tense forms of the modal verbs *dürfen, müssen* and *mögen* and explains that, as with the three modal verbs already met, these are used with an infinitive at the end of the sentence or clause. Students could search for sentences which include a modal verb in the text in activity 1, or make up simple sentences of their own using these three modal verbs. The panel also suggests that students revise how to use *man*, referring them to p.29.

2 G Copy the sentences and fill in the gaps with the correct form of *müssen* or *dürfen*.

This activity involves using the correct present tense form of either *müssen* or *dürfen* to fill gaps in sentences.

Before they do this activity, refer students to the *Grammatik* panel. Make sure they understand the difference in meaning between *müssen* and *dürfen*, and point out the *Tipp* about saying 'must not' in German.

Answers:

a darf   b müssen   c darf
d Darfst   e muss   f müssen

Tipp

Use simple example sentences about alcohol or drugs to model the use of *dürfen nicht* to mean 'must not' in German.

3 🎥 *Transcript:*

Interviewerin: Hallo und willkommen bei der Anna Brinkmann Show! Ich bin die Anna und heute Abend habe ich für Sie ein richtiges Vernügen vorbereitet. Wir haben im Studio den Rockstar „Blitz", von der Gruppe „Herr Schmidt"... Also Blitz, herzlich willkommen bei der Anna Brinkmann Show. Es freut mich sehr, dass Sie heute bei uns im Studio sind.
Blitz: Kein Problem.
Interviewerin: Wie geht's Ihnen heutzutage? Eigentlich sehen Sie ganz toll aus.
Blitz: Es geht mir viel besser als früher, muss ich sagen.
Interviewerin: Und wie war es früher?
Blitz: Naja, wie die meisten Leute schon wissen, habe ich Probleme mit Alkohol gehabt. Vor einem Jahr habe ich regelmäßig eine Flasche Whiskey und viel Bier nach jedem Konzert getrunken. Als Band waren wir sehr erfolgreich – Nummer eins in Deutschland und Österreich – aber ich war schon total kaputt, hatte mein Leben gar nicht im Griff.
Interviewerin: Und jedoch wußte keiner damals, dass es Ihnen so schlecht ging. Und mit den Drogen auch ...
Blitz: Ich habe alles genommen: Ich habe Cannabis geraucht, Ecstasytabletten genommen und Kokain gesnifft. Ich habe sogar Heroin gespritzt. Drogen waren ein normaler Teil meines Lebens als Rockstar.
Interviewerin: Warum haben Sie denn damit aufgehört? Gab es einen besonderen Auslöser?

Blitz:	Letzes Jahr hat die Band in Südamerika gespielt. Nach dem Konzert gab es natürlich eine Party im Hotelzimmer. Axel, der Bassgitarrenspieler, hat leider eine Überdosis genommen und ist gestorben. Das war schrecklich, weil wir immer Freunde waren.
Interviewerin:	Und dann haben Sie mit den Drogen aufgehört. Es ist aber schwer, Drogen aufzugeben, oder?
Blitz:	Da haben Sie Recht. Ich war drei Monate in einer privaten Klinik und ich habe eine Entziehungskur gemacht. Das war schlimm, aber jetzt bin ich wieder gesund. Ich darf nie wieder Alkohol trinken und Drogen sind einfach verboten.
Interviewerin:	Und jetzt, wie sieht die Zukunft aus?
Blitz:	Jetzt muss ich dieses alte Leben hinter mir lassen. Ich kann meine Familie auch wieder kennenlernen, was mich sehr freut. Und die Band bringt nächsten Monat ein neues Lied heraus. Dann im nächstem Jahr macht die Band eine Welttour. Für uns sieht die Zukunft ganz toll aus!
Interviewerin:	Blitz, herzlichen Dank. Ich wünsche Ihnen viel Spaß und natürlich viel Erfolg!
Blitz:	Danke!

3 Watch the interview with the rock star, Blitz, and fill in the gaps in the sentences below.

The video of an interview with a rock star includes key vocabulary relating to alcohol and drug consumption. It also includes examples of modal verbs.

After students have watched the interview, they fill the gaps in the sentences with one of the words given. They could then watch again, or use the transcript, to check their answers. You could follow this up with some 'harvesting' of useful vocabulary for talking about drugs and alcohol from the text. Make a list of English words and phrases, and ask students to find the German, or simply ask them to pick 10 nouns or verbs from the transcript which they think are useful for this Context.

Answers:

a Alkohol b besser c normal
d Hotel e Überdosis f Entziehungskur
g darf h Monat

4 Work in pairs to conduct interviews similar to those in the video. One of you is the interviewer while the other is either a hard-living celebrity or a clean-living sportsperson. Then swap roles.

Students prepare and then conduct interviews in pairs. They could use some of the questions from the video, or create their own. Less confident students could prepare simple questions using modal verbs (you could provide basic structures for this and sample answers). Refer students back to the *Grammatik* panel and suggest that they make use of vocabulary from activities 1 and 3, and perhaps also from the structure grid in activity 5.

> **Strategie**
> To demonstrate the strategy of understanding word order, use example sentences to help the class understand the word order in sentences where *weil* is used with a modal verb. More confident students could make up similar sentences using *wenn* or *dass*.

5 Write up your interview for a magazine, describing your interviewee's attitude to drugs and alcohol using the third person.

Before students start this activity, refer them to the *Strategie* panel. Ensure that the meanings of the vocabulary given in the structure grid are clear, and point out that using *weil* (or other subordinating conjunctions) with a modal verb is a good way of gaining marks for range of language in the Speaking and Writing units.

Plenary activity

Ask all students to write down three things they must not or should not do, relating to drink or alcohol. Less confident students could produce a simple list using *ich darf nicht*, others could include use of *ich sollte nicht* from the previous subtopic, and/or extend their sentences using *weil* and language from the texts in this subtopic. Elicit an example from each student if time allows (you could stand by the door and hear these as students pass you to leave at the end of the lesson).

Pages 26–27

Reading and listening

Health

kerboodle!
- Audio file for core reading text
- Audio file and transcript for listening activity 2

Um länger zu leben, muss man richtig leben!

The reading stimulus text consists of comments and tips from German school pupils about health-related issues. These cover smoking and its effects, treatment for drug addiction, limiting salt intake, the problems associated with alcohol consumption, anorexia, and the importance of exercise. The text includes examples of present tense verbs, inversion, modal verbs and near-cognates.

The reading text is also available online as an audio file.

1a Read the students' tips, then read the following sentences. For each sentence write T (true) or F (false), in accordance with what the students advise.

All students should be able to attempt the true/false activity 1a. Activity 1b involves a deeper understanding of the text's content and is more challenging. After they have finished, refer students to the *Grammatik* panel. Then ask more confident students to find examples of complex word order in the text, such as use of subordinating conjunctions with modal verbs. They could also pick out useful words and phrases and note them down for use in their own work.

Answers:

a F – you should exercise every day
b T
c F – anorexia affects more girls than boys
d F – alcoholism is a growing problem
e F – you should eat no more than 6g of salt per day
f T

1b 📖 🎧 Read the tips again and answer the following questions in English.

Answers:

a Dirk	b Ulrika	c Helga
d Andreas	e Dieter	f Wilhelm

> This panel asks students to find examples of inversion and present tense modal verbs in the text and refers them back to pages 21 and 25 where these grammar points were explained. Elicit and discuss some of the examples found, taking the opportunity to recap these two features with less confident students.

Grammatik

2a 🎧 *Transcript:*

1 Karla, du darfst keinen Alkohol trinken – du bist viel zu jung.
2 Du musst jeden Tag Bewegung haben, zum Beispiel Federball spielen oder so was.
3 Schlank bleiben ist wichtig, aber bitte nicht zu schlank.
4 Rauchen darfst du natürlich nicht – es ist so ungesund.
5 Zu Hause bekommst du gutes Essen. Also darfst du nur ab und zu Fastfood essen.
6 Du darfst nie Drogen nehmen – sie sind viel zu gefährlich.
7 Stress macht krank – du sollst dich jeden Abend entspannen.
8 Du musst jede Nacht sieben bis acht Stunden schlafen.

2a 🎧 Listen to Karla getting advice from her mother about living healthily. Put the pictures in the correct order.

The audio extract consists of eight short pieces of advice relating to health issues. It includes examples of present tense modal verbs, inversion and near-cognates, and is accessible for less confident students.

After listening to the extract and sequencing the pictures correctly, students could listen again and pick out particular language items, for example specific modal verbs and examples of inversion or near-cognates.

Answers:

d, g, f, c, a, h, e, b

2b 🎧 *Transcript:*

Part 1

Mit vierzehn Jahren habe ich angefangen, mit meinen Freunden Cannabis zu rauchen. Das hat mir gut gefallen, aber meine Eltern waren total dagegen. Ich musste ein paar Wochen lang abends zu Hause bleiben und durfte nicht ausgehen. Dann habe ich wieder Cannabis geraucht und meistens bin ich dann einfach nicht zur Schule gegangen.

Part 2

Ein Jahr später habe ich ein Mädchen kennen gelernt. Sie heißt Sonja und ist sehr hübsch. Sie hat Cannabis geraucht, aber sie hat auch Ecstasy genommen und ich wollte es auch probieren. Für mich war es toll, aber leider brauchten wir bald immer mehr davon. Nach sechs Monaten sind wir von zu Hause weggelaufen und wir wohnen jetzt in Hamburg. Unsere Eltern wissen nicht, wo wir sind, aber sie wollen uns nicht helfen und wollen nichts von uns wissen.

Part 3

Wir haben keinen Job und müssen Handys oder Geld stehlen, um Drogen zu kaufen. Wir schlafen auf der Straße und das finden wir furchtbar. Aber was sollen wir denn machen? Alle unsere Freunde nehmen Drogen und viele nehmen harte Drogen wie zum Beispiel Heroin. Ich habe Angst davor, dass wir eines Tages vielleicht Heroin probieren werden.

2b 🎧 Listen to Kurt talking about taking drugs then answer the following questions in English.

This audio extract contains longer and more complex sentences to challenge more confident students. Most should listen to it one section at a time, and complete the corresponding activity, but the most able could listen to the whole extract and then attempt all three activities. The extract includes examples of inversion, modal verbs, subordinating conjunctions, the present, perfect and imperfect tenses, and other structures such as *zu* + infinitive.

Point out to students that when comprehension questions are written in English, they should always be answered in English. Less confident students could tackle just the first one or two parts of the audio text and the related questions, or could work collaboratively with others to cover the whole audio text between them. They may also need to refer to the transcript for support.

Answers:

Part 1
a 14
b His parents grounded him for a few weeks.
c He didn't go to school.

Part 2
d 15
e Kurt wanted to try Ecstasy.
f After six months Kurt and Sonja ran away.

Part 3
g Kurt and Sonja make money by stealing mobile phones or money.
h They find sleeping on the street awful.
i Kurt is afraid that he and Sonja might try heroin one day.

Pages 28–29

Grammar practice

G Health

Using the indefinite article and the accusative case

This is the subsidiary grammar point linked to Spread 1.1, *Gesund essen, gesund leben!* Students will first encounter examples of the indefinite article followed by the accusative in Klaus's text on page 18. They will later need to use forms correctly in productive activities 4a and 4b on page 19.
Students may be referred to this grammar box while going through Klaus's text, before completing the activity on page 28 as homework in preparation for activities 4a and 4b.

1 Underline all the indefinite articles in the accusative case. Take care because not every article is in the accusative!

This reading activity requires students to identify indefinite articles and decide whether they are in the accusative case.

You might wish to discuss with students the difference between the subject and the object of a sentence, giving and eliciting examples, before they start this activity. When discussing the answers afterwards, ask students to explain why the article they've selected is in the accusative, and what the gender is of the noun it relates to.

Answers:

a Ich trinke gern <u>eine</u> Cola, aber ein Orangensaft schmeckt besser.
b In der Pause isst sie <u>ein</u> Käsebrot oder <u>einen</u> Apfel.
c Zu Mittag isst sie <u>einen</u> Hamburger mit Pommes und trinkt <u>ein</u> Glas Limonade.
d Mein Lieblingsessen ist ein halbes Hähnchen mit Kartoffelsalat.
e Zum Abendessen esse ich normalerweise <u>eine</u> Portion Fleisch mit Gemüse.
f Der Junge hat <u>eine</u> Zigarette in der Hand, aber er sieht nicht cool aus.

Using adverbs of frequency

This is the subsidiary grammar point linked to Spread 1.2, *Ich bin in Form!*
Students will encounter examples of adverbs of frequency in the *Gesundheitsquiz* on page 20. They will later need to use them in grammar activity 2 as part of their work on inversion and in productive activities 4a and 4b on page 21. Students may be referred to the subsidiary grammar box and activities at any point during their work on the spread.

2a Translate the following sentences into English.
This reading activity practises understanding of the adverbs of frequency given in the *Grammatik* panel.

Accept any correct variation in wording in students' English translations.
Answers:

1 Now and again I go to the cinema with my friends.
2 My family and I often go bowling because it's fun.
3 I never eat meat because I'm a vegetarian.

2b Now translate these sentences into German. Be careful with the word order!

This writing activity practises writing sentences with adverbs of frequency.

Remind students that the adverb comes after the verb. After discussing the answers, you could encourage students to try creating alternative versions starting with the adverb – remind them to use inversion so that the verb remains as second idea.

Answers:

1 Ich esse selten Käse oder Butter.
2 Wir spielen ab und zu Tischtennis.
3 Ich gehe manchmal am Wochenende schwimmen.

2c Work with a partner: one partner asks the questions on the clipboard and another answers, using full sentences and a different adverb each time. Then swap roles. (Remember to use inversion if you start the sentence with an adverb.)

This speaking activity gives more extended practice of using a range of adverbs of frequency.

Encourage more confident students to vary word order by sometimes starting with the adverb, followed by inversion. The activity could be extended into a survey, and students could create extra questions of their own to ask. They could then write up their findings.

Forming negative phrases using '*nicht*' and '*kein*'

This is the subsidiary grammar point linked to Spread 1.3, *Rauchen ist doch ungesund!*
Students will encounter examples of different negative forms in the opinions on smoking on page 22.
Invite students to identify the different forms in Kirsten, Jörg and Stefan's texts. With more able students, you may wish to elicit explanations as to why one form is used rather than another before referring them to the grammar box and activities on page 29.

3a Write a suitable negative response to each of the following questions. You need to work out whether to use *nicht* or *kein* each time.

This writing activity practises the formation of negative phrases, and requires students to decide if they should use *nicht* or *kein*.

Support less confident students by discussing the correct option for each sentence before they start. Point out that for sentences with *kein*, they will need to check the gender of the noun it relates to, in order to add the correct ending.

Context 1 Lifestyle **27**

Answers:
A Ich esse nicht gern Spinat.
B Ich habe keine Banane.
C Ich rauche nicht.
D Ich trinke keinen Alkohol.
E Ich habe keine Angst vor Krankheiten.
F Ich bin kein Raucher / keine Raucherin / Nichtraucher / Nichtraucherin.

3b Say in German what your friend has / hasn't got in her shopping basket, based on the pictures below.

This speaking activity gives more extended practice of using *ein/kein*.

Again, make sure students check the genders of the nouns involved so that they can add the correct endings to *ein/kein*. You may wish to provide the nouns and genders in advance for less confident students.

Answers:

a Sie hat keine Wurst.
b Sie hat Obst.
c Sie hat einen Salat.
d Sie hat keine Schokolade.
e Sie hat keinen Kuchen.
f Sie hat ein Hähnchen.

> **Using 'man'**
> This is the subsidiary grammar point linked to Spread 1.4, *Alkohol und Drogen brauchen wir nicht!* *Man* is not used extensively in the activities on the spread, but reinforcement of how and when it is used should complement work on talking about drugs and alcohol, and on using modal verbs (particularly *dürfen*). For instance, students may be invited to answer general questions such as *Darf man Drogen nehmen? Ab wann darf man Alkohol trinken?* etc. as part of a class discussion.
>
> *Grammatik*

4a Re-write the following sentences replacing *du* with *man*. You will need to make sure you change the verb ending too!

This writing activity gives practice in applying the correct endings to present tense modal verbs for *man*.

Refer less confident students back to pages 23 and 25, where the present tense forms of modal verbs are explained, and elicit the fact that the *er/sie/es/man* form is the same as the *ich* form, and involves simply dropping the *st* from the *du* form in the original sentences of this activity. After discussing the answers, you could elicit translations of the new sentences to make sure that the meaning of *man* is understood.

Answers:
1 Man soll keine Drogen nehmen.
2 Man muss jeden Tag spazieren gehen.
3 Darf man hier rauchen?
4 In der Schule muss man eine Uniform tragen.
5 Pro Tag soll man fünf Portionen Obst und Gemüse essen.

4b Now translate these sentences into German using *man*.

This writing activity gives more challenging practice of writing sentences using *man* with present tense modal verbs.

Help less confident students to prepare by discussing with them which modal verb should be used for each sentence. Point out that they will need to think about whether to use *nicht* or *kein* in the negative sentences.

Answers:
1 Man soll oft Obst essen.
2 Man darf nicht in Restaurants rauchen.
3 Man muss sich mehr bewegen.
4 In der Schule darf man keine Sportschuhe tragen.
5 Man kann hier nicht schlafen, weil es zu laut ist.

Pages 30–31

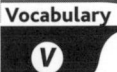

Vocabulary

V Health

kerboodle! • MP3 files for each vocabulary list

The essential vocabulary used within Topic 1, Context 1 is presented on this vocabulary spread.

Here students can learn the key words for the topic area *Health*. You may also want to direct students to the online audio files of these vocabulary lists, so they can hear how the words are pronounced by a native speaker.

Some words are in light grey on the vocabulary spreads in the Student Book. This indicates items that are not included in the GCSE specification vocabulary list, so students do not need to learn these items for Listening and Reading assessment. However, you may wish students to use them in Speaking and Writing Controlled Assessments.

Pages 32–33

1.5 Familie und Freunde – zu Hause

Relationships with family and friends

Subject	Discussing different family situations
G 1	Using the present tense of *haben* and *sein*
G 2	Using *ihr*
	Identifying patterns between German and English

kerboodle!
• Audio file for core reading text
• Audio file and transcript for listening activity 3
• Listening activity and transcript: *Gibt es Probleme zu Hause?*
• Grammar activity: Using the present tense of *haben* and *sein*
• Writing worksheet
• Foundation listening worksheet
• Extension reading worksheet
• Audio file and transcript for foundation listening worksheet

Starter activity

Display a group of four or five family-related German nouns for five seconds for students to memorise, then hide them. All of the words except one should have a link with English. For example, *Mutter, Vater, Bruder, Tante*.

Ask students which one of the words they think has no link with an English word, elicit what the remaining words were, reveal them all again, and discuss the links they can see.

Wie ist es in deiner Familie?

This transcript of an extended interview with two teenagers about their families includes key vocabulary for discussing family situations, examples of present tense forms of *haben* and *sein*, and of words which have links with English.

The reading text is also available online as an audio file.

> 📖 Ask students to read this panel on identifying patterns between German and English, then ask them to find examples of words which they think have links with English in the text for activity 1.
>
> *Strategie*

1 📖 🎧 🌐 In the text find the German for these phrases.

Students read and/or listen to the interview, then find the German for each of the English sentences given. They could then be asked to find other items of key vocabulary from the text. Before starting the activity, refer students to the *Strategie* panel.

Answers:

a Normalerweise essen wir alle zusammen.
b Vor drei Jahren haben sich meine Eltern scheiden lassen.
c Jedes zweite Wochenende verbringe ich bei meiner Mutter in Hamburg.
d Ich fühle mich manchmal einsam.
e Die Leute sagen, dass wir sehr ähnlich sind.
f Ab und zu ist sie ein bisschen eifersüchtig.
g Ich finde sie sehr lieb und immer großzügig.
h Damals waren mein Bruder und ich sehr traurig.

> This panel shows students the present tense forms of the verbs *haben* and *sein*. Point out that these are very useful verbs that students should learn by heart. Make sure weaker students understand the meanings of all of the pronouns listed – they could make up simple sentences of their own to practise these.
> The panel also suggests that students learn how to use *ihr*, referring them to p.46.
>
> *Grammatik*

2 🅖 Read the interview with Jutta and fill in the gaps with the correct form of *haben* or *sein*.

A gap-filling task practising present tense forms of *haben* and *sein* in the context of a young person talking about her family.

Before starting the activity, refer students to the *Grammatik* panel and the *Tipp*. When discussing the answers, ask students to translate the interview and to note any useful words and phrases.

Answers:

a ist	b sind	c habe	d ist
e hat	f ist	g ist	h habe

> Show students a few simple examples of sentences in the perfect tense using *haben* and *sein* to reinforce the point made in this *Tipp*. Stress that a good knowledge of these two key verbs will help to increase their accuracy marks in the Speaking and Writing units.
>
> *Tipp*

3 🎧 *Transcript:*

Paul: Servus, ich heiße Paul und bin fünfzehn Jahre alt. Ich habe drei Brüder, aber keine Schwestern. Wir wohnen bei unseren Eltern in Passau in Süddeutschland. Mein Opa wohnt auch bei uns. Er ist achtundsechzig Jahre alt und ist immer freundlich.

Julia: Guten Tag. Mein Name ist Julia. Mein Haus ist in Magdeburg in Ostdeutschland. In meiner Familie gibt es fünf Personen: meinen Vater, meine zwei Brüder Hannes und Erich, meine ältere Schwester Karin und mich. Karin ist verlobt. Leider ist meine Mutter gestorben, als ich ganz klein war. Mein Vater hat aber nie wieder geheiratet. Deswegen helfen wir alle im Haushalt, zum Beispiel beim Abwaschen, beim Aufräumen, und so weiter.

Michael: Hallo, ich bin der Michael. Ich bin vierzehn und komme aus Seefeld in Österreich. Mein Vater wohnt nicht bei uns, weil meine Eltern geschieden sind. Hier wohne ich zusammen mit meiner Mutter und meinem Stiefvater. Ich habe eine Schwester und einen Halbbruder, der Tobias heißt. Er ist erst sechs Monate alt.

3 🎧 Paul, Julia and Michael are talking about their families. First make notes on each person. Then answer the questions below with the name of the relevant person.

This audio extract consists of three young people talking about their families. It includes useful vocabulary for giving information about family situations, examples of present tense forms of *haben* and *sein*, and words which have links with English.

Students should listen to each person speaking, and make brief notes of key details they can understand. They then answer the comprehension questions, and could listen again to check their answers or to find any missing information.

Answers:

a Michael	b Julia	c Paul	d Michael
e Michael	f Paul	g Julia	h Julia

4 💬 Work in pairs. Using the interviews above as examples, interview your partner about his or her family, before swapping roles. Here are some questions to get you started.

Students interview each other about their families. Sample questions are given, and further ideas can be taken from the interviews in activities 1 and 2. The structure grid gives key vocabulary for possible answers. This could be followed up by writing an email or blog entry about their family.

Plenary activity

Tell students to take the role of a mystery celebrity of their choice, and to write down five or so statements about their family situation (e.g. *ich bin geschieden, ich habe drei Kinder, meine Freundin ist 20 Jahre alt*). They should then read these out, one at a time, to a partner, who has to guess the name of the celebrity as soon as possible. Alternatively, the 'celebrity' could be interviewed by their partner, until enough information has been obtained to guess the identity.

Pages 34–35

1.6 Familie und Freunde – Beziehungen

Relationships with family and friends	
Subject	Describing different relationship scenarios
G 1	Using possessive adjectives
G 2	Using adjectives after nouns and using quantifiers / intensifiers
🔧	Using your knowledge of grammatical categories

kerboodle!
- Audio file for core reading text
- Audio file and transcript for listening activity 3
- Reading activity: *Wie verstehst du dich mit deiner Familie und deinen Freunden?*
- Grammar activity: Using possessive adjectives
- Speaking worksheet
- Extension listening worksheet
- Audio file and transcript for extension listening worksheet (same as for activity 3)

Starter activity

Display five jumbled German sentences relating to families, to recap vocabulary from previous subtopics which will be useful for this one. For example: *trinkt Stiefbruder oft mein Alkohol,* or *fühle ich weil mich Einzelkind einsam bin ich.* Students work individually or in pairs to rearrange the words in the correct order and translate each sentence into English.

Probleme zu Hause

The reading stimulus text consists of statements by three teenagers about their relationships with different members of their families. It includes possessive adjectives and vocabulary for describing people and how well you get on with them.

The reading text is also available online as an audio file.

Strategie

📖 Explain to the class that this strategy of using knowledge of grammatical categories will help them to work out the possible meanings of new words, which could increase their marks in the Reading unit. Make sure that less confident students understand what the three grammatical categories mean. Practise identifying words from each category by asking pupils to find a certain number of nouns, verbs and adjectives in the stimulus reading text.

1 📖 🎧 🌐 Decide if these statements are true (T) or false (F).

Students read and/or listen to the three statements, then read the seven statements about the young people and decide if each is true or false. Refer them to the *Strategie* panel.

Answers:

a F	b T	c T	d T
e T	f F	g F	

Grammatik

This panel on possessive adjectives shows students the basic words for 'my', 'your', 'his' etc, then explains that they often need an ending, depending on the gender and case of the noun which follows. Endings for the nominative and accusative cases are shown, and students are referred to pages 28 and 39 for a reminder about cases and gender. Encourage students to learn the meanings of these possessive adjectives – you could test them, or practise them in class.
The panel also suggests that students learn how to use adjectives after nouns, referring them to p.46.

Tipp

This *Tipp* reminds students that the possessive adjective must agree with the person or thing it refers to, and gives examples. Use vocabulary from this subtopic to practise this with further examples. Point out to students that they can increase their accuracy mark in the Writing and Speaking units with correct agreements.

2 G Copy out the sentences and fill in the missing possessive adjective.

This activity practises agreement of possessive adjectives.

Before starting the activity, refer students to the *Grammatik* and *Tipp* panels. Remind them to check the gender of the person/noun that the possessive adjective must agree with, before selecting which is the correct version from those provided. Afterwards, elicit English translations of the sentences to ensure the meanings of the possessive adjectives are clear.

Answers:

a <u>Mein</u> bester Freund heißt Felix.
b <u>Meine</u> Familie wohnt in Köln.
c Ich treffe <u>seinen</u> Bruder in der Stadtmitte.
d Am Wochenende gehen <u>ihre</u> Freunde einkaufen.
e Karl und ich besuchen am Samstag <u>unseren</u> Onkel.
f Beate muss <u>ihre</u> Hausaufgaben machen.
g Hat <u>dein</u> Vater ein deutsches Auto?

3 🎧 Transcript:

Guten Tag. Ich heiße Matthias, ich bin sechzehn Jahre alt und ich komme aus Hannover. Meine Familie ist ziemlich groß: es gibt meinen Stiefvater, meine Mutter, meinen Bruder, meine Schwester und mich. Ich bin der Jüngste. Leider arbeitet mein Stiefvater nicht. Also muss meine Mutter dreimal pro Woche in einem Supermarkt arbeiten, aber das bringt nicht viel Geld. Ich verstehe mich ziemlich gut mit meinem Bruder, aber er bringt seine Freunde oft nach Hause und sie sind zu laut. Das ärgert mich, wenn ich fernsehen oder Musik hören will. Einmal im Monat besuchen wir unseren Vater in Augsburg, aber das gefällt uns nicht. Er hat jetzt eine neue Familie und deswegen hat er nicht so viel Zeit für uns. Das ist wirklich schade.

Hallo. Mein Name ist Karla. Ich bin vierzehn Jahre alt und wohne in Zürich in der Schweiz. Meine beste Freundin heißt Antonia und wir verstehen uns sehr gut. Ich kenne sie seit drei Jahren und wir sind in derselben Schulklasse. Antonia ist immer lustig, freundlich und treu. Das ist mir so wichtig. Wir sehen uns jeden Tag und wir haben dieselben Interessen: Schwimmen, Musik und Kino. Jeden Samstag gehen wir in die Stadtmitte und kaufen Kleidung oder Makeup. Antonia wohnt in der Nähe von mir und ab und zu dürfen wir eine Übernachtungsparty haben. Das macht so viel Spaß!

3 🎧 Read the statements below then listen to Matthias and Karla describing relationships important to them. Who says what? Write down the name of the person concerned.

In the audio extract, a teenage boy and girl each describe relationships which are important to them – family or friends. The extract includes words for describing feelings and how well you get on with someone, and examples of possessive adjectives in the nominative and accusative cases.

After reading and making sure they understand the eight short statements on the page, students listen to the extract and decide who says each of them.

Answers:

a	Matthias	b	Karla	c	Matthias	d	Matthias
e	Matthias	f	Karla	g	Matthias	h	Karla

4 ✏️ Using the language support box, write an article about a fictional family (e.g. from a book or TV soap) and its problems.

Students think of a family from a fictional setting, or create one from scratch, and write about them using the language support box given, and other language from the texts and audio extract in this subtopic. Remind them to make sure they include all of the required points. Refer them back to the *Grammatik* and *Tipp* panels for use of third person possessive adjectives.

Plenary activity

Students could read out their written work, or an extract from it, to the class or to groups of other students. Encourage the audience to give positive feedback in German afterwards. If families from TV soaps or books have been used, the family name could be left out and the audience guesses which family it is.

Pages 36–37

1.7 Zukunftspläne – Heiraten, ja oder nein?

Future plans regarding: marriage / partnership

Subject	Talking about future relationships
G 1	Using the present tense to talk about the future
G 2	Using adverbial phrases of time
🔊	Asking for help when unsure

kerboodle!
- Audio file for core reading text
- Audio file and transcript for listening activity 3
- Listening activity and transcript: *Heiraten ist wichtig, oder?*
- Grammar activity: Using the present tense to talk about the future
- Writing worksheet
- Extension reading worksheet

Starter activity

Display five or six pairs of words which are related to each other, listed in random order. Students must find the pairs. Use words relating to this topic, perhaps from the stimulus reading text. For example: *verheiratet / ledig, früh / spät, Verlobungsring / Hochzeit, Karriere / Geschäftsfrau, streiten / unglücklich.*

Willst du heiraten oder ledig bleiben?

Four teenagers say whether they want to marry or stay unmarried. Their statements include vocabulary relating to future relationships and plans.

The reading text is also available online as an audio file.

1 📖 🎧 Find the following sentences in the German text above.

After reading and/or listening to the text, students look for the German equivalents of the English sentences given.

Answers:

a Ich möchte auf jeden Fall Single bleiben.
b Meine Karriere ist sehr wichtig für mich.
c Für mich ist Familie das Wichtigste.
d Meine Eltern streiten sich so viel und sind immer unglücklich.
e Ich möchte mit einer Freundin zusammenleben.
f Ich muss ein schnelles Auto und eine Luxuswohnung haben.
g Ich möchte eine traditionelle Hochzeit.
h Deswegen will ich viel Spaß in meinem Leben.

Context 1 Lifestyle   31

> **Grammatik**
> This panel shows students how to use the present tense, with a future indicator, to talk about the future. Point out that this is a useful and simple way of introducing a different tense into their written and spoken German. Elicit some examples of future indicator phrases. The panel also suggests that students learn about adverbial phrases of time, referring them to p.46.

> **Strategie**
> Encourage students to use this strategy of asking for help when unsure, when working in class, including during speaking activity 4. You might want to take the opportunity to give them additional useful phrases for seeking help or clarification (*Wie bitte? / Langsamer bitte / ich verstehe nicht* etc).

2 **G** Unscramble the statements about the future so that they make sense. Start with the underlined word. Take care with the word order.

Students re-write the jumbled sentences, starting with the underlined word. The resulting sentences provide examples of present tense sentences about the future. After completing the activity, ask students to translate the sentences into English, then refer to the *Grammatik* panel. Ask them to identify the future indicator in each of the sentences.

Answers:

a Hoffentlich habe ich einen guten Beruf.
b Ich heirate in 10 Jahren.
c Im September studiere ich Mathe und Englisch. / Im September studiere ich Englisch und Mathe.
d Heute Abend treffen wir unsere Freunde.
e Im Sommer besucht sie ihre Freundin.
f Heute Nachmittag haben sie Biologie und Sport. / Heute Nachmittag haben sie Sport und Biologie.
g Nächsten Samstag machen meine Schwestern und ich eine Radtour.

3 🎧 *Transcript:*

1 Guten Tag. Ich bin die Petra. Ich finde Heiraten eine gute Idee, aber ich will keine Kinder haben, weil ich sie nicht mag.
2 Hallo. Ich heiße Lars. Ich will mit dreißig Jahren heiraten. Vorher will ich aber in Amerika arbeiten.
3 Mein Name ist Sophie. Ich möchte ein schönes weißes Kleid tragen und in einer Kirche heiraten. Später will ich einen Sohn und zwei Töchter haben.
4 Tag. Ich heiße Achim. Ich möchte ledig bleiben, weil ich abends mit meinen Freunden ausgehen will. Ich will nicht jeden Abend mit meiner Frau verbringen.
5 Hallo. Ich bin die Elke. Mein Freund und ich wollen zuerst zusammenleben und erst später heiraten. Meine Eltern sind seit 2 oder 3 Jahren geschieden. Das will ich nicht für uns.

In the audio extract, five young people say whether they want to get married or have children.

3 🎧 Listen to five young people talking about whether they want to get married and have children. Decide whether the sentences are true (T) or false (F).

Students listen to the extract and decide whether the sentences on the page are true or false. Remind weaker students that *will* is part of the verb *wollen* and should not be confused with the future tense.

Answers:

| a T | b T | c F | d T | e T |
| f F | g T | h F | i F | j T |

4 💬 ✏️ 🌐 Class survey. Using the questions below, find out people's views on marriage. Use the table to help you give your own responses. When you have completed the survey, you can write up people's different viewpoints (but remember to use the third person!).

Make sure less confident students understand the suggested answers in the language structure box, and point out the difference in word order after *weil* and *da*, compared with *denn*. Refer to the *Tipp* to assist with pronunciation of *ei* and *ie*.

> **Tipp**
> Practise pronunciation of words containing *ei* or *ie* by displaying several relevant German words and asking the class to say them.

Plenary activity

Language trawl. Consolidate language of this subtopic by asking students to tell you the German for various words, parts of sentences or whole sentences from the texts and activities. More confident students could try to respond without referring to their book.

Pages 38–39

1.8 Gleichheit für Männer und Frauen?

Social issues and equality

Subject	Learning about gender issues
G 1	Understanding nouns and gender
G 2	Using the correct word for 'it'
🌐	Matching German and English phrases

kerboodle!
- Audio file for core reading text
- Audio file and transcript for listening activity 3
- Reading activity: *Das ist keine Stelle für dich, oder?*
- Grammar activity: Understanding nouns and gender
- Writing worksheet
- Extension listening worksheet
- Audio file and transcript for extension listening worksheet (same as for activity 3)

Starter activity

Display a list of German words for jobs – a mixture of male and female versions. These should be familiar from previous work in KS3, and could include examples from the texts in this subtopic. For example: *Journalistin, Feherwehrmann, Hausfrau, Tänzer, Sekretärin, Bauer,*

Arzt. Students must decide if each is the male or female version, and convert each to the opposite gender.

Das ist keine Stelle für dich, oder?

In the reading stimulus text, four young people tell of an unusual (for their gender) job which one of their family members does. It includes language for jobs, associated tasks, reactions and some examples of nouns with endings that indicate their gender.

The reading text is also available online as an audio file.

> **Tipp**
> Elicit examples of male and female versions of German job words. Students may be interested to discuss whether we use gender-based versions of these less in English than we used to, and why that might be.

1a 📖 🎧 Read the text above and match the photos to the correct paragraphs.

Students read and/or listen to the text, and decide which person is shown in each of the four photographs.

Answers:

a 2   b 3   c 1   d 4

> **Strategie**
> 📖 Explain to students the strategy of matching German and English phrases. Knowing that equivalent phrases may be of differing lengths in German and English can help students to identify the correct phrase in activities like 1b, and therefore increase their marks in the Reading unit. A simple example would be *Er ist Sekretär* (unlike the English, there is no article before the job word in German).

1b 📖 🎧 🌐 Read the text again and find the German for these phrases.

Refer students to the *Strategie* panel for help with matching German and English phrases.

Answers:

a ein[en] gut bezalht[en] Beruf
b manchmal gefährlich
c organisiert Geschäftsreisen
d den ganzen Tag
e am Anfang
f Einige Leute finden das komisch.

> **Grammatik**
> This panel on understanding nouns and gender shows students how they can often work out the gender of a noun from its ending, or the letters *ge* at the start. Usual endings for each gender are shown. Encourage students to learn these. Practise the technique, by asking them to think of examples of words they already know with some of the endings, to predict the gender, then to check by looking it up.
> The panel also suggests that students learn how to use the correct word for 'it', referring them to p.47.

2 **G** Add the correct definite article for each of these nouns.

This activity requires students to work out the genders of nouns, using their endings or starts as indicators.

Before starting the activity, refer to the *Grammatik* panel.

Answers:

a die Limonade   b der Körper
c die Gesundheit   d das Gehirn
e die Meinung   f das Auge
g das Lineal   h der Teppich
i der Lehrer   j die Freundin

3 🎧 *Transcript:*

Interviewer: Herzlich willkommen im Studio, Frau Braun.
Frau Braun: Danke schön.
Interviewer: Wie ist es heute mit der Diskriminierung zwischen Männern und Frauen?
Frau Braun: Sowohl in England als auch in Deutschland ist die Diskriminierung zwischen Männern und Frauen illegal. In Deutschland sind mehr Männer als Frauen arbeitslos!
Interviewer: Warum?
Frau Braun: Weil Frauen die Schule mit besseren Qualifikationen verlassen. Aber sie verdienen etwa dreißig Prozent weniger als Männer.
Interviewer: Gibt es dieses Problem nur in England und Deutschland?
Frau Braun: Nein, Das ist ein internationales Problem. Männer und Frauen sollen den gleichen Lohn für die gleiche Arbeit bekommen, aber das passiert nicht immer.
Interviewer: Wieso?
Frau Braun: Frauen müssen oft zu Hause bleiben und auf die Kinder aufpassen. Auch haben Frauen mehr Teilzeitjobs und es gibt mehr Männer als Manager. Männer haben die besseren Stellen und die meisten Frauen sind Angestellte.
Interviewer: Und wie finden Sie diese Situation?
Frau Braun: Diese Diskriminierung ist ungerecht und muss sofort enden.

3 🎧 Listen to the radio report about gender discrimination in Germany and the UK. Complete the gaps in the sentences, using the words on the right.

The audio extract consists of an interview about gender discrimination in the workplace in Germany and England, and internationally. It includes examples of nouns with endings which indicate their gender, and useful vocabulary for talking about discrimination.

Students listen to the extract and fill the gaps in the sentences given, using words from the right of the page. Point out that they might not hear exactly the same word order in the audio text. More confident students could then be asked whether they see evidence of the discrimination discussed in their own lives (e.g. more women with part-time jobs, more men as managers).

Answers:

a illegal   b arbeitslos   c besseren   d weniger
e müssen   f mehr   g enden

Context 1 Lifestyle 33

4 Study the Austrian poster about unequal pay and discuss it in pairs. Use the questions and table below to help you.

Make sure that less confident students understand the content of the poster, and the language in the questions and table, before starting the activity. They might prefer to prepare their answer to each question before the discussion. After discussing the poster, students write up their answers, with opinions.

Plenary activity

To practise further the language used for discussing and expressing opinions on gender issues in activity 4, display a series of brief and controversial statements relating to gender issues or stereotypes: students must agree or disagree and say why (using *da* or *weil*).

Pages 40–41

1.9 Ethnische Probleme

Social issues and equality

Subject	Discussing racial issues
G 1	Using coordinating conjunctions
G 2	Using adverbs of place
	Speaking and writing creatively

kerboodle!
- Audio file for core reading text
- Audio file and transcript for listening activity 3
- Listening activity and transcript: *Hier wollen wir keinen Rassismus!*
- Grammar activity: Using coordinating conjunctions
- Speaking worksheet
- Extension reading worksheet

Starter activity

Display a list of eight to ten languages in German, to include *Deutsch, Englisch, Türkisch*. Students work individually or in pairs within a time limit, and write down the/a country in German where each language is usually spoken – allow access to dictionaries for research if necessary. Award a point for each correct answer when discussing afterwards.

Hat Ahmet keine Chance?

The reading stimulus text is an interview with a boy of Turkish origin who comes from Berlin. It includes vocabulary for social issues and examples of coordinating conjunctions. The reading text is also available online as an audio file.

1 Read the interview with Ahmet and answer these multiple-choice questions.

Students read and/or listen to the interview and answer the multiple-choice questions. You might wish to explain to the class the history of many Turkish people originally coming to Germany as *Gastarbeiter*.

Answers:

a 1   b 2   c 3   d 1   e 2   f 3

> **Grammatik**
> This panel explains how to use coordinating conjunctions, and points out that they are easy to use as no change to word order is required. The most common of these: *und, aber* and *denn,* are shown as examples. Students could search for sentences which include a coordinating conjunction in the text in activity 1.
> The panel also suggests that students revise how to use adverbs of place, referring them to p.47.

2a Join the two sentences together to form one new sentence by using the conjunction given in brackets.

This activity practises use of coordinating conjunctions. Before starting the activity, refer students to the *Grammatik* panel.

Answers:

a Ich kenne ein paar Leute in der Schule, <u>aber</u> wir sind keine richtigen Freunde.
b Dort ist es nicht so schön, <u>denn</u> es gibt Probleme mit Rassismus.
c Wir besuchen eine Schule am Stadtrand <u>und</u> sie ist nicht sehr groß.
d Meine Eltern bleiben meistens zu Hause, <u>denn</u> sie haben Probleme mit der Sprache.

2b Choose your own coordinating conjunctions for these sentences.

In this activity, students select an appropriate coordinating conjunction to join each pair of sentences given.

Again, they should refer to the *Grammatik* panel.

Answers:

a Ich möchte auf die Uni gehen, aber ich bin nicht intelligent genug.
b Meine Eltern kommen aus der Türkei und / , aber sie wohnen seit 20 Jahren hier.

> **Tipp**
> Use example sentences to reinforce the need for inversion where an adverbial phrase follows *und*.

3 *Transcript:*

Interviewer: Guten Tag, liebe Zuhörer. Wir haben heute im Studio die Schuldirektorin Frau Ilse König von der Hugo-Schmidt-Hauptschule. Herzlich willkommen! Die Schule hat den Titel „Schule ohne Rassismus". Können Sie das bitte erklären?

Frau König: Ja, gerne. Es ist ein Projekt von und für Schüler und Schülerinnen, die gegen alle Formen von Diskriminierung, insbesondere Rassismus, sind. Sie wollen eine Gesellschaft ohne Gewalttätigkeit haben. Hautfarbe und Religion sind für sie nicht wichtig.

Interviewer:	Seit wann existiert das Projekt?
Frau König:	Das Projekt, das „Schulen ohne Rassismus" heißt, existiert seit 1995 in Deutschland. Es hat 1988 in Belgien begonnen. In Deutschland gibt es jetzt mehr als 400 Schulen mit diesem Titel.
Interviewer:	Und seit wann in ihre Schule?
Frau König:	Seit zwei Jahren.
Interviewer:	Wie bekommt eine Schule diesen Titel?
Frau König:	Siebzig Prozent der Schüler und Lehrer müssen zeigen, dass sie total gegen Diskriminierung sind.
Interviewer:	Und was für Aktivitäten gibt es in der Schule?
Frau König:	Die Schüler organisieren Filme, Diskussionen und Konzerte. Auch treffen sie Schüler von anderen Schulen. Letzte Woche hatten wir sogar ein Sportfest für alle Familien in der Gegend. Es war ganz toll.
Interviewer:	Und ist das Projekt erfolgreich?
Frau König:	Ja, bestimmt. Es gibt jetzt weniger Angst. Ausländer, Einwanderer und Deutsche beginnen, in Harmonie zusammen zu leben. Das freut mich sehr.
Interviewer:	Frau König, recht vielen Dank.
Frau König:	Bitte schön.

3 🎧 Listen to this radio report about a project in Germany called "Schule ohne Rassismus – Schule mit Courage". Then match the sentence beginnings and endings.

The audio extract consists of an interview about an anti-racism project in German schools. It includes useful vocabulary relating to this subtopic.

After listening to the interview, students match the sentence halves according to what they have heard. Alternatively, they could try matching them first, based on logic and grammar, and then listen to check. Make sure the meanings of the final sentences are clear to all.

Answers:

a 5	b 1	c 7	d 8
e 2	f 3	g 6	h 4

> ✏️ 💬 Help students with the strategy for writing and speaking creatively by pointing out that making things up, or finding a different way of phrasing something, can enable them to say or write far more in German, by showing off as many words and structures that they know as possible. *Strategie*

4 ✏️ 🌐 Imagine that you have just moved to a new country. Write an email to friends and / or family in your home country describing the issues you now face living abroad. Use the table below to help you.

Before starting the activity, refer students to the *Strategie* panel and with less confident students, collect possible ideas for inclusion together. Encourage them to not only make use of the table to help them, but also to find ideas in the text for activity 1.

Plenary activity

Students work in pairs, and using ideas from their written work in activity 4 (but not simply reading it out), each tries to speak for 30 seconds in the role of a young person who has just moved to a new country. Partners time them and offer prompts and positive feedback in German. With more confident learners, the time could be extended.

Pages 42–43

1.10 Armut

Social issues and equality

Subject	Talking about poverty
G 1	Using subordinating conjunctions
G 2	Using *um ... zu ...*
🎧	Identifying compound nouns

kerboodle!
- Audio file for core reading text
- Audio file and transcript for listening activity 3
- Reading activity: *Ist Geld wichtig, um glücklich zu sein?*
- Grammar activity: Using subordinating conjunctions
- Writing worksheet
- Extension listening worksheet
- Audio file and transcript for extension listening worksheet (same as for activity 3)
- Foundation reading worksheet

Starter activity

Write the title of this subtopic, *Armut*, on the board, at the centre of an as yet empty spider chart or similar. Elicit or give the meaning, and give the class two minutes to jot down in their own draft spider charts any German words and phrases they can think of associated with poverty (these can be simple, such as *kein Geld, keine Arbeit, krank*). Then collate their answers on the 'master chart' on the board.

Zwei junge Leute, zwei verschiedene Lebensstile

In the reading stimulus text, two young people, one very wealthy and privileged and the other deprived and homeless, describe their lifestyles. The text includes examples of subordinating conjunctions and compound nouns.

The reading text is also available online as an audio file.

> 📖 Advice on identifying compound nouns. Ask students to find examples of compound nouns in the text. Write these on the board, and discuss the meaning of each part, and the whole, with the class. Encourage them to feel confident about working out the meanings of long German words. *Strategie*

Context 1 Lifestyle 35

1 📖 🎧 🌐 Read the article above and decide if the following sentences are true (T) or false (F).

Before reading and/or listening to the text, you could ask the class to look at the title and pictures, and to predict what the two different lifestyles depicted are. After reading about the two young people, students decide if the sentences given are true or false. Refer them to the *Strategie* panel.

Answers:

| a F | b T | c F | d F |
| e F | f F | g T | h T |

> **Grammatik**
> This panel explains how to use subordinating conjunctions, with the verb going to the end of the sentence. The most common of these: *weil, wenn, obwohl, dass* and *da* are shown as examples. Students could make up a simple sentence of their own to demonstrate each one, and could search for sentences which include a subordinating conjunction in the text in activity 1.
> The panel also suggests that students learn how to use *um … zu …*, referring them to p.47.

2a Ⓖ Join the sentences together to form one new sentence by using the subordinating conjunction given in brackets.

This activity practises joining two sentences with a subordinating conjunction, sending the verb to the end of the sentence.
Before starting the activity, refer students to the *Grammatik* panel.

Answers:

a Nachts kann ich nicht gut schlafen, weil ich Angst habe.
b Meine Freunde und ich gehen ins Kino, wenn wir genug Geld haben.
c Ich kaufe ein neues Handy, obwohl es sehr teuer ist.
d Meine Schwester geht sehr gern schwimmen, wenn sie gestresst ist.
e Ich darf nicht ausgehen, da ich zu viele Hausaufgaben habe.
f Sie arbeitet oft ehrenamtlich, obwohl sie sehr viel zu tun hat.

2b Ⓖ Once your teacher has checked your answers, re-write the sentences starting with the subordinate clause.

In this activity, the technique of starting a sentence with a subordinate clause is practised.
Refer students to the *Tipp*. They then re-combine the pairs of sentences from 2a, starting with the subordinate clause and with inversion after the comma.

Answers:

a Weil ich Angst habe, kann ich nachts nicht gut schlafen.
b Wenn wir genug Geld haben, gehen meine Freunde und ich ins Kino.
c Obwohl es sehr teuer ich, kaufe ich ein neues Handy.
d Wenn sie gestresst ist, geht meine Schwester sehr gern schwimmen.
e Da ich zu viele Hausaufgaben habe, darf ich nicht ausgehen.
f Obwohl sie sehr viel zu tun hat, arbeitet sie oft ehrenamtlich.

> **Tipp**
> Demonstrate starting sentences with a subordinate clause with a few examples, including the example sentence from activity 2b. Ask students what they think the difference is in terms of emphasis between the two different versions. Point out that demonstrating both types of structure can increase their range and accuracy marks in the Writing and Speaking units.

3 🎧 *Transcript:*

Interviewer: Hallo, Renate. Was machst du für die Obdachlosen?
Renate: Meine Freunde und ich kochen einmal in der Woche für sie. Die Lebensmittel kommen von Supermärkten und privaten Spenden.
Interviewer: Und wie findest du das?
Renate: Es macht sehr viel Spaß. Wir haben so viele Bedürftige in der Gesellschaft und wir können ihnen helfen.
Interviewer: Und Benjamin, wie hilfst du?
Benjamin: Meine Schule organisiert dreimal pro Monat eine Wohltätigkeitsveranstaltung. Meine Mitschüler und ich helfen ehrenamtlich mit – wir verkaufen Kuchen.
Interviewer: Warum macht ihr das?
Benjamin: Es ist wichtig, anderen Leuten zu helfen. Obwohl wir nur ein bisschen Geld bekommen, können wir es für die Obdachlosen spenden.
Interviewer: Und zuletzt, Bettina?
Bettina: Aufstehen, Duschen, Frühstücken – das ist Routine für die meisten Leute, aber für obdachlose Menschen ist das Luxus. Alle zwei Wochen kommen die zu uns in die Schule.
Interviewer: Und was passiert?
Bettina: Es gibt ein großes Frühstücksbüffet und sie können duschen und sich frisch einkleiden. Auch ein Friseur ist dabei.
Interviewer: Also. Danke schön.

Pages 44–45

3a 🎧 Listen to these three young people being interviewed about their voluntary work for the homeless. Match these words and phrases to the English translations.

The audio extract consists of an interview with three young people, each of whom talks about their voluntary work with the homeless. It includes useful vocabulary relating to homelessness, compound nouns, and an example of a sentence starting with a subordinate clause. Students listen to the interview and match key vocabulary items from it with the correct English meaning. Remind the class that German phrases do not always contain the same number of words as their English equivalents, and to look for clues such as capital letters indicating nouns.

Answers:

| a 4 | b 8 | c 2 | d 5 |
| e 7 | f 3 | g 1 | h 6 |

3b 🎧 Now write down what voluntary work each person does. Give any extra details that you pick up.

Students now listen in greater detail and make notes about the voluntary work each person does, in English. Encourage more confident students to write as many details as they can.

Answers:

Renate – cooks for homeless people once a week. Extra details: cooks with a friend, obtains food from supermarkets and private donations, finds it fun.

Benjamin – takes part in charity events at school three times a month. Extra details: sells cakes, money goes to homeless people.

Bettina – homeless people come to her school. Extra details: happens every two weeks, there's a breakfast buffet, showers, fresh clothes and a hairdresser.

4a ✏️ Imagine that you are either very rich or very poor. Write about your lifestyle – *Ein Tag in meinem Leben*.

Encourage students to include subordinating conjunctions, and remind them to be creative in this task – making up information and details in order to use more German. As well as the language structure box, they can look for ideas in the text for activity 1.

4b 💬 Use what you have written to give a presentation.

Students could give their presentation to a partner, to a small group, or to the whole class. Rather than them simply reading out their written work, give time for preparation and writing of brief prompt notes. Encourage the audience to give supportive feedback in German.

Plenary activity

Pronunciation practice: use some of the compound nouns from the reading and listening texts in this subtopic, or particular words which students have had difficulty pronouncing in their presentations. Display each one and demonstrate correct pronunciation, then students repeat in pairs and correct each other.

Reading and listening
📖🎧 Relationships and choices

Zwei Brüder, zwei verschiedene Meinungen!

The reading stimulus text consists of emails written by two brothers who have chosen very different lifestyles and don't get on well together. The text includes examples of coordinating and subordinating conjunctions, possessive adjectives and compound nouns.

All students should be able to attempt activity 1a. Activity 1b involves a deeper understanding of the text's content and is more challenging. After they have finished, refer students to the *Grammatik* panel. Then ask more confident students to pick out additional useful words and phrases from the text and note them down for use in their own work.

The reading text is also available online as an audio file.

1a 📖🎧 Read the blog entries and answer the questions below, giving the name of the correct person each time.

Answers:

| a Petru | b Andrei | c Andrei |
| d Petru | e Andrei | f Andrei |

1b 📖🎧 Read the blogs again and answer the following questions in English.

Answers:

a Their father is a head of a company and their mother has a boutique in the town centre.
b Andrei works with homeless people next to the bus station every weekend.
c Petru doesn't need to work because his parents are rich and generous.
d Eventually Petru wants to marry a rich woman who will look after him.
e Petru thinks Andrei is boring and needs to have more fun.
f Andrei thinks the family are lucky to have money and a nice lifestyle, and that they mustn't forget this.

> **Grammatik**
> This panel asks students to find examples of coordinating and subordinating conjunctions in the text, and refers them back to pages 41 and 43 where these grammar points were explained. Elicit and discuss some of the examples found, taking the opportunity to recap these two types of conjunction, and word order after them, with less confident students.

2a 🎧 *Transcript:*
a In der Zukunft will ich heiraten, aber keine Kinder haben.
b Ich habe keine Wohnung und muss in einem Park schlafen.
c Meine Schwester arbeitet seit sechs Jahren als Feuerwehrfrau.
d Meine Oma wohnt bei uns. Sie findet es manchmal schwer, weil sie im Rollstuhl ist.

Context 1 Lifestyle 37

2a 🎧 Listen to these people talking about their families or life problems, before selecting the correct picture for each question.

The audio extract consists of four short statements by young people relating to their families or life problems. It includes examples of coordinating and subordinating conjunctions and is accessible for less confident students. After listening to the extract and choosing the correct picture to represent each statement, students could listen again and be asked to pick out particular language items, for example specific modal verbs and conjunctions.

Answers:

a 2   b 2   c 3   d 2

2b 🎧 *Transcript:*

Part 1
Hallo. Ich heiße Anna und wohne zusammen mit meiner Mutter, meinem Stiefvater und meinem Stiefbruder in Nürnberg in Deutschland. Meine Eltern haben sich vor vier Jahren scheiden lassen. Jetzt wohnt mein Vater bei seiner Freundin im Ausland. Deshalb sehe ich ihn selten.

Part 2
Ich komme ziemlich gut mit meinem Stiefvater aus, obwohl er manchmal streng ist, besonders wenn ich meine Musik zu laut spiele. Am Wochenende gehen wir aber normalerweise kegeln. Das Wichtigste ist, meine Mutter ist mit ihm glücklich.

Part 3
Leider verstehe ich mich nicht sehr gut mit meinem Stiefbruder Günther. Er ist siebzehn, also zwei Jahre älter als ich, aber er bekommt viel mehr Taschengeld als ich, was ich sehr unfair finde. Manchmal kommt er mitten in der Nacht betrunken nach Hause, aber mein Vater lacht nur darüber und sagt absolut nichts. Ich muss jeden Abend zu Hause sitzen und für die Schule lernen!

2b 🎧 Listen to Anna talking about her family and answer the questions below.

This audio extract contains longer and more complex sentences to challenge more confident students. Most should listen to it one section at a time, and complete the corresponding activity, but the most able could listen to the whole extract and then attempt all three activities. The extract includes examples of coordinating and subordinating conjunctions, the present, and perfect tenses, and a range of other structures.

Less confident students could tackle just the first one or two parts of the audio text, and the related questions, or could work collaboratively with others to cover the whole audio text between them. They may also need to refer to the transcript for support.

Answers:

Part 1
a Anna's parents divorced four years ago.
b Her father lives abroad.

Part 2
c Anna gets on quite well with her stepfather, although he's sometimes strict.
d Anna feels the important thing is that her mother's happy with her stepfather.

Part 3
e 15
f He laughs about it and doesn't say anything.

Pages 46–47

Grammar practice

G **Relationships and choices**

Using *ihr*

This is the subsidiary grammar point linked to Spread 1.5, *Familie und Freunde – zu Hause!*
Students will encounter examples of *ihr* in Thomas's interview on page 32, and in Jutta's interview on page 33.
Students may be referred to this grammar box while going through Thomas's text. Elicit the meaning from them. The activities on page 46 need not be used just when working through Spread 1.5, but at any point when revision of pronouns for 'you' seems appropriate.

1a ✏️ Complete the following questions using the correct word for 'you' (*du*, *Sie* or *ihr*) and the appropriate form of the verb given in brackets.

This writing activity practises distinguishing between the use of *du*, *Sie* and *ihr* and applying the correct verb ending for each.

Make sure that less confident students understand the difference between the three forms of 'you' before starting the activity, and that they realise how to find clues in the sentences from the names given. Explain that if someone is referred to by their surname, *Sie* should be used. You may also need to revise the relevant verb endings with them.

Answers:

a <u>Geht ihr</u> heute schwimmen, Peter und Ute?
b Was <u>macht ihr</u>, Kinder?
c <u>Hast du</u> einen Bruder, Lisa?
d Frau Bachmann, <u>kommen Sie</u> aus Österreich oder aus der Schweiz?
e Marion und Klaus, <u>habt ihr</u> eine Stiefschwester?
f <u>Wohnst du</u> in Nürnberg, Charlotte?

1b 💬 Work in groups of three or four. One person must ask the others a question using *ihr*. The others give answers, then swap roles.

This speaking activity gives more extended practice of using *ihr* in questions.

Students could be asked to prepare some questions before starting this activity.

Adjectives after nouns, Quantifiers / intensifiers

'Adjectives after nouns' is the subsidiary grammar point linked to Spread 1.6, *Familie und Freunde – Beziehungen*. Students encounter several examples of adjectives used after nouns in Jasmin, Lutz and Natascha's texts on page 34. They will later need to use different adjectives to talk about families for productive activity 4. Highlight the different adjectives in the texts on page 34 – *eifersüchtig, eingebildet, sympathisch* etc. – and invite students to describe their role before referring them to this grammar point.

'Quantifiers / intensifiers' is the second subsidiary grammar point linked to Spread 1.6, *Familie und Freunde – Beziehungen*.

Students encounter examples of quantifiers / intensifiers in Jasmin, Lutz and Natascha's texts on page 34. More able students should be encouraged to use them in their productive work for activity 4. Highlight the different intensifiers / quantifiers in the texts on page 34 – *sehr, so* – and invite students to describe their role before referring them to this grammar point. You may also wish to point out that they are a subset of adverbs such as *gut, manchmal* etc. which also appear in the text (although if some students find the terminology confusing, this could be avoided in order to concentrate on reinforcing the vocabulary itself).

2 📖 Read the following sentences and note down all the adjectives and quantifiers / intensifiers. Write 'A' or 'Q' above each one.

This reading activity practises identifying adjectives and quantifiers / intensifiers.

Make sure all students are clear about what these are before starting the activity.

Answers:

a eifersüchtig = A, besonders = Q, freundlich = A
b ziemlich = Q, groß = A, modern = A
c ganz = Q, toll = A
d laut = A, sehr = Q, süß = A
e schnell = A, so = Q, teuer = A
f blond = A, lang = A, ziemlich = Q, lockig = A

Adverbial phrases of time

'Adverbial phrases of time' is the subsidiary grammar point linked to Spread 1.7, *Zukunftspläne – Heiraten, ja oder nein?*

This grammar point complements the grammar work on the main spread, where students practise using the present tense to talk about the future (activity 2, pages 36–37). However, the activity on page 46 will also make students aware that adverbial phrases of time are not just used to talk about future events, but also general occurrences (you may also wish to mention some examples where the past is referred to e.g. *letztes Jahr*).

3 📖 Note down the adverbial time phrase in the following sentences. Then translate the sentences into English.

This reading activity practises identifying adverbial time phrases.

Explain to students that the phrases they are noting down are useful to learn, so that they can include them in their own German. When discussing their translations, ask students to identify which time phrases refer to the future.

Answers:

a In fünf Jahren – I'm getting married in five years' time.
b nächste Woche – My father is going to France next week.
c Im Winter – In winter I like to go skiing.
d Diesen Monat – She has exams this month.

Using the word 'it'

Using the word 'it' is the subsidiary grammar point linked to Spread 1.8, *Gleichheit für Männer und Frauen?* On Spread 1.8 students revise work on nouns and gender in German. Work on how to say 'it' reinforces this by tackling a common stumbling block, namely the fact that words for 'he' and 'she' can also mean 'it' in German. Students may be referred to this grammar box after completing activity 2 on page 39. You may also invite them to look at each of the nouns in activity 2 again and in each case identify how 'it' would be translated.

4 ✏️ Complete the following sentences using the correct word for 'it'.

This writing activity practises selecting the correct word for 'it', depending on the gender of the noun.

Remind students to follow the advice in the *Grammatik* panel on page 38 to help them work out genders of nouns, and to check any that they are unsure of.

Answers:

a Ich esse einen Hamburger. <u>Er</u> ist ungesund, aber schmeckt sehr gut.
b Meine Familie wohnt in einer Wohnung. <u>Sie</u> ist klein, aber schön.
c Mein Bruder hat ein Handy gekauft. <u>Es</u> ist einfach klasse!
d Meine Oma hat einen Rollstuhl, aber <u>er</u> ist nicht sehr bequem.
e Das Mädchen hat eine Katze. <u>Sie</u> ist braun und schwarz.
f Ich mag die Arbeit. <u>Sie</u> ist wirklich interessant.

Adverbs of place

'Adverbs of place' is the subsidiary grammar point linked to Spread 1.9, *Ethnische Probleme*.

Reinforcement of how and when to use *hier* and *dort* should complement work on comparing different places and cultures.

The activities on page 47 need not be used when working through Spread 1.9, but at any point when revision of adverbs of place seems appropriate.

Context 1 Lifestyle

5a Match the following adverbs of place with the correct English translations.

This reading activity practises understanding adverbs of place.

After finishing the activity, encourage students to write out the pairs of words in German and English and to learn them.

Answers:

| a 3 | b 5 | c 7 | d 6 |
| e 8 | f 4 | g 2 | h 1 |

5b Work in pairs. One person names a classroom item that both people can locate and the other says where it is, using an adverb of place. Then swap roles.

This speaking activity gives students the opportunity to practise using adverbs for place in context.

You may wish to practise pronunciation of some of the adverbs before starting the activity (particularly *nirgendwo/irgendwo*). For less confident students, you could provide a list of items with genders for them to ask about.

Possible answers:

Wo ist die Lehrerin?
Sie ist dort. Wo sind die Schüler der Klasse 10C?
Sie sind draußen. Wo ist ...

Using *um* ... *zu* ...

Learning how to use *um* ... *zu* ... is the subsidiary grammar point linked to Spread 1.10, *Armut*. It should complement and consolidate work throughout the Lifestyle topic, both in talking about what to do in order to live a healthy life and in describing things which can be done to help others in society.

This grammar box can be referred to at this stage in the course, or later if students still need to consolidate more basic syntax work. Later on work on *um* ... *zu* ... is accompanied by work on *ohne* ... *zu* ... and *anstatt* ... *zu* ... (page 84).

---

6 Match the pictures below to the sentences. Then rewrite each pair of sentences as one sentence, using *um* ... *zu* ... .

This reading activity firstly checks general comprehension of the sentences to be used, by asking students to match a picture to each. They then practise using *um* ... *zu* ... .

Point out to students that they must understand both sentences in each pair, and decide in which half the *um* ... *zu* ... should be put. When discussing the answers, elicit translations of the new sentences.

Answers:

a 5 – Ich spende Geld, um den Obdachlosen zu helfen.
b 4 – Sie muss sehr fit sein, um Feuerwehrfrau zu werden.
c 3 – Am Samstag gehen wir ins Stadtzentrum, um ein Geschenk für Mutti zu kaufen.
d 1 – Ich gehe dreimal pro Woche einkaufen, um meiner Mutter zu helfen.
e 2 – Die Jugendlichen stehlen Handys, um Geld für Drogen zu bekommen.

Pages 48–49

Vocabulary

V Relationships and choices

- MP3 files for each vocabulary list

The essential vocabulary used within Topic 2, Context 1 is presented on this vocabulary spread.

Here students can learn the key words for the topic area *Relationships and choices*. You may also want to direct students to the online audio files of these vocabulary lists, so they can hear how the words are pronounced by a native speaker.

Some words are in light grey on the vocabulary spreads in the Student Book. This indicates items that are not included in the GCSE specification vocabulary list, so students do not need to learn these items for Listening and Reading assessment. However, you may wish students to use them in Speaking and Writing Controlled Assessments.

Pages 50–53

Controlled Assessment

Please refer to the section on Controlled Assessment, pages 113–119 in this Teacher's Book.

Page 54

1 Context summary

- Interactive multiple-choice quiz

The closing page for Context 1, Lifestyle provides a multiple-choice quiz which tests the key language learnt in the preceding chapter.

A longer version of this quiz is also available online as an interactive, self-marking multiple-choice test.

Answers:

1 Gemüse
2 er läuft
3 e.g. die Bratwurst, das Hähnchen, der Schinken
4 Ich will mich entspannen.
5 7–8 (sieben bis acht) Stunden
6 sie darf
7 sprechen
8 dass
9 He does voluntary work. / He is a volunteer worker.
10 Ich kann meinen Bruder nicht leiden, da er so laut ist.

2 Leisure

Free time and the media
- Free time activities

KS3 Revision:
Sports and leisure, clothes; Transport; Places in town

Online materials
- Audio files for core reading texts

2.1 Was hast du gestern gemacht?
- Using the perfect tense with *haben*
- Reusing questions when giving answers

- Audio file for core reading text
- Audio file and transcript for listening activity 2
- Listening activity and transcript: *Anjas Freitag*
- Grammar activity: Using the perfect tense with *haben*
- Writing worksheet
- Foundation reading worksheet
- Extension reading worksheet

2.2 Ich bin in die Stadt gegangen
- Using the perfect tense with *sein*
- Understanding questions

- Audio file for core reading text
- Audio file and transcript for listening activity 3
- Reading activity: *Letztes Wochenende*
- Grammar activity: Using the perfect tense with *sein*
- Writing worksheet
- Extension reading worksheet

Shopping, money, fashion and trends

2.3 Wir bekommen nicht genug Taschengeld!
- Using the perfect tense with *haben* or *sein*
- Checking auxiliary verbs

- Audio file for core reading text
- Audio file and transcript for listening activity 3
- Listening activity and transcript: *Mein Taschengeld reicht mir nicht*
- Grammar activity: Using the perfect tense with *haben* or *sein*
- Writing worksheet
- Extension listening worksheet
- Audio file and transcript for extension listening worksheet

2.4 Wir waren im Einkaufszentrum
- Using the imperfect tense
- Paraphrasing

- Audio file for core reading text
- Audio file and transcript for listening activity 3
- Listening activity and transcript: *Wir sind einkaufen gegangen*
- Grammar activity: Using the imperfect tense
- Writing worksheet
- Foundation listening worksheet
- Audio file and transcript for foundation listening worksheet
- Extension listening worksheet
- Audio file and transcript for extension listening worksheet

Advantages and disadvantages of new technology

2.5 Ich lebe im Internet
- Using different tenses (past and present)
- Using notes when making a presentation

- Audio file for core reading text
- Audio file and transcript for listening activity 3
- Reading activity: *Das Internet*
- Grammar activity: Using different tenses (past and present)
- Speaking worksheet
- Extension reading worksheet

Reading and listening

- Audio file for core reading texts
- Audio files and transcripts for listening activity 2

Grammar

Free time and the media
- Separable verbs
- The perfect tense with irregular verbs
- The imperfect tenses of *haben* and *sein*
- Modal verbs (revision)
- Using *wann*, *wenn* and *als*

Vocabulary

Free time and the media
- MP3 files for each vocabulary list

Holidays
Plans, preferences, experiences

What to see and getting around

Reading and listening

Grammar

Vocabulary

Summative assessment

2.6 Ich möchte mal nach …
- Using correct word order (time – manner – place)
- Recognising information presented in different ways

- Audio file for core reading text
- Audio file and transcript for listening activity 2
- Listening activity and transcript: *Grüße aus …*
- Grammar activity: Using correct word order (time – manner – place)
- Writing worksheet
- Foundation reading worksheet
- Extension reading worksheet

2.7 Urlaubspläne
- Using the future tense with *werden*
- Applying rules in new situations

- Audio file for core reading text
- Audio file and transcript for listening activity 3
- Reading activity: *Konstantins Urlaubspläne*
- Grammar activity: Using the future tense with *werden*
- Speaking worksheet
- Foundation listening worksheet
- Audio file and transcript for foundation listening worksheet
- Extension listening worksheet
- Audio file and transcript for extension listening worksheet

2.8 Berlin ist cool!
- Using different tenses (past, present and future)
- Tackling longer texts

- Audio file for core reading text
- Audio file and transcript for listening activity 2
- Listening activity and transcript: *Tina am Apparat!*
- Grammar activity: Using different tenses (past, present and future)
- Speaking worksheet
- Extension listening worksheet
- Audio file and transcript for extension listening worksheet

2.9 Auf Achse
- Asking questions using interrogatives
- Making vocabulary lists

- Audio file for core reading text
- Video and transcript for video activity 3
- Grammar activity: Using interrogatives
- Writing worksheet
- Extension listening worksheet
- Audio file and transcript for extension listening worksheet

- Audio file for core reading text
- Audio files and transcripts for listening activity 2

Holidays
- *Ich möchte…*
- Using *um … zu …, ohne … zu …* and *anstatt … zu …*

- Using adjectives after *etwas, nichts, viel, wenig* and *alles*
- The nominative and accusative cases (revision)

Holidays
- MP3 files for each vocabulary list

Leisure
- Interactive multiple-choice quiz

The opening page for Context 2, Leisure provides a quick-reference overview of how the teaching spreads, grammar and strategies within this Context in the Student Book map to the Topics and Purposes of Context 2 in the GCSE specification. Also included here is an overview of the online resources available for each of these spreads in the Student Book.

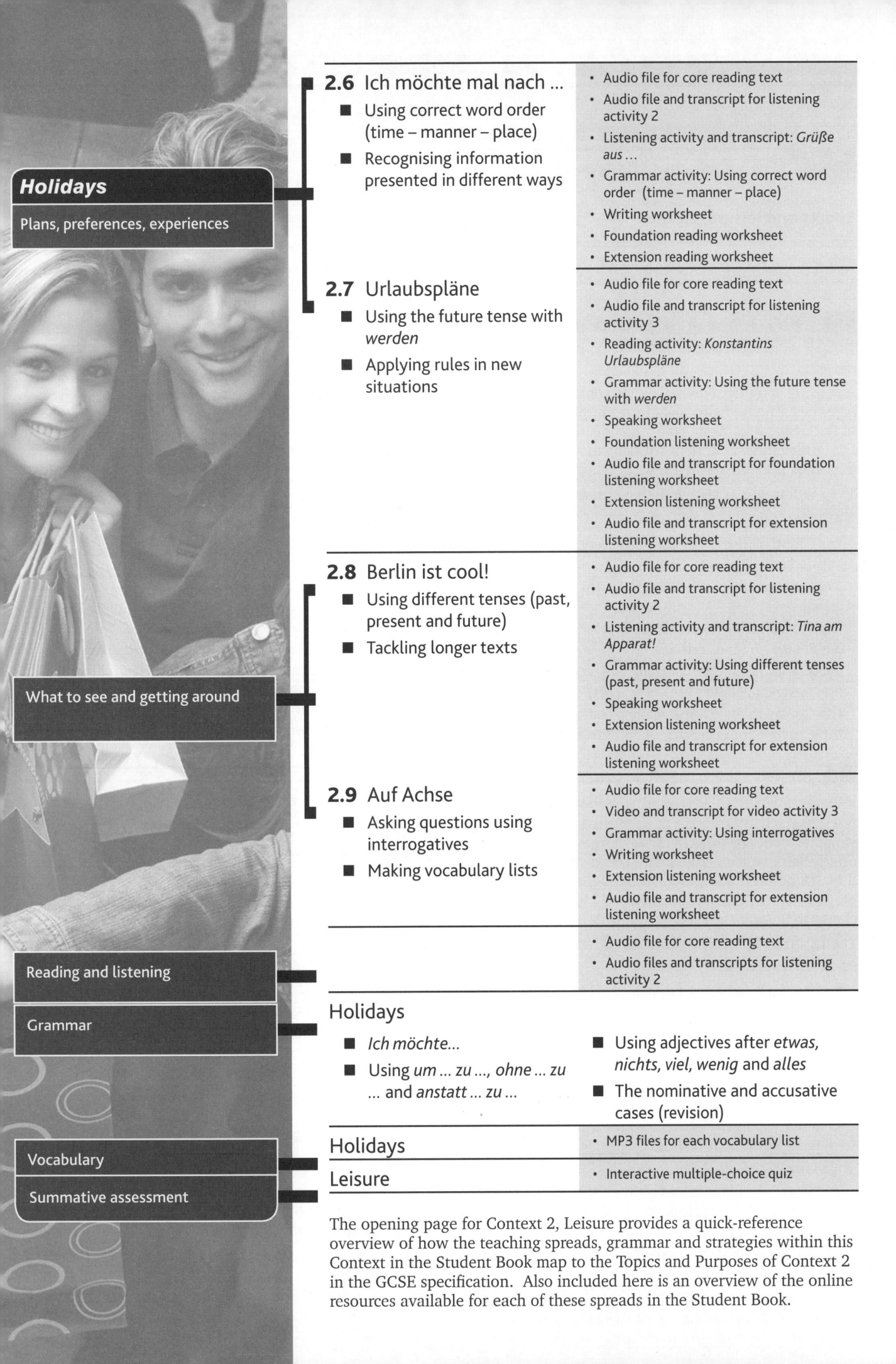

Pages 56–57

Revision

Free time and the media

Sports and leisure, clothes

kerboodle!
- Audio files for core reading texts

1a Read the texts above and note down in English what each person likes doing, adding any extra details.

A reading activity to revise key vocabulary for leisure activities. The text also includes examples of expressions of frequency and use of *gern / nicht gern / am liebsten*. Encourage more confident students to add as many extra details as possible to their answers.

The reading text is also available online as an audio file.

Answers:

Erik – football (extra details: plays every weekend, doesn't like basketball).
Jana – swimming (extra detail: favourite stroke is front crawl).
Frauke – shopping (extra details: brother plays the guitar, but Frauke isn't musical).
Tobias – lazing around, watching TV (extra details: does this every evening, doesn't like doing sport).
Lisa – going to the cinema, reading (extra details: reads three to four books per month, finds television boring).

1b Write down the answers to the following questions, using the texts above to help you.

A writing activity to practise answering questions about students' own leisure activities. This could firstly be done orally. Refer weaker students to the vocabulary list before they start, and remind them of frequency expressions they could use. Encourage use of *weil* with a subordinate clause to answer the final question.

The reading text is also available online as an audio file.

Possible answers:

Was machst du gern in deiner Freizeit?
Ich lese gern. / Ich faulenze. / Ich gehe schwimmen.
Wie oft machst du das?
Das mache ich dreimal pro Woche. / jeden Tag. / nur einmal im Monat.
Was machst du nicht gern?
Ich treibe nicht gern Sport. / Ich höre nicht so gern Musik. / Ich finde Fußball schrecklich.
Warum nicht?
Ich bin gar nicht fit. / Ich bin nicht musikalisch. / Fußball ist echt langweilig – ich spiele lieber Tennis.

2a Match the statements below to the items of clothing.

A reading activity to revise German words for items of clothing. Point out the use of the accusative case in the statements, and refer to the *Grammatik* panel. If necessary, you could follow this activity with revision of additional words for clothing, encouraging students to note them with genders and practise forming similar statements using them.

The reading text is also available online as an audio file.

Answers:

| a 7 | b 6 | c 3 | d 8 |
| e 2 | f 4 | g 1 | h 5 |

2b Work in pairs. Take it in turns to say what you would wear for each of the following occasions.

A speaking activity to practise using the accusative case with words for items of clothing, by forming statements similar to those in activity 1a. Afterwards, students could work with a different partner, and start with a statement of what they wear – partners listen and guess on which of the occasions given it would be worn.

Possible answers:

Was trägst du auf einer Party?
Ich trage ein schönes Kleid. Was trägst du im Winter?
Ich trage immer eine Jacke und einen Hut.

> **Grammatik**
> This panel reminds students about use of the accusative case for the direct object in a sentence. With a weaker group, you may need to practise identifying the direct object in example sentences, to make sure that all students are clear on what it is. They will need to use the accusative case in activity 2b – you could try one or two sample answers together to help them. The panel also refers students to page 85 for further information about the accusative case.

Transport, places in town

kerboodle!
- Audio files for core reading texts

1a Read the text about Jochen's home town. Read the following statements and for each, write T (true), F (false) or ? (Not in the Text).

A reading activity to revise places in a town. The text includes examples of *es gibt*. Refer students to the vocabulary list before they start, and remind weaker learners that they will not necessarily need to understand every single word of the text, but should focus on what they need to decide if each statement is true, false or not in the text.

The reading text is also available online as an audio file.

Answers:

| a T | b T | c T |
| d F | e T | f ? |

1b Using Jochen's text as a model, write about what there is and isn't in your area.

A writing activity to practise using vocabulary for places in a town or area, and *es gibt*. Refer to the *Grammatik* panel. Encourage more confident learners to extend their writing by using other phrases and structures from Jochen's text (e.g. *man kann,* subordinate clauses).

Context 2 Leisure **43**

This panel explains how to use *es gibt ein / kein* followed by the accusative case to say what there is in a place. Students will need to use this structure in activity 1b – you could try one or two sample answers together to help them, using words from the vocabulary list. Point out use of *es gibt* in the text for activity 1a, showing how it is used with plural nouns or the definite article.

Grammatik

2a 📖 🎧 Read the statements below. For each find a matching picture. Note down any additional details in English.

A reading activity to revise phrases for talking about types of transport. Remind students of the difference in use between *fahren* and *gehen*.

The reading text is also available online as an audio file.

Answers:

- a 2 (extra details: usually cycles to school).
- b 4 (extra details: flies to Spain every year).
- c 3 (extra details: mostly travels into town on the underground).
- d 5 (extra detail: walks to visit female friend / girlfriend).
- e 1 (extra details: travels by car at the weekend to visit grandparents).

2b 💬 Work in pairs. One person asks the following questions and the other answers. Then swap roles.

A speaking activity to practise using transport phrases. Refer to the vocabulary list, and encourage more confident learners to extend their answers. Students could then ask further questions using their own ideas – remind them that *nach* is used for 'to' with named places only.

Possible answers:

Wie fährst du zur Schule?
Ich fahre mit dem Rad. / Ich fahre mit dem Rad zur Schule. / Ich fahre immer mit dem Rad zur Schule.
Wie fährst du zu deinen Freunden?
Ich fahre mit dem Bus. / Ich fahre mit dem Bus zu meinen Freunden. / Ich fahre oft mit dem Bus zu meinen Freunden.
Wie fährst du zum Einkaufen?
Ich fahre mit der U-Bahn. / Ich fahre mit der U-Bahn zum Einkaufen. / Ich fahre normalerweise mit der U-Bahn zum Einkaufen.
Wie fährst du in die Stadt?
Ich gehe zu Fuß. / Ich gehe zu Fuß in die Stadt. / Ich gehe jeden Tag zu Fuß in die Stadt.

Pages 58–59

2.1 Was hast du gestern gemacht?

Free time activities

Subject	Talking about free time activities
G 1	Using the perfect tense with *haben*
G 2	Using separable verbs with the perfect tense
🌐	Reusing questions to give answers

kerboodle!
- Audio file for core reading text
- Audio file and transcript for listening activity 2
- Listening activity and transcript: *Anjas Freitag*
- Grammar activity: Using the perfect tense with *haben*
- Writing worksheet
- Foundation reading worksheet
- Extension reading worksheet

Starter activity

Display familiar infinitives relating to this subtopic, and nouns or phrases used with them – either as two lists, or scattered on the board. Students must find pairs and say them or write them down (e.g. *in die Disko – gehen, einen Freund – treffen, einen Film – sehen*).

Jetzt chatten!

A reading text consisting of five chatroom messages about free time activities. The text includes examples of the perfect tense with *haben*, including some separable verbs.

The reading text is also available online as an audio file.

1 📖 🎧 Copy the sentences and fill in the gaps with one of the words on the right.

Students read/listen to the text and fill the gaps in sentences about its content, selecting from the words given.

Answers:

a Kino	b gefallen	c Geld	d Disko
e Freund	f teuer	g Hause	h Idee

2 🎧 *Transcript:*

Was hast du gemacht, Anna?
Ich habe letzten Montag Freunde getroffen. Wir haben uns den neuen Film mit Will Smith angesehen, aber er hat mir nicht so gut gefallen.
Was hast du am Wochenende gemacht, Stefan?
Ich habe nicht viel gemacht. Ich habe nur ein neues Computerspiel gekauft und habe es mit ein paar Freunden gespielt. Das hat Spaß gemacht.
Michaela, was hast du gestern Abend gemacht?
Ich habe nur ein paar Freundinnen angerufen und gequatscht. Meine Eltern haben gesagt, ich darf nicht ausgehen – sowas Blödes.
Nuri, was hast du gemacht?
Ich bin in einem Orchester und habe letztes Wochenende in einem Konzert gespielt. Ich spiele Geige. Das war mir viel zu anstrengend.

Was hast du am Wochenende gemacht, Maik?
Am Wochenende habe ich meinem Bruder mit seinen Mathehausaufgaben geholfen, weil er am Montag eine Prüfung hat. Ich habe dabei selbst viel gelernt. Das habe ich nützlich gefunden.

2 What did these people do last week? Did they enjoy it or not?

This audio extract consists of five young people being asked what they have done in their free time recently. Their replies include use of the perfect tense with *haben*, with some examples of separable verbs. The last speaker re-uses language from the question in their answer.

Students listen to the audio extract, then note what each speaker did, and whether they enjoyed it. Before listening, refer them to the *Tipp*. Less confident students should do this in two stages – they could firstly note down the activities, then listen again to decide whether each was enjoyed and write it in the correct column of the grid. Prepare for the second stage by picking out some of the relevant opinion-giving vocabulary (e.g. *Spaß, anstrengend, nützlich*) and getting them to check the meanings.

Answers:

	☺	☹
Anna		saw film (new Will Smith film)
Stefan	bought new computer game and played it with friends	
Michaela		rang a few friends and chatted (parents won't let her go out)
Nuri		played violin in a concert (too exhausting)
Maik	helped brother with maths homework (brother had exam on Monday, learned a lot himself, found it useful)	

Tipp
Use this box to assist students before doing the listening activity. After reading it with them, you could illustrate the technique of listening for stems of verbs within past participles by playing a small part of the listening extract and analysing the participles heard with the class. Alternatively, read out a short list of participles and get students to work out which verb they come from. Point out that this is a useful technique for the listening exam.

Grammatik
This panel explains how to find the stem of a regular verb before adding present tense endings, and changes to the stem for irregular verbs. With weaker students, clarify their understanding of what the present tense is by using simple examples in English. If necessary, revise with students the meanings of the pronouns *ich, du, er/sie/es* etc, and look up the correct endings for each in the Grammar section. Practise finding the stem and applying the correct endings with several regular verbs. The reading and listening materials in activities 1 and 3 provide examples of present tense verb forms.
This *Grammatik* panel also refers students to p.28 for information on saying 'I eat a/an...' using the accusative indefinite article.

3 G Copy the sentences and fill in the gaps with the correct form of *haben*.

A grammar activity to practise forms of the auxiliary verb *haben* in perfect tense sentences.

Before they start the activity, refer students to the *Grammatik* panel. Afterwards, you could ask them to translate the sentences into English. Discuss the past participles involved – some are irregular (this will be covered in the next subtopic), and some are separable verbs.

Answers:

a habe b haben c haben
d Hast e hat f haben, haben

Strategie
Discuss the 'reusing questions' strategy with students before they start speaking activity 4, and ask for volunteers to give example answers when you ask a question.

4 Practise dialogues about what you did and give opinions.

Students use the suggested question and answer structures to ask and answer questions about their recent free time activities. This could be done in pairs, small groups, or as a survey. Refer to the *Strategie* panel and encourage more confident students to answer with as much detail in their sentences as possible. Weaker students could prepare for this activity by noting down in advance the activities and opinions they wish to say.

5 You are describing last weekend to friends. Write down what you did following the prompts. Now describe what someone else did.

Students follow the prompts and the language structures given to write about their free time activities last weekend, and those of someone else. More confident students should include additional ideas of their own, and could then write further sentences using other pronouns (*wir / ihr / sie / Sie*). Refer them back to the *Grammatik* panel.

Context 2 Leisure 45

Plenary activity

Build perfect tense sentences with *haben* about free time activities around the class: each student says one word when you point at them to add to the sentence. When a sentence has reached its logical conclusion, the next student pointed at should say *Punkt* and the following one starts a new sentence.

Pages 60–61

2.2 Ich bin in die Stadt gegangen

Free time activities

Subject	Talking about going out
G 1	Using the perfect tense with *sein*
G 2	Learning about irregular past participles
🎧	Understanding question words in German

kerboodle!
- Audio file for core reading text
- Audio file and transcript for listening activity 3
- Reading activity: *Letztes Wochenende*
- Grammar activity: Using the perfect tense with *sein*
- Writing worksheet
- Extension reading worksheet

Starter activity

Identifying the perfect tense. Read out a series of sentences, some in the perfect tense (you could use sentences from texts in this and the previous subtopics). Students must listen, and stand up or step forward when they hear the perfect tense. They could perform an additional action when the perfect tense with *sein* is used.

Ich bin in die Stadt gefahren

In this reading text, five teenagers give details of what they did at the weekend. The text includes examples of the perfect tense with *sein*.

The reading text is also available online as an audio file.

1 📖 🎧 Read what the teenagers say about their weekends then answer the following questions.

Students read/listen to the text, and decide which person each of the questions relates to. Afterwards, you could use vocabulary from the text, such as *Schwimmverein, Wettkampf, Wochenende, Vorgestern,* to practise German pronunciation of 'w' and 'v' with weaker students (which will be useful when using question words later in this subtopic).

Answers:

a Natascha	b Erika	c Kornelia
d Andreas	e Kai	f Kornelia
g Andreas	h Natascha	i Erika

> **Grammatik**
> This panel explains that certain verbs use the auxiliary verb *sein* with a past participle to form the perfect tense. It shows common examples of these (you could suggest that students memorise this list), and points out that all such verbs have irregular past participles. Students could search for examples in the text for activity 1. With weaker students, revise the present tense forms of *sein*.
> The panel also refers students to page 70 to learn more about irregular participles.

2 **G** Copy and complete each sentence, using the correct form of *sein*. If you need extra help, look for the different examples of *sein* elsewhere on the page.

This grammar activity practises use of the different forms of the auxiliary verb *sein* in perfect tense sentences.

Refer students to the *Grammatik* panel. They then select the correct form of *sein* to fill the gap in each of the sentences given. Afterwards, elicit translations of the sentences.

Answers:

| a bin | b sind | c sind |
| d ist | e sind | f bist |

> **Tipp**
> After reading the panel with students, ask them to find examples of irregular past participles in the text. Point out that many English verbs also have irregular past participles.

3 🎧 *Transcript:*

Fabian: Hi. Ich heiße Fabian. Ich bin am Freitagabend mit meinen Eltern in die Stadt gefahren. Wir sind mit dem Auto gefahren, weil das bequem ist. In der Stadt sind wir ins Kino gegangen. Es hat wirklich Spaß gemacht.

Max: Hallo. Mein Name ist Max. Was ich am Wochenende gemacht habe? Absolut gar nichts. Ich bin nirgendwo hingegangen. Ich bin zu Hause geblieben. Meine Eltern waren nicht hier und ich war ganz allein. Das war ja so langweilig.

Charlotte: Hallo. Ich bin die Charlotte. Ich wohne in der Stadtmitte, aber man kann hier viel machen. Ich bin am Sonntag mit meinen Freunden in den Park gegangen. Der Park ist in der Nähe und darum sind wir zu Fuß gegangen. Im Park gibt es eine Skateanlage und dort sind wir ein bisschen Skateboard gefahren. Das war cool, aber später hat es dann geregnet.

Denise: Ich heiße Denise und das ist meine beste Freundin Julia. Ich und meine Freundin Julia sind am Samstag ins Freibad gegangen, weil es sonnig war. Wir sind mit dem Bus gefahren, weil das viel billiger ist als mit dem Auto.

3 🎧 Listen to the following interviews and write down the correct letters for Fabian, Max, Charlotte and Denise. You need to listen for where they went, when, with whom and, for three of them, how they got there.

This audio extract consists of four young people saying what they did at the weekend, using the perfect tense with *sein*.

Students listen to the extract and look at a series of pictures. They must decide which pictures relate to each speaker. Less confident students could tackle the activity in stages, firstly listening for where the person went, then with whom, and finally how they got there.

Answers:

Fabian	c, d, f, m
Max	e, h, n
Charlotte	i, j, l, o
Denise	a, b, g, k

> **Strategie**
> To reinforce this strategy for understanding questions, practise the pronunciation of the question words given, and stress the importance of knowing and remembering their meanings – point out that these words will be useful for the Reading, Listening and Speaking units (potentially also the Writing).

4 💬 🌐 Work in pairs: one partner asks questions and the other answers. Then swap roles. Use the pictures in Activity 3.

Students interview each other about what they did, using the pictures to direct which answer is required, and the language structures given for support. Refer to the *Strategie* panel.

Plenary activity

Display German sentences and questions relating to the content of this subtopic, each of which contains one error (e.g. incorrect question word, incorrect past participle). Students must spot and correct the errors, either working in pairs or individually.

Pages 62–63

2.3 Wir bekommen nicht genug Taschengeld!

Shopping, money, fashion and trends	
Subject	Talking about money and shopping
G 1	Using the perfect tense with *haben* or *sein*
G 2	Recognising the imperfect tenses of *haben* and *sein*
🌐	Checking auxiliary verbs

kerboodle!
- Audio file for core reading text
- Audio file and transcript for listening activity 3
- Listening activity and transcript: *Mein Taschengeld reicht mir nicht*
- Grammar activity: Using the perfect tense with *haben* or *sein*
- Writing worksheet
- Extension listening worksheet
- Audio file and transcript for extension listening worksheet

Starter activity

Firstly display a list of previously familiar German words for types of shop (e.g. those used in activity 1), with the letters jumbled. Students must unjumble them and give their English meaning.

1 V Identify the items below. Match them up with the correct shop.

Students then do activity 1, matching pictures of products to the correct word for a shop.

Answers:

| a 1 | b 6 | c 3 |
| d 2 | e 5 | f 4 |

Mein Geld

In the reading text, three young people say how much pocket money they receive, whether they think it's enough, and what they spend it on. It includes examples of the perfect tense with *haben* and *sein*, and useful shopping-related vocabulary.

The reading text is also available online as an audio file.

2a 📖 🎧 Read the paragraphs above and decide whether the statements are True (T), False (F) or not in the text (NT).

Students read/listen to the text and decide if each English statement is true, false, or not in the text. They then do the same for the German statements. You might wish to take the opportunity to practise numbers (of Euros) with weaker students.

Answers:

| a T | b F | c T |
| d NT | e F | f T |

Context 2 Leisure 47

2b Now do the same with the sentences in German.

Answers:

a T b T c F d NT

3 Transcript: _____

Wie viel Taschengeld bekommst du Ahmet?
Ich bekomme zehn Euro pro Woche. Ich habe zwei Monate gespart und mir dann letzte Woche neue Turnschuhe gekauft, weil sie zur Zeit in sind. Ich finde, mein Taschengeld ist nicht genug, weil ich öfter einkaufen gehen möchte.

Bekommst du Taschengeld, Serena?
Meine Eltern geben mir fünfzig Euro pro Monat. Ich bin letztes Wochenende in die Stadt gegangen und habe mir für dreißig Euro Make-up und ein paar Modezeitschriften gekauft.

Reicht dir dein Taschengeld?
Ja, mir reicht mein Taschengeld. Ja, ich bekomme genug Taschengeld.

Wie viel Taschengeld bekommst du Ralf?
Ich bekomme fünfzehn Euro pro Woche. Ich habe schon lange nichts mehr gekauft. Ich habe die letzten Jahre mein Geld gespart, weil ich in Zukunft reisen möchte. Ich war vor drei Jahren in Amerika und möchte wieder dorthinfahren. Aber mein Taschengeld reicht mir.

Patrick, du bekommst viel Taschengeld, nicht wahr?
Ich bekomme einhundertfünfzig Euro im Monat. Ich weiß, das ist sehr viel, aber ich muss alles damit kaufen. Letzte Woche habe ich neue Hefte, neue Schuhe, eine neue Hose und Kredit für mein Handy gekauft, weil ich so viel telefoniere. Ich finde also, dass es nicht genug ist.

Bekommst du genug Taschengeld, Anja?
Hmm, mein Taschengeld reicht mir eigentlich. Ich bekomme nur acht Euro in der Woche, aber ich bekomme immer extra Geld, wenn ich es brauche. Ich war zum Beispiel letzte Woche in der Stadt und habe eine CD gekauft, und ich bin mit Freundinnen ins Schwimmbad gegangen. Meine Mutter hat mir das Geld für beides gegeben.

3 Listen to the interviews and complete the table.
This audio extract consists of interviews with five young people, who say how much pocket money they get, what they have spent it on recently, and whether they think it's enough. It includes examples of the perfect tense with *haben* and *sein*.
Students listen to the extract and complete the table with the necessary details in English. Encourage more confident students to note as many extra details as possible.

Answers:

Name	Pocket money received	Spent on...? Saved?	Enough?	Extra details
Ahmet	10 Euros per week	trainers	No	wants to go shopping more often
Serena	50 Euros per month	make-up, fashion magazines	Yes	bought the items in town last week
Ralf	15 Euros per week	saving up to go travelling	Yes	has been saving for the last three years, went to America then and wants to go again
Patrick	150 Euros per month	exercise books, new shoes, new trousers, credit for mobile phone	No	knows he gets a lot of money but has to buy everything with it, uses his mobile a lot
Anja	8 Euros per week	CD, going swimming	Yes	gets extra money when she needs it – mother gave her money for CDs and swimming trip

> **Grammatik**
> This panel reminds students that they need to know whether a verb takes *haben* or *sein* as its auxiliary in the perfect tense, and refers them to the verb tables at the back of their textbook to check this. It also reminds them of the importance of learning the different forms of *haben* and *sein*. You might want to practise identifying verbs of motion or change of state using a few examples.
> The panel also refers students to page 71 to learn to recognise the imperfect tenses of *haben* and *sein*.

4a Copy out the sentences and choose the correct auxiliary verb to go in the gaps.
This grammar activity practises selecting the correct auxiliary verb in perfect tense sentences.
Refer to the *Grammatik* panel. When discussing the answers, ask students to translate the sentences into English to check that meanings are clear.

Answers:

a bin   b sind   c haben
d ist   e haben

G To practise checking auxiliary verbs, use sample sentences that include some with deliberate errors, to help students gain skills in checking subject-verb agreement of the auxiliary verb. Point out that this will help to increase their accuracy mark in the Speaking and Writing units.

Strategie

4b **G** 🌐 Now add the correct form of *haben* or *sein*.

This grammar activity practises selecting the correct auxiliary verb and the correct form of *haben* or *sein*.

If necessary, revise the forms of both auxiliary verbs before students do this task. Refer to the *Grammatik* and *Strategie* panels.

Answers:

a ist   b hat   c habe

5 💬 ✏️ Carry out a pocket money survey in class. Ask the questions below and use the box to help you with your answers. Then write up the results of your survey, using the worksheet to help you (you will need to use verbs in the third person!).

Support less confident students by practising pronunciation of the four questions before they start the activity, and helping them to prepare their answers using the language structures box. Refer all students to the *Tipp*.

Point out to students that ability to switch between tenses will improve their range of language marks in the Speaking and Writing units.

Tipp

Plenary activity

Students work in pairs, and each tries to speak in German for 30 seconds on the subject of their pocket money (you could extend the time for more confident students). Partners listen, time them and give supportive feedback. Encourage them to use their answers from activity 5, to find ideas in the activities of this subtopic, and to give lots of examples of the things they buy with their pocket money, including some they have recently bought – using the perfect tense. You may wish to give a short period of preparation time for making notes before they start.

Pages 64–65

2.4 Wir waren im Einkaufszentrum

Shopping, money, fashion and trends

Subject	Talking about fashion and trends
G 1	Using the imperfect tense
G 2	Revising modal verbs (present tense)
🌐	Paraphrasing

kerboodle!
- Audio file for core reading text
- Audio file and transcript for listening activity 3
- Listening activity and transcript: *Wir sind einkaufen gegangen*
- Grammar activity: Using the imperfect tense
- Writing worksheet
- Foundation listening worksheet
- Audio file and transcript for foundation listening worksheet
- Extension listening worksheet
- Audio file and transcript for extension listening worksheet

Starter activity

Ask students to work in pairs, and give them two minutes to 'brainstorm' and write a list of all the German words for items of clothing they can remember. Collate their findings on the board and elicit meanings.

Ich kaufe Klamotten

The reading text consists of statements by five people about their clothes buying preferences and recent purchases. It includes examples of the imperfect tense of regular and irregular verbs, and useful vocabulary for items of clothing and shops.

The reading text is also available online as an audio file.

1 📖 🎧 Put the correct name in each of the gaps.

Students read/listen to the text and identify the correct name to fill the gap in each sentence given. They could then re-read the text aloud with a partner, each taking the roles of some of the young people and translating the statements into English.

Answers:

a Lars   b Selima   c Uli
d Frau Peters   e Lars   f Katharina

This panel explains use of the imperfect tense. It shows how to form the imperfect for regular verbs – you might wish to practise with the class using further examples related to the topic of clothes shopping (e.g. *passen*). It also gives the irregular forms for the common verbs *sein*, *haben* and *geben*.
The panel also refers students to page 71 to revise modal verbs in the present tense.

Grammatik

Context 2 Leisure 49

2 **G** Fill in the gaps with the correct form of the imperfect.

Refer to the *Grammatik* panel. After completing the activity, students could look for examples of the imperfect tense in the text for activity 1.

Answers:

a war	b hatte	c kaufte
d waren	e hatte	f sagtest

3 🎧 *Transcript:*

a Ich war in einem Kaufhaus und habe eine gelbe Jacke für meinen Bruder gekauft. Zu Hause habe ich bemerkt, dass die Jacke viel zu lang war.

b Ich war mit Freundinnen auf dem Markt. Ich hatte etwas Geld dabei und habe mir einen Rock gekauft, aber ich habe den Rock nicht anprobiert. Zu Hause merkte ich, dass der Rock zu weit war. Ich muss ihn umtauschen.

c Meine Eltern und ich waren gestern in einer Boutique, weil es mein Geburtstag war und ich als Geschenk einen Pulli kaufen durfte. Ich habe also einen Designerpulli gekauft. Er passt wirklich gut.

d Ich war gestern im Kaufhaus und habe mir einen Schal gekauft und eine Kappe für meine Schwester. Mit dem Schal gab es natürlich keine Probleme, aber die Kappe hatte die falsche Farbe. Schade.

3 🎧 Listen to the recordings. Note down where each person went, what they bought and whether there were any problems. Include any extra details you pick up.

This audio extract consists of statements by five young people who have recently been shopping for clothes. They say which shop they went to, what they bought, and whether there were any problems with it. The extract includes examples of the imperfect tense of regular and irregular verbs. The final speaker uses *es gab* (see *Tipp*).

Students listen to the extract and make notes in English about the content as required. Encourage more confident students to note as many extra details as possible.

Answers:

a department store, yellow jacket, too long. Extra details: jacket is for brother, noticed problem at home.

b market, skirt, too big. Extra details: shopping with friends, didn't try skirt on, has to exchange it.

c boutique, pullover, no problems. Extra details: birthday, with parents, pullover is present, it's designer, fits really well.

d department store, scarf and cap, cap is the wrong colour. Extra details: cap is for sister, scarf for speaker.

✏️ Point out to students that paraphrasing is a useful strategy when writing or speaking in German. You might want to practise with the whole class using one or two examples.

Strategie

Tipp: Advise students to learn the useful expression *Es gab*, and suggest some ways they could make use of it in their email writing for activity 4.

4 ✏️ 🌐 Write an email to a friend about a shopping trip.

Before students start their email, refer them to the *Strategie* panel and the *Tipp*. Remind them to make sure they include all the points required and to make up details if necessary. Encourage more confident students to add as much detail as they can, rather than restricting themselves to the language structure box given. Remind them to include the imperfect tense.

Plenary activity

Consolidate the language learnt in this subtopic by asking students to do a language trawl: display a list of things that they must find by looking at the two pages of this subtopic in their textbook. For example, 2 regular imperfect verbs, 2 irregular imperfect verbs, 4 items of clothing etc. Set a time limit, and ask students to work individually or in pairs. Then elicit a range of their answers.

Pages 66–67

2.5   Ich lebe im Internet

Advantages and disadvantages of new technology

Subject	Talking about new technology
G 1	Using different tenses (past and present)
G 2	Distinguishing between *als* and *wenn*
🔧	Using notes when making a presentation

kerboodle!
- Audio file for core reading text
- Audio file and transcript for listening activity 3
- Reading activity: *Das Internet*
- Grammar activity: Using different tenses (past and present)
- Speaking worksheet
- Extension reading worksheet

Starter activity

Read out a series of sentences using familiar language which are either in the present, perfect or imperfect tense. Students must perform a specific action, e.g. stand up/sit down/put their hands on their head, depending upon which tense they hear (a repeat of the starter activity suggested for subtopic 2.2, this time with an action for each of three tenses). For a more confident class, you could suggest a supplementary action (e.g. touching their nose) when the verb they hear is irregular!

Surfen, chatten und SMSen

The reading texts consists of emails, text and chat messages from young people about their use of the internet. They include examples of the present, imperfect and perfect tenses.

The reading text is also available online as an audio file.

1 📖 🎧 **Read the texts above. Copy and complete each sentence, using the words below.**

Students read/listen to the texts and fill gaps in sentences about their content, selecting from the words given. You could then analyse the texts further, eliciting comments from students about the international use of English words relating to the internet, and harvesting useful vocabulary.

Answers:

a teuer	b Stunden	c Hilfe	d finden
e Fotos	f glaubte	g waren	h hat

> **Grammatik**
>
> This panel reminds students that it is important to try and use different tenses to talk about the past and the present, and when to use the two types of past tense in German. It refers students back to the pages where formation of the perfect and imperfect tenses is explained.
> The panel also refers students to page 71 to learn how to distinguish between *als* and *wenn*.

2 **G** **Re-read the texts on page 66 and for each person, identify and note down the verbs and tenses he or she uses.**

This grammar activity practises identifying verbs and their tenses.

Refer to the *Grammatik* panel. Support less confident students by showing them where to find the verb in a sentence, and suggesting or eliciting clues as to which tense it is in. Remind them to follow the references given in the *Grammatik* panel to revise formation of the perfect and imperfect tenses.

Answers:

	Present	Imperfect	Perfect	Infinitive
Benny	simse, ist			
Antonia	weiss, bin, chatte, ist, kann	war	bin geworden	helfen
Martina	heiße, finde, habe, kann, hat, suche		habe gemailt	recherchieren, schicken
Simon	findest, findet, weiß, finde	hatte, ausprobierte, fand, glaubte	haben begonnen, haben gemobbt	chatten
Karina	lade (runter), kostet, kann, will	kaufte, fand	habe gekauft	brennen, synchronisieren

3 🎧 *Transcript:*

Großmutter: Norbert. Jetzt bist du schon wieder im Internet und zur gleichen Zeit am Handy. Du bist jetzt schon vier Stunden am Computer. Als ich jünger war hatte ich nicht mal ein Telefon im Haus. Ich musste zum Nachbarn gehen zum telefonieren. Ich mache mir Sorgen, dass du deine Freunde nicht triffst. Ich finde du solltest deine Freunde öfter besuchen und nicht nur schreiben. Ausserdem ist das viel zu teuer. Deine Eltern geben dir zu viel Taschengeld.

Norbert: Ach Oma, beruhige dich doch. So schlimm ist das nicht. Meine Hausaufgaben sind schon lange fertig. Ich finde das Internet auch praktisch. Ich spreche zum Beispiel mit Freunden im Ausland und übe mein Englisch. Das ist doch gut, oder? Weisst du Oma, möchtest du nicht auch etwas über das Internet lernen? Ich helfe dir dabei. Du findest das sicherlich gut.

> **Tipp**
>
> Practise this technique with the class by looking at the first few questions for activity 3 before listening, and discussing what they should be preparing to listen out for.

3 🎧 **Listen to the conversation between Norbert and his grandmother. Choose the correct answers from the options below.**

The audio extract consists of a conversation between a concerned grandmother and her grandson who is spending a lot of time at his computer. It includes examples of the present and imperfect tenses, and *als*.

Students listen to the extract and answer the multiple-choice comprehension questions. Refer them to the *Tipp* before starting.

Answers:

a 2	b 1	c 1	d 3
e 2	f 3	g 1	

> **Strategie**
>
> Read through this panel with the class. Point out that following this strategy of using notes when making a presentation, rather than simply reading from a sheet, will help them to practise speaking fluently without being dependent on reading, and eventually to increase their marks in the Speaking unit.

4 ✏️ 💬 🌐 **Make a presentation on the advantages or disadvantages of modern technology. Choose one particular item (mobile phone, MP3 player etc.). Make notes then present your arguments to the class or a partner.**

Allow plenty of time for students to prepare their presentation, perhaps partly as a homework task. Refer to the *Strategie* panel, and consider giving students feedback afterwards on the notes they used. Remind them to be creative, and encourage the more confident to include as much detail and information as possible.

Context 2 Leisure 51

Plenary activity

If students made their presentation in activity 3 to a partner, you might wish to ask for volunteers to make theirs to the whole class for your plenary. Alternatively, use a quick fire quiz to consolidate learning from this subtopic: read out five to ten questions relating to the vocabulary and grammar content of the subtopic and award points for correct answers. Students could participate individually or collaborate in pairs.

Pages 68–69

Reading and listening

Free time and the media

kerboodle!
- Audio files for core reading texts
- Audio files and transcripts for listening activity 2

Tokio Hotel

The reading stimulus text consists of a profile of a German band. The first two paragraphs are mainly in the present tense, and are more accessible for weaker learners. They are followed by *Steckbrief* type details about each of the four young band members. The second two paragraphs, mainly in the imperfect tense, include more complex structures.

The reading text is also available online as an audio file.

1a Read the article about the group "Tokio Hotel" and answer the questions below, giving the name of the correct person each time.

Refer to the vocabulary list. All students should be able to tackle the comprehension activity 1a, which can be done without reading the final two paragraphs.

Answers:

a Tom	b Georg	c Bill
d Gustav	e Georg	

1b Read the article again, then read the following sentences. For each sentence, write T (true), F (false) or ? (Not in the Text).

Activity 1b involves a deeper understanding of the text's content and is more challenging. Afterwards, refer to the *Grammatik* panel. Point out that this text, as often in written German, contains many examples of the imperfect tense.

Answers:

a T	b T	c F
d ?	e F	f ?

> **Grammatik**
> This panel reminds students of the types of past tense they have learnt about: the perfect with *haben* or *sein*, and the imperfect. It asks them to find examples of these tenses in the reading text, and refers them to page 182 in the grammar section. Elicit and discuss some of the examples found, taking the opportunity to recap the features of these tenses with less confident students.

2a *Transcript:* _____

Part 1

Was ist deine Lieblingsband?
Meine Lieblingsband ist "Juli".
Juli ist eine Band?
Ja, "Juli" ist eine Rockband aus Deutschland.
Wie lange gibt es "Juli" schon?
"Juli" gibt es seit 2001.
Und wieviele Bandmitglieder hat "Juli"?
Es gibt fünf Personen in "Juli". Die Sängerin heißt Eva Briegel. Das schreibt man E-V-A B-R-I-E-G-E-L

Part 2

Und welche Musik hörst du gern?
Ich mag die "Fantastischen Vier".
Das ist aber ein komischer Name.
Naja, es gibt eben vier Personen in dieser Gruppe.
Und welche Musik machen sie?
Also, sie sind besonders, weil es die erste Gruppe war, die in Deutschland Hip Hop und Rap auf Deutsch gesungen hat.
Wie lange gibt es die "Fantastischen Vier" schon?
Sie sind schon seit 1991 zusammen.
Seit 1991? Das ist aber lange. Wann hatten sie den letzten Hit?
Das war 2007. Die Single hieß „Einfach sein".
OK. Danke. Ich hoffe, ich kann mal etwas von den Fantastischen Vier hören.

Part 3

Hallo, Frau Maier. Was hören Sie denn gern?
Also, ich mag Marlene Dietrich sehr gern.
Marlene Dietrich – singt sie Rap?
Nein, nein. Marlene Dietrich wurde am 27. Dezember 1901 in Berlin geboren.
Hat sie immer in Berlin gewohnt?
Nein, sie war auch in Amerika und Frankreich und ist dann 1992 in Paris gestorben.
Hat sie noch etwas Anderes gemacht?
Ja, sie war auch Schauspielerin in vielen Filmen.
War sie erfolgreich?
Ja, sie hat Filme in Amerika gemacht und 1930 wurde sie für den Film "Morocco" für einen Oscar nominiert.

2a Listen to the interviews, then answer the following questions in English.

The audio extract consists of three short interviews with people about their favourite music. It includes examples of the present, perfect and imperfect tenses, and is accessible for less confident students.

Before starting, refer to the Examiner's tip. Students should listen to each part and answer the relevant questions before moving on to the next one. They could then listen all the way through to check their answers. Afterwards, you could ask them to pick out examples of the different tenses used.

Answers:

Part 1
a Rock music
b 2001
c Five
d Eva Briegel

Part 2
e The Fantastic Four
f They were the first group in Germany to do hip-hop and rap in German.
g 1991
h 2007

Part 3
i 27 December 1901 in Berlin
j America and France
k She was an actress and appeared in many films.
l She was nominated for an Oscar for her role in the film "Morocco".

2b 🎧 *Transcript:*

Große Einzugsparty für Bill. Bill zieht ins Wachsfigurenkabinett bei Madame Tussauds ein! Nicht das Madame Tussauds in London, sondern Madame Tussauds in Berlin. Am 30. September findet die Einzugsparty bei Madame Tussauds statt, dann wird die einzigartige Figur enthüllt. Und hier ist die große Überraschung für Fans von Tokio Hotel. Die ersten 20 Fans, die mit einem Geschenk für Bill Kaulitz am 30. September um 9:30 Uhr zu Madame Tussauds Berlin kommen, erhalten freien Eintritt und dürfen live bei der Enthüllung sein. Bill und die anderen Bandmitglieder werden natürlich auch dabei sein.

2b 🎧 Listen to the report about a special event for a member of "Tokio Hotel". Choose the correct answers.

This audio extract contains longer and more complex sentences to challenge more confident students. It consists of a news report about a party to celebrate the installation of a model of the lead singer of Tokio Hotel in Madame Tussauds, Berlin.

Refer to the Examiner's tip and the vocabulary given. Start by asking students to listen once through for gist, and to tell you what they have understood so far (if they do this without first reading the multiple-choice questions, it will be more challenging). When answering the questions, less confident students could work collaboratively with others, or refer to the transcript for support. Remind them that the information needed will be heard in the same order as the questions, and that they should listen for key indicators such as times and dates.

Answers:

a 2 b 3 c 1
d 2 e 3

Pages 70–71

Grammar practice

G Free time and the media

Separable verbs

'Separable verbs' is the subsidiary grammar point linked to Spread 2.1, *Was hast du gestern gemacht?* Students encounter examples of separable past participles (*ausgegeben, eingekauft*) in the core reading text, *Jetzt chatten!*, on page 58. Further examples (*ferngesehen, eingebrochen, ausgetrunken*) appear on page 59.
This grammar box deals with separable verbs in both the present and perfect tenses. Students may be referred to it at any point over the course of the spread.

1a 📖 ✏️ Unjumble the sentences below. Sentences a–c are in the present tense and sentences d–f are in the perfect tense.

This reading and writing activity requires students to decide on the correct word order for sentences containing separable verbs, in the present and perfect tenses.

Before they start the activity, discuss with weaker students key points of word order they must remember, and elicit the fact that the first three sentences will have a separable prefix at the end, while the second three will have a participle.

Answers:

a Ich mache mein Buch zu.
b Sie macht ihr Geschenk auf.
c Ihr hört selten richtig zu.
d Er hat bei Spielen nie mitgemacht.
e Sie hat im Kaufhaus eingekauft.
f Sie haben die ganze Nacht ferngesehen.

1b 💬 Work in pairs. You will need a dice. Roll the dice once to pick a pronoun and a second time to pick an activity. Then say the sentence in either the present or perfect tense.

This speaking activity practises using present tense and perfect tense forms of separable verbs, with a range of pronouns.

Less confident students could focus firstly just on the present tense forms of the separable verbs given, and you may wish to discuss these with them first in preparation. The more confident students could be asked to give both tenses each time.

Possible answers:

3 + 5 = Er gibt Geld aus. / Er hat Geld ausgegeben.
1 + 6 = Ich kaufe ein. / Ich habe eingekauft.
6 + 4 = Sie rufen an. / Sie haben angerufen.

Context 2 Leisure 53

The perfect tense with irregular verbs

The perfect tense of irregular verbs is the subsidiary grammar point linked to Spread 2.2, *Ich bin in die Stadt gegangen*.

Students will encounter many different types of irregular past participle in this spread – *geschwommen, geblieben, gegangen,* etc.

This grammar box complements the main spread grammar box on using the perfect tense with *sein*. Work on the subsidiary grammar point may follow on from students' main spread work on activity 2.

2a Read the following sentences. Either using your knowledge or referring to the verb table on pages 191–194, correct the mistakes in the past participles.

This reading activity requires students to check past participles for accuracy, and to practise using the verb table in their book.

Encourage them to rely firstly on their knowledge to make a guess, then to use the verb table to check. Stress the importance of learning irregular past participles, as many of the most useful verbs are irregular (and point out that the same is true in English!)

Answers:

a Er ist in den Ferien im Meer geschwommen.
b Wir haben von Madrid viele Postkarten geschrieben.
c Manchmal sind wir am Abend ins Kino gegangen.
d Die Familie Peters ist wie jedes Jahr nach Mallorca geflogen.
e Als ich jünger war, habe ich in einem Chor gesungen.
f Ich bin heute morgen sehr spät aufgestanden.

2b After your teacher has checked your answers, write six sentences of your own using the irregular past participles.

This writing activity practises using irregular past participles in students' own work.

Suggest that they find examples of verbs in the verb table to use and encourage creativity!

The imperfect tenses of *haben* and *sein*

The imperfect of *haben* and *sein* is the subsidiary grammar point linked to Spread 2.3, *Wir bekommen nicht genug Taschengeld!*

The imperfect tense of *haben* and *sein* feature in the core reading text on page 62, *Mein Geld*. Students should be able to work out the meanings of *war* and *hatte* from context.

The next spreads in the Free time and the media topic cover the imperfect tense in more detail. This grammar box serves as an introduction to these common forms, with the accompanying activity requiring receptive rather than productive work.

3 Choose the correct imperfect forms of *haben* and *sein* in each sentence.

This reading activity requires students to distinguish between *haben* and *sein* in the imperfect tense, choosing the correct verb according to meaning.

Point out that the imperfect forms of these two verbs are easy to understand and use, being similar to the English, and stress their usefulness as a way of adding a past tense in the Speaking and Writing units.

Answers:

a Wo warst du letztes Wochenende? Hattest du gutes Wetter?
b Ich war gestern im Park und meine kleine Schwester war dabei.
c Wir hatten wenig Zeit, als wir letztes Wochenende beim Einkaufen waren.
d Peter und Angelika waren sehr enttäuscht, dass es zu spät fürs Kino war.
e Wart ihr in den Ferien? Hattet ihr gutes Wetter? Ihr seht so braun aus.

Modal verbs (revision)

The revision of modal verbs is the subsidiary grammar point linked to Spread 2.4, *Wir waren im Einkaufszentrum*.

The core reading text on page 64, *Ich kaufe Klamotten*, features examples of present tense modal verbs in use (*nur darf ich das nicht meinen Eltern sagen, ich muss sie jetzt umtauschen, ich kann mir das jetzt nicht mehr leisten* etc.).

Students can be referred to this grammar box to refresh their memories on modal verbs, which they first worked on in Context 1 (pages 23 and 25).

4a Translate the following sentences into English.

This reading activity requires students to understand modal verbs and locate the infinitives which go with them at the end of the sentences, in order to translate the sentences into English.

For additional practice, students could then make up four sentences of their own starting with the same pronouns and modal verbs as these.

Answers (suggested):

a I have to save my money for an MP3 player.
b He's not allowed to go out for too long.
c We can meet in town at the weekend.
d We should visit my grandma next weekend.

4b Now translate these sentences into German.

This writing activity requires students to select the correct modal verb and form and to use correct word order, in order to translate the sentences into German.

Accept any suitable slight variations in wording in their answers. You may wish to supply one or two items of key vocabulary for weaker students.

Answers:

a Ich will neue Sportschuhe kaufen.
b Wir dürfen nicht zu spät ausbleiben.
c Sie kann mich nicht verstehen.
d Könnt ihr Oma am Wochenende besuchen?

> **Using *wann*, *wenn* and *als***   *Grammatik*
>
> This is the subsidiary grammar point linked to Spread 2.5, *Ich lebe im Internet*.
> Activity 2 on page 67 involves comparisons of past and present, with the use of *als*. The wider topic of different ways of saying 'when' in German may be introduced at this point, as a way into further discussions of technologies of today and yesterday.

5a Read the sentences and fill in the gaps with *wann*, *wenn* or *als*.

In this activity, students must distinguish between the uses of the three different words for 'when', in order to select the correct one for each gap.

Remind students to look for grammatical clues: verb tenses and word order. They could then translate the sentences into English to show they have understood them.

Answers:

a Wann   b wenn   c Wenn
d als   e wann / wenn   f als

5b Now write five sentences of your own, using *wann*, *wenn* and *als*.

This writing activity challenges students to make active use of *wann*, *wenn* and *als*, and to structure their sentences correctly accordingly.

For less confident students, you could firstly provide simple sentences in English, with familiar vocabulary, for them to translate into German – perhaps focusing on *wenn* and *als* initially. They could then replace words in these sentences to make them their own.

Pages 72–73

Vocabulary

V   **Free time and the media**

kerboodle! • MP3 files for each vocabulary list

The essential vocabulary used within Topic 1, Context 2 is presented on this vocabulary spread.

Here students can learn the key words for the topic area *Free time and the media*. You may also want to direct students to the online audio files of these vocabulary lists, so they can hear how the words are pronounced by a native speaker.

Some words are in light grey on the vocabulary spreads in the Student Book. This indicates items that are not included in the GCSE specification vocabulary list, so

students do not need to learn these items for Listening and Reading assessment. However, you may wish students to use them in Speaking and Writing Controlled Assessments.

Pages 74–75

2.6   Ich möchte mal nach …

Plans, preferences, experiences

Subject	Talking about holiday preferences and experiences
G 1	Using correct word order (time – manner – place)
G 2	Using *ich möchte …*
	Recognising information presented in different ways

kerboodle!
- Audio file for core reading text
- Audio file and transcript for listening activity 2
- Listening activity and transcript: *Grüße aus …*
- Grammar activity: Using correct word order (time – manner – place)
- Writing worksheet
- Foundation reading worksheet
- Extension reading worksheet

Starter activity

To introduce this subtopic and revise German words for countries, display five to ten anagrams of familiar names of countries, and ask students to solve them. Alternatively, use a computer-generated wordsearch or crossword puzzle.

Urlaubsgrüsse

The two holiday postcards which make up the reading stimulus text include examples of varied word order (inversion and subordinating conjunctions). They also include use of *ich möchte*.

The reading text is also available online as an audio file.

> Explain that if students can learn to recognise information presented in different ways they will feel more confident in understanding complicated-looking phrases. They should also remember in their own speaking and writing that there will always be an alternative way of saying something if they can't remember a precise phrase.   *Strategie*

1 Match up the two sentence halves.

Students read/listen to the postcards and work out which sentence halves should be joined to reflect the content. Refer to the *Strategie* panel. Afterwards, you could read the postcards in detail with the class, analysing word order and picking out useful holiday-related words and phrases. Refer also to the *Tipp*.

Answers:

a 3   b 7   c 4   d 6
e 1   f 5   g 2   h 8

Context 2 Leisure 55

Look at this box with students and elicit their ideas on where they have previously encountered *ich möchte*. Ask them to look at the examples in the reading text and tell you how it is used (with an infinitive). Point out that it is an easy to use and very useful expression. *Tipp*

2 🎧 Transcript:

1 Hallo! Ich bin der Felix. Ich fahre im Winter normalerweise mit meiner Schule zum Skifahren in die Schweiz. Ich mache das gern, weil ich sportlich bin.
2 Tag! Ich heiße Nadja. Im Sommer reise ich normalerweise mit meinen Eltern nach Frankreich, weil wir Familie dort haben. Wir fahren meistens mit dem Auto, aber das dauert sehr lange. Ich möchte lieber alleine fahren.
3 Hi! Ich heiße Luis. Am Wochenende fahre ich oft mit meiner Freundin nach London zum einkaufen. Wir nehmen den Zug. Leider kann das ein bisschen teuer sein.
4 Hallo! Mein Name ist Marcus. Ich möchte nächste Woche sieben Tage in Spanien verbringen. Ich lerne in der Schule Englisch und Spanisch und will mein Spanisch üben. Ich möchte mit dem Flugzeug nach Spanien fliegen, weil es schneller ist.
5 Ich bin die Anita. Ich bleibe dieses Jahr in den Herbstferien zu Hause. Meine Eltern fahren in Urlaub. Ich bleibe mit meinem kleinen Bruder zu Hause. Ich bin schon achtzehn. Ich mag das nicht, aber meine Eltern geben mir auch etwas Geld.

2 🎧 Listen to the five people discussing holidays. For each person, choose three pictures to illlustrate any of the following: destination, season, length of stay, transport, which people he or she went with. Each person will only mention three of the five things, but there may be additional details for you to note down.

The audio extract consists of five young people talking about where they usually holiday, or what they will be doing this year. It includes examples of time – manner – place word order and of *ich möchte*.

Students listen to the recording and select three relevant pictures from those given. Encourage more confident learners to note as many additional details as possible (the listening could be done in two stages, with this as the second stage). With weaker students, you may need to interpret the pictures before they listen: ask them to suggest/guess what each one represents.

Answers:

Felix	i, k, n	Additional details: going skiing, likes it because he's sporty.
Nadja	b, c, m	Additional details: going with family, has relatives in France, car journey takes a long time, would rather go alone.
Luis	e, j, o	Additional details: going with girlfriend, going shopping, train can be a bit expensive.
Marcus	d, h, l	Additional details: wants to go next week, learns English and Spanish at school, wants to practise his Spanish, wants to travel by plane because it's quicker.
Anita	a, f, g	Additional details: parents are going on holiday, is 18, doesn't like being left at home but parents give her some money.

This panel explains use of the time – manner – place rule for word order. It shows how to form sentences following this rule, and reminds students that the verb must remain as second idea. You might wish to practise this further by building example sentences together with the class, and arranging components of a sentence in the correct order. This could be made more physical by asking for volunteers to stand at the front of the class holding cards with parts of the sentence on, and others to move them so that they are standing in the correct order.
The panel also refers students to page 84 to learn the use of the different forms of *ich möchte* etc. *Grammatik*

3a G Put the words in each sentence in the correct order.

This grammar activity practises using time – manner – place word order.

Refer to the *Grammatik* panel. Students look at the component parts provided for each sentence, and arrange them in the correct order according to the time – manner – place rule. You may wish to point out afterwards that *nach* (to) is only used with named places/countries.

Answers:

a In den Ferien fahre ich mit dem Auto nach Spanien.
b Meine Eltern reisen im Sommer alleine nach Italien.
c Nächstes Jahr möchte ich mit Freunden in die Schweiz fliegen.
d Mein Bruder und ich möchten im Winter mit dem Zug nach Holland fahren.
e Er ist im Sommer mit seiner Schulklasse nach Deutschland gefahren.

3b G Now write some sentences of your own using the time – manner – place rule.

This grammar activity provides supported practice in constructing new sentences following the time – manner – place rule. If necessary, refer again to the *Grammatik* panel.

Students use the language structure grid to create sentences with the correct word order. More confident students could be encouraged to branch out and make up entirely new sentences.

4 💬 Work in pairs. You are at a travel agent's. One of you plays the role of the client explaining what your holiday preferences are, while the other plays the role of the agent trying to find the perfect holiday. Include the following questions, using the *Sie* form of address. The person playing the agent should make a suggestion before you swap roles.

The student playing the role of the client can use the language structure grid for support. More confident learners should be able to use *ich möchte* with exciting holiday ideas of their own – encourage creativity!

Plenary activity

Ask all students to write down three things about their own usual holidays (using language from this subtopic), and one sentence to say where they would really like to go (using *ich möchte*). They could then read these out to a partner (a different one from activity 4), or to the whole class.

Pages 76–77

2.7 Urlaubspläne

Plans, preferences, experiences	
Subject	Talking about holiday plans
G 1	Using the future tense with *werden*
G 2	Using *um … zu …*, *ohne … zu …* and *anstatt … zu …*
🌐	Applying rules in new situations

kerboodle!
- Audio file for core reading text
- Audio file and transcript for listening activity 3
- Reading activity: *Konstantins Urlaubspläne*
- Grammar activity: Using the future tense with *werden*
- Speaking worksheet
- Foundation listening worksheet
- Audio file and transcript for foundation listening worksheet
- Extension listening worksheet
- Audio file and transcript for extension listening worksheet

Starter activity

Briefly revise the concept of time – manner – place to assist students in applying it in this subtopic (see the *Strategie* panel on p.77): give students a collection of phrases relating to holidays to classify into three groups – time, manner and place. This could be done on the board/screen, as a worksheet, or as a physical activity using word cards.

Das werde ich machen

The reading stimulus text consists of six young people describing their future holiday plans. It includes examples of the future tense with *werden*, and of *wenn … dann …* and *um … zu …* .

The reading text is also available online as an audio file.

1 📖 🎧 Read the holiday plans. Are the following statements true (T), false (F) or not in the text (?)?

Students read/listen to the text, then decide if the sentences given are true, false or not in the text. Afterwards, elicit the fact that the future tense is used, and see if students can explain how it is formed before they look at the *Grammatik* panel. Also refer to the *Tipp*.

Answers:

| a T | b T | c F | d F |
| e T | f ? | g T | h F |

> **Tipp**
> Read the content of this box with the class, and discuss how to use these constructions in terms of word order. Point out to students that 'showing off' that they can use these could increase their range of language and accuracy marks in the Speaking and Writing units.

> **Grammatik**
> This panel explains how to form the future tense, and gives the present tense forms of *werden*. Point out that this construction, with an infinitive at the end of the sentence, is the same as they have already used with modal verbs (and most recently with *ich möchte* in the previous subtopic). Remind students that the ability to use a range of tenses will improve their marks in the Speaking and Writing units.
> The panel also refers students to page 84 to learn about using *ohne … zu …*, *anstatt … zu …* and *um … zu …* .

2 **G** Write the correct form of *werden* and add the infinitive in German of the word in brackets.

This grammar activity practises use of the future tense with *werden*.

Refer firstly to the *Grammatik* panel. Make sure students have noted that *werden* is irregular, and that they are clear about the use of an infinitive at the end of the sentence. They then fill the gaps in the sentences given, with the correct form of *werden* and infinitive.

Answers:

a Ich <u>werde</u> nach Frankreich <u>reisen</u>.
b Wir <u>werden</u> meine Oma und meinen Opa <u>besuchen</u>.
c Lara und Tobias <u>werden</u> mit dem Flugzeug <u>fliegen</u>.
d <u>Wirst</u> du mit mir nach Amerika <u>kommen</u>?
e Sie <u>wird</u> sich am Strand <u>ausruhen</u>.

3 🎧 *Transcript:*

> Grüß Gott. Ich heiße Lukas. Ich habe schon viele Pläne für meine Sommerferien. Ich werde in der ersten Woche meiner Ferien zu meinen Großeltern gehen. Dann, in der zweiten Woche, werden meine Eltern und ich mit dem Wohnwagen nach Italien fahren. In Italien werden wir zuerst in Venedig mit einer Gondel auf den Kanälen fahren. Dann fahren wir weiter und verbringen noch zwei Wochen an der Küste. Wenn das Wetter gut ist, werde ich im Meer baden, Beachvolleyball spielen und am Abend viel Pizza essen.

3 🎧 Listen to Lukas talking about his holiday plans and fill in the gaps.

In this audio extract, a young person describes his holiday plans for this summer. The extract includes examples of the future tense with *werden* and the time – manner – place rule, as well as useful vocabulary relating to holiday activities.

Students listen to the extract and fill the gaps in the transcript. They should then listen again to check, and could be asked to translate what Lukas says into English.

Answers:

a Pläne	b Woche	c Großeltern
d Wohnwagen	e Italien	f werden
g fahren	h zwei	i Wetter
j baden	k spielen	l Abend

> 💭 Point out to students that it is always important to try and include previously-learned knowledge of grammar in their speaking and writing. Show them how the language structure grid for activities 4 and 5 is set out following time – manner – place word order to help them. Emphasise that this is just one example of the strategy of applying rules that they already know, to new situations.
>
> *Strategie*

4 💭 🔊 Work in pairs. You are planning a holiday. Choose at least three pictures, point at them and tell your partner your plans, using the future tense with *werden*. Use the following questions as a starting point.

Support weaker learners by practising in advance how they could respond for each picture, using the language structure grid. Refer to the *Strategie* panel and ask students to check whether their partner is following the time – manner – place rule in their answers. You could then re-run the activity, with students trying to give their own real-life answers if they wish. Encourage more confident students to include as much detail as possible, perhaps eliciting and collating additional vocabulary for destinations and holiday activities before they start. Partners will need to make brief notes on what their partner says in preparation for the writing activity which follows.

5 ✏️ Write up both your plans and your partner's.

Students should make use of the language structure grid to maximise their accuracy in this activity, and will also need to refer back to the *Grammatik* and *Strategie* panels. More confident learners should be encouraged to include use of *wenn … dann*, *um … zu …* etc. if appropriate.

Plenary activity

Ask volunteers to read out what they have written about their holiday plans to the class, and encourage positive comments in German. Alternatively, you could collect in the texts and select some to read aloud, asking the class to listen and guess who each one is about.

Pages 78–79

2.8 Berlin ist cool!

What to see and getting around

Subject	Talking about holiday activities and attractions
G 1	Using different tenses (past, present and future)
G 2	Using adjectives after *etwas*, *nichts*, *viel*, *wenig* and *alles*
🔊	Tackling longer texts

kerboodle!
- Audio file for core reading text
- Audio file and transcript for listening activity 2
- Listening activity and transcript: *Tina am Apparat!*
- Grammar activity: Using different tenses (past, present and future)
- Speaking worksheet
- Extension listening worksheet
- Audio file and transcript for extension listening worksheet

Starter activity

Engage students' interest in the city of Berlin in preparation for the reading text in this subtopic by giving them a few general knowledge quiz questions about the city to answer. These could have multiple-choice answers, and for weaker groups could be in English if you prefer. For example, ask them to locate the city on a map, establish that it's Germany's capital city, ask about the former Berlin Wall, the German Parliament, or the name of any German politician they've heard of.

Daniels Urlaub

This longer reading stimulus text is a description of how a young person from Berlin spends his holiday time in the city. It includes examples of the present, perfect, imperfect and future tenses.

Before they start this reading activity, refer students to the *Strategie* panel about tackling longer texts. Encourage them to look for visual clues as to what the text is about, and point out that titles, subtitles and captions of pictures often give a good idea of what is in the text. Advise them to start by reading the text once through for gist before trying to answer the questions. They should also be aware that the information needed for the answers is likely to be found in the same order within the text as the order of the questions. They then firstly answer the multiple-choice comprehension questions, followed by more difficult comprehension questions requiring full answers.

The reading text is also available online as an audio file.

> 📖 You could demonstrate this strategy for tackling longer texts by looking at the first part of the text for activity 1 with the class, and asking them to pick out words they know, to guess some from context, and thus to work out as much as they can about the meaning.
>
> *Strategie*

1a 📖 🎧 Read Daniel's article then choose the correct answers for each question.

Answers:

| a 2 | b 1 | c 1 |
| d 3 | e 2 | |

1b 📖 🎧 Read the article again and answer these questions in German.

Answers:

a Er ist zum Bundestagsgebäude gegangen.
b Er wird mit ein paar Freunden grillen.
c [Answers may vary – teacher to check]: Man kann ins Kino gehen, einkaufen gehen, zum Museum am Checkpoint Charlie gehen …

2 🎧 *Transcript:*

1 *Hallo, wie heißt du?*
Ich heiße Jutta und komme aus der Schweiz.
Was machst du gerade?
Im Moment bin ich im Naturkundemuseum, weil ich mich für Erdkunde und Geschichte interessiere.
Wie lange bist du schon hier in München?
Ich bin schon drei Tage hier und bin schon einkaufen gegangen und habe mich im Englischen Garten gesonnt. Heute Nachmittag werde ich noch Souvenirs kaufen und morgen fahre ich nach Hause.

2 *Hallo, wie heißt du?*
Ich bin der Bernd.
Bist du hier auf Urlaub?
Ja, ich komme eigentlich aus Germering in Süddeutschland, aber ich mache Urlaub hier in Hamburg. Ich mache gerade eine Bootsfahrt, weil die Sonne scheint. Gestern war das Wetter schlecht und wir sind einkaufen gegangen. Heute Abend werden wir in einem italienischen Restaurant essen, weil ich Pizza lecker finde.

3 *Grüß dich. Wie heißt du?*
Ich bin Mareike und komme aus Norddeutschland.
Oh, und was machst du hier in Köln?
Also im Moment kaufe ich Souvenirs für meine Familie ein, aber gestern habe ich die Sehenswürdigkeiten besichtigt, der Kölner Dom ist ja sehr imposant. Morgen werde ich dann noch ein paar Museen besuchen. Ich finde es wirklich toll hier!

4 *Hallo. Wer bist du?*
Ich bin Klara und verbringe meine Ferien hier an der Nordseeküste. Ich nutze das schöne Wetter und sonne mich hier am Strand. In den nächsten paar Tagen werde ich noch eine Bootsfahrt machen und das kleine Schifffahrtsmuseum besuchen.
Hast du schon etwas anderes hier gemacht?
Ja, gestern haben wir im Restaurant gegessen und ich bin im Meer geschwommen.

5 *Wir sind hier in Dresden. Hallo, Entschuldigung. Wie heißt du? Wohnst du hier?*
Mein Name ist Konstantin und ich bin hier auf Urlaub.
Was hast du schon gemacht?
Ich habe schon die Sehenswürdigkeiten wie die Dresdner Oper besucht. Im Moment kaufe ich ein paar Souvenirs, aber ich treffe in ein paar Minuten meine Freunde und dann werden wir noch ein Museum besuchen.

2 🎧 Five teenagers are being interviewed on holiday. They each mention what they are doing, what they have done and what they are going to do. Copy and complete the table.

The audio extract consists of five young people being interviewed on holiday. It includes examples of the present, perfect and future tenses.

Before students listen to the recording, discuss which tenses they will be listening out for, and what the indicators for these will be. More confident students could listen a second time and note down any additional information they can understand. They could also report their answers in German third person sentences.

Answers:

	macht	schon gemacht	wird machen
Jutta	b	d, f	d
Bernd	a	d	c
Mareike	d	e	b
Klara	f	c, g	a, b
Konstantin	d	e	b

3 🌀 Throw a dice and, using the pictures from the previous activity, practise the present tense, perfect tense and future tense (blue = present tense, orange = perfect tense, green = future tense).

This activity practises formation of the present, perfect and future tenses.

Before they start this speaking activity, refer students to the *Grammatik* panel, and as necessary back to the pages where formation of the three tenses is explained. You might wish to practise forming the tenses for each, or some, of the pictures they will be using, and to display visual support of this for weaker students. Students should work in pairs or small groups and use a counter to move along the squares as they throw the dice.

> This panel reminds students to include different tenses in their German speaking and writing. It refers them back to the pages where formation of each tense was explained. You could ask them to find examples of each tense in the reading text for activity 1. Remind them that using different tenses will increase their marks in the Speaking and Writing units.

Grammatik

4 **G** Where do the sentences start and finish? Are the sentences in the perfect tense, present tense or future tense?

This grammar activity practises identifying the present, perfect and future tenses, and word order associated with them.

Students identify the start and finish of each sentence, and write them out correctly with gaps between each word. They note which tense each sentence is in. Refer to the *Grammatik* panel and the *Tipp*. Quick finishers could write some similar sentences for another student to solve.

Context 2 Leisure 59

Answers:

Ich fahre in den Ferien oft nach Amerika. – present tense

Letztes Jahr bin ich auch nach Amerika gefahren. – perfect tense

Wir sind nach Orlando geflogen. – perfect tense

Ich liebe Orlando. – present tense

Mein Bruder und ich lieben die Vergnügungsparks und Wasserparks. – present tense

Wir sind viel schwimmen gegangen und haben oft in Fastfood-Restaurants gegessen. – perfect tense

Wir werden nächstes Jahr nicht nach Amerika fliegen. – future tense

Ich werde meinen Brieffreund in der Türkei besuchen und meine Eltern werden hier bleiben. – future tense

> **Tipp**
> After looking at this box with the class, you could elicit and collate further examples of time indicators for each tense, and ask students to learn them as a homework task.

Plenary activity

Provide five to ten sentences, in a range of tenses, for students to expand – they must identify the tense and select and insert a suitable time indicator. Remind them that if they start their sentence with the time indicator, the verb must remain as second idea. Elicit a few examples for each sentence afterwards.

Pages 80–81

2.9 Auf Achse

What to see and getting around

Subject	Talking about travel
G 1	Asking questions using interrogatives
G 2	Revising different cases (nominative and accusative)
🌐	Making vocab lists

kerboodle!
- Audio file for core reading text
- Video and transcript for video activity 3
- Grammar activity: Using interrogatives
- Writing worksheet
- Extension listening worksheet
- Audio file and transcript for extension listening worksheet

Starter activity

Revise familiar transport-related vocabulary in preparation for this subtopic: display lists of words and ask students to find the odd one out in each case. The lists could for example include modes of transport, signs at a station, types of ticket or timetable-related words.

1 **V** You see the following signs at a train station. Where would you go if you wanted to …

Students look at the train station signs and match each to the correct meaning.

a Gepäckaufbewahrung
b Imbiss
c Ausgang
d Auskunft
e Reservierungen
f Bahnsteig

Core reading text

The reading stimulus text consists of five short personal statements about modes of transport when on holiday. It includes examples of the present, perfect, imperfect and future tenses.

The reading text is also available online as an audio file.

2 📖 🎧 Read what these people have to say about different modes of transport.

Students read/listen to the statements and find the required information. Encourage more confident learners to provide as many additional details as possible.

Answers:

Herr und Frau Schiller: car/hire car, positive because they were independent, wanted to discover the surroundings, want to do it again in future

Tatjana: flying, negative because she wants to protect the environment and the CO_2 emissions are so high, is quite active in her environmental protection group at school, wants to travel round Europe next year

Olaf: tour bus, negative because it was exhausting, was in South America for three weeks with family and had originally wanted to rent a car, will stay at home next year and go to the lake

Esther: train (Interrailing), positive because it's cheap for young people, will be touring Eastern Europe with her sister this year, neither of them have a driver's licence

Karsten: sponsored bike ride in the Alps, positive as it's for a good cause and keeps him fit, has to raise 500 Euros and train a lot.

3 🎬 *Transcript:*

A
Katja	Entschuldigung! Wie komme ich am besten zum Bahnhof?
Frank	Wie bitte?
Katja	Wie komme ich am besten zum Bahnhof, bitte?
Frank	Naja, das kommt darauf an … Möchtest du zum Hauptbahnhof oder zum Ostbahnhof?
Katja	Zum Hauptbahnhof, bitte.
Frank	Tja, dann gehst du am besten zu Fuß.
Katja	Zu Fuß? Ich bin aber eigentlich schon sehr müde und würde lieber mit dem Bus fahren. Wie lange dauert das, wenn ich zu Fuß gehe?
Frank	Nur fünf Minuten. Der Bahnhof is gleich um die Ecke.
Katja	Danke sehr.

B
Lorenz	Entschuldigen Sie, bitte. Wo ist die Stephanskirche? Ich habe gehört, dass sie sehr schön ist.

Frau Müller	Die Stephanskirche? Ja, die ist wunderschön. Nun, wenn du dorthin fahren willst, dann nimmst du am besten den Bus, Nummer sieben oder zweiunddreißig.
Lorenz	Was kostet eine Busfahrt? Vielleicht muss ich doch zu Fuß gehen, denn ich habe nur fünf Euro.
Frau Müller	Keine Angst, eine Fahrt für Jugendliche kostet nur drei Euro.
Lorenz	Ach, das ist gut. Danke. Auf Wiedersehen!
Frau Müller	Auf Wiedersehen!
C	
Anja	Entschuldigung. Ich suche das Museum.
Herr Becker	Also, Museen gibt es hier viele. Welches Museum meinst du denn? Es gibt das Völkerkundemuseum, das historische Museum und das Stadtmuseum …
Anja	Nein, keines von denen. Ich meinte das Technikmuseum.
Herr Becker	Moment mal, das Technikmuseum … mmmh … ach ja. Nimm den Zug Richtung Karlsplatz und steig dort um. Von da nimm die Straßenbahn.
Anja	Ich nehme den Zug … oh, das ist aber kompliziert. Können Sie das nochmal wiederholen?
Herr Becker	Also, fahr zuerst mit dem Zug zum Karlsplatz und dort musst du umsteigen. Dann nimm die Straßenbahn.
Anja	Danke. Und wann öffnet das Museum?
Herr Becker	Alle Museen öffnen um neun Uhr.
Anja	Danke. Tschüss.
D	
Frank	Oh! Entschuldigen Sie! Wie komme ich am besten zur Post?
Frau Müller	Da fährst du am besten mit dem Bus. Das dauert nur zehn Minuten … Aber moment mal. Es ist ja schon siebzehn Uhr! Die Post ist jetzt geschlossen.
Frank	Ach, nein. Das gibt's doch nicht. Morgen ist der Geburtstag meiner Oma, und ich habe vergessen, ihr eine Karte zu schreiben. Jetzt bekommt sie ihre Geburtstagskarte nicht mehr rechtzeitig.

3 Watch and listen to the dialogues. Where does each person want to go? How will they get there? Note down any extra information you pick up.

This video clip shows four people asking how to get to places in the town. It includes examples of interrogatives, as well as useful vocabulary for directions and transport.

Students watch the video and note the required information. Encourage more confident learners to note as much additional information as possible. Before moving on to activity four, they could watch the clip again and make a note of any question words they hear.

Answers:

a main railway station, walk. Extra details: person is very tired and would rather take the bus but it's only five minutes away, just around the corner

b church, bus. Extra details: Stephanskirche, very beautiful, bus number 7 or 32, traveller only has 5 Euros but journey only costs 3 Euros for young people

c technology museum, train then tram. Extra details: take train to Karlsplatz and change to tram there, museum opens at 9

d post office, bus. Extra details: journey is only 10 minutes but it's 5pm already so post office will be closed, it's the speaker's grandma's birthday tomorrow so she won't get her card on time

> **Grammatik**
> This panel explains how to use interrogatives at the start of a question in German, and lists the most common interrogatives. Make sure all meanings are clear to the class, and practise pronunciation of the more difficult ones (e.g. *Welche / Warum / Woher*). Elicit the reason for the varying endings of *Welche(r/s)*, and demonstrate its use with nouns of different genders. The panel also refers students to page 85 to revise the nominative and accusative cases.

4a **G** Fill the gaps with the correct question word.

This grammar activity practises the selection and use of question words.

Refer to the *Grammatik* panel. Point out that students must read each question carefully to ensure they use the correct question word.

Answers:

a <u>Wann</u> kommt der Zug aus Salzburg an?
b <u>Wie</u> finde ich bitte einen Supermarkt?
c <u>Wohin</u> fährt dieser Bus – nach Augsburg oder Nürnberg?
d <u>Was</u> kostet eine Karte für einen Erwachsenen?

4b **G** Now try to ask the correct question for the underlined part of each sentence.

This grammar activity practises question formation. Again refer students to the *Grammatik* panel. Make sure all are clear on the difference between *wohin?* and *woher?*

Answers:

a Wie viel kostet eine Karte für Jugendliche?
b Wo ist / Wie finde ich die Bushaltestelle? / Wie komme ich am besten zur Bushaltestelle?
c Wohin fährt der Zug?
d Woher kommt der Zug?

> **Strategie**
> This list-making strategy should help students to expand their vocabulary. Encourage them to look up the words they need, and note them down methodically (genders with nouns, infinitives of verbs). If they haven't already done so, this might be a good point for students to start keeping a vocabulary notebook or list which they regularly add to and learn from.

Context 2 Leisure 61

5a You and a friend are planning a trip. It could be a weekend trip or a journey around the world. Answer your friend's questions.

In preparation for this activity, refer students to the *Strategie* panel and allow time for preparation of vocab lists. You may need to elicit or make some suggestions of the types of words that will be useful for this activity. Encourage students to be creative in their replies to the questions and to try and have a real discussion, where both contribute opinions and they reach decisions together. They should use the language structure box for support. Refer also to the *Tipp*. By reusing the questions when giving answers, they should aim to extend their sentences beyond the bare minimum.

> *Tipp*
> Remind students that this is a good way of extending their sentences, and thus the range and quality of their German. You could practise the technique using some of the questions from activity 5a.

5b Now write about your plans.

Students use the language structure grid to help them write sentences about the plan they decided upon. More confident students should include as much extra detail as possible. Afterwards, volunteers could read their plan out to the class.

Plenary activity

Students could finish this subtopic by adding to the vocab list they started for activity 5a (or starting one, if not already done). Suggest a number of nouns, verbs and adjectives they should aim to collect by looking back through the texts on the two pages of the subtopic, or also going a little further back if you prefer. They could then select the ten most interesting or useful words to learn as part of their homework. At the end of the allotted time, you could ask for examples of the most interesting / difficult / strange word they have noted.

Pages 82–83

Reading and listening

Holidays

kerboodle!
- Audio file for core reading text
- Audio files and transcripts for listening activity 2

Zell am See und Kaprun

The reading stimulus text consists of information from a tourism website about leisure activities in two Austrian resorts, both in winter and in summer. It contains useful vocabulary relating to leisure activities, and examples of a range of structures including *wenn…dann, es gibt, man kann…*

The reading text is also available online as an audio file.

1a Read the texts on Zell am See and Kaprun, then answer the following questions in English.

All students should be able to attempt activity 1a. Remind them to look at pictures and headings for clues about the content, and ask them firstly to read each of the two parts for gist, using the vocabulary list for support, then to think about what types of words they are looking for to answer each of the questions.

Answers:

a Austria
b Blue
c English, French, Italian, Polish and German
d 10
e Swimming, surfing, sailing and waterskiing
f 4 km long and 1.3 km wide
g 40

1b Read the texts again and match up the sentence halves.

Activity 1b involves a deeper understanding of the text than 1a and is more challenging. Refer students to the Examiner's tip before they start.

Answers:

a 3   b 7   c 4   d 1
e 6   f 5   g 2

> *Grammatik*
> This panel explains the use of *oder?* and *nicht wahr?* at the end of a statement to make it into a question, as heard in the interview with Herr Weber. It also suggests that students note down the question words they hear in the interview (see activities 2a and 2b), and refers them forward to page 187 in the grammar section for further information about interrogatives. Elicit and discuss some of the examples found, taking the opportunity to remind students that asking questions is a useful way of keeping a conversation going.

2a *Transcript:*

Interviewer: Grüß Gott, Herr Weber. Man sagt doch 'Grüß Gott' in dieser Gegend nicht 'Guten Tag', oder?
Herr Weber: Ja, das ist richtig. Man sagt hier 'Grüß Gott' oder 'Servus'.
Interviewer: Sie arbeiten hier im Fremdenverkehrsamt in Zell am See. Darf ich ihnen ein paar Fragen stellen?
Herr Weber: Ja, sicher. Fragen Sie nur.
Interviewer: Also, die erste Frage: Wie komme ich als Tourist am besten nach Zell am See?
Herr Weber: Nun, wenn sie nicht so weit weg wohnen, dann fahren Sie mit dem Auto. Wir haben hier auch einen Bahnhof. Sie können also auch mit dem Zug fahren. Aber, wenn sie weit weg wohnen, dann fliegen Sie am besten. Der nächste Flughafen ist in Salzburg.
Interviewer: Danke.

2a 🎧 Listen to the interview with Herr Weber and answer the following questions in English.

The audio extract consists of the first part of an interview with Herr Weber, who works in the tourist information office in Zell am See. The questions and answers are mainly short, and not complex, making the extract accessible for less confident students.

After listening to the extract and answering the questions, students could listen again and be asked to pick out particular language items, for example the use of *oder* at the end of a statement, and question words. Refer to the *Grammatik* panel.

Answers:

a Grüß Gott and Servus.
b The tourist information office in Zell.
c Car, train or plane.

2b 🎧 *Transcript:*

Interviewer:	Herr Weber. Ich habe noch andere Fragen. Wie viele Einwohner hat Zell am See?
Herr Weber:	Hier gibt es circa zehntausend Einwohner, aber wir haben viele Touristen. Deshalb gibt es hier immer mehr Leute.
Interviewer:	OK. Hier ist meine nächste Frage: Zell ist berühmt für seinen See. Wie tief ist der Zeller See?
Herr Weber:	Moment. Da muss ich nachdenken. Mmh..ach ja..er ist achtundsechzig Meter tief.
Interviewer:	Achtundsechzig Meter … das ist aber tief. Danke. Und wie hoch ist der höchste Berg hier in Österreich?
Herr Weber:	Also, der höchste Berg ist nicht hier in Zell am See, aber er ist in der Nähe. Er heißt Großglockner und ist dreitausendsiebenhundertachtundneunzig Meter hoch.
Interviewer:	Moment, ich schreibe das auf – dreitausendsiebenhundertachtundneunzig Meter. OK. Wenn ich als Jugendlicher nach Zell komme, wo kann ich hier übernachten? Ist es sehr teuer?
Herr Weber:	Nein, wir haben Jugendherbergen. Sie kosten zwischen zehn und dreißig Euro pro Nacht.
Interviewer:	Und was gibt es in diesen Jugendherbergen?
Herr Weber:	Das kommt darauf an, aber alle unsere Jugendherbergen haben eine Dusche im Zimmer. Hier in der Nähe gibt es die Jugendherberge ‚Seeblick'. Sie ist nur fünf Minuten vom See entfernt und hat auch einen Fußball- und Basketballplatz. Am Abend kann man in den Fernsehraum gehen und es gibt auch ein kleines Kino. Gar nicht schlecht für eine Jugendherberge.
Interviewer:	Danke, Herr Weber. Das ist dann alles. Auf Wiedersehen.

2b 🎧 Listen to the next part of the interview and answer the following questions in English.

This second part of the interview with Herr Weber contains longer and more complex sentences to challenge more confident students. The extract includes examples of question words and *es gibt*.

Less confident students could work collaboratively with others to answer the questions. They may also need to refer to the transcript for support. Afterwards, ask the class to pick out question words heard, and refer to the *Grammatik* panel if you have not already done so. More confident learners could be asked to 'harvest' other useful phrases from the recording, for example *es kommt darauf an / gar nicht schlecht*.

Answers:

a About 10,000
b 68 metres
c It's not in Zell am See, but is nearby. It's called Großglockner and is 3,798 metres high.
d Between 10 and 30 Euros
e Any three of: football pitch, basketball court, TV room, small cinema

Pages 84–85

Grammar practice

G Holidays

> *Ich möchte …*
>
> Using *Ich möchte* is the subsidiary grammar point linked to Spread 2.6, *Ich möchte mal nach …*
> *Ich möchte …* is used in the postcards on page 74, and is highlighted in the Tipp box. Students are later encouraged to use *ich möchte …* in their productive work on page 75.
> Students may be referred to this grammar box before starting work on activity 4 on page 75.

1a 💬 Work in pairs. Ask your partner the following questions about a future holiday. He or she answers. Then swap roles.

This speaking activity enables students to practise using different forms of *möchten* with an infinitive, rather than limiting themselves to *ich möchte*.

Insist on full sentences for their answers, as in the example, and remind them to take the form of the verb, and often also the infinitive, from those used in the question.

Possible answers:

Wohin möchtest du fahren?
Ich möchte nach Deutschland / in die Schweiz / nach Schottland fahren.
Mit wem möchtest du fahren?
Ich möchte mit meiner Familie / mit meinen Freunden / allein fahren.
Wie möchtet ihr fahren?

Wir möchten mit dem Bus / mit dem Auto / mit dem Schiff fahren.

Wo möchtet ihr übernachten?
Wir möchten in einem Hotel / in einer Pension / in unserem Wohnwagen übernachten.

Was möchtest du machen?
Ich möchte Eis essen. / mich sonnen. / die Sehenswürdigkeiten besichtigen.

Was möchte deine Freundin / dein Freund machen?
Er / Sie möchte Sport treiben. / einkaufen gehen. / das Museum besuchen.

Wie viel Geld möchtest du ausgeben?
Ich möchte wenig Geld / viel Geld / 500 Euro ausgeben.

1b Using your work in the previous activity as a starting point, write up your holiday plans. Present your plans to the class (using pictures to illustrate, if wished).

This writing and speaking activity requires students to write sentences, or a more detailed paragraph, using different forms of *möchten* with infinitives.

Encourage them to use the same variety of verb forms as in the previous activity. After the holiday plans have been presented orally, the class could ask further questions about them, again using forms of *möchten*.

> **Using *um … zu …*, *ohne … zu …* and *anstatt … zu …***
>
> This is the subsidiary grammar point linked to Spread 2.7, *Urlaubspläne*.
> Students have already encountered *um … zu …* in Context 1 (page 47). There are several examples of *um … zu …* in the core reading text on page 76, *Das werde ich machen*.
> This grammar box expands on this work by adding other constructions following the same pattern, and may be referred to at any point in the spread.

2a Put the second half of the following sentences into the right order.

This activity requires students to think about word order in sentences with *um … zu …*, *ohne … zu …*, and *anstatt … zu …* .

Refer to the examples in the *Grammatik* panel to guide students, and afterwards elicit English translations of the sentences to ensure meanings of these structures are clear.

Answers:

a Ich werde nach Italien fahren, um Italienisch zu lernen.
b Ich werde nach Paris fahren, ohne den Eiffelturm zu sehen.
c Wir werden meine Großmutter besuchen, um ihren Geburtstag zu feiern.
d Sie wird dieses Jahr ans Meer fahren, anstatt in die Berge zu gehen.
e Sie werden eine Weltreise machen, anstatt das Geld zu sparen.
f Er wird mit Freunden nach Spanien fahren, ohne seine Eltern zu fragen.

2b Now complete the following sentences, using *um … zu …*, *ohne … zu …* or *anstatt … zu …* . Use as many words as possible from the box (but you can also add your own ideas!).

Students are now required to use the three structures more actively, choosing suitable words from those given and arranging them in the correct order to complete each sentence.

Accept any correct alternatives to the answers, and give particular credit for students' own additional ideas. More confident learners could then write whole new sentences of their own, perhaps based on other holiday destinations.

Possible answers:

a Ich werde nach Irland fahren, ohne Dublin zu besuchen.
b Ich werde zu Hause bleiben, um mir eine DVD anzusehen.
c Wir werden ins italienische Restaurant gehen, um eine Pizza zu essen.
d Wir werden nach China fliegen, anstatt Chinesisch zu lernen.
e Sie werden ins Geschäft gehen, ohne Souvenirs zu kaufen.
f Sie werden an den Strand gehen, um im Meer zu schwimmen.

> **Using adjectives after *etwas*, *nichts*, *viel*, *wenig* and *alles***
>
> This is the subsidiary grammar point linked to Spread 2.8, *Berlin ist cool!*
> In his text on Berlin (page 78) Daniel mentions *etwas Kulturelles*. Although this use of adjectives is not extensive on this spread, more able students may wish to explore this point in more detail at this stage.

3a Translate the following phrases into German.

This writing activity practises using adjectives after *etwas, nichts, viel, wenig* and *alles*.

Point out to students that these are useful structures to add variety to their German, and that it might be useful to learn one or two phrases of this type by heart (for example *nichts Interessantes, etwas Neues*), to use later in the Speaking or Writing units.

Answers:

a etwas Großes
b etwas Größeres
c nichts Interessantes
d nichts Blaues
e wenig Interessantes
f viel Gutes
g alles Moderne

3b Once your teacher has checked your work on the previous activity, write six sentences, each one containing one of the phrases you have translated.

This writing activity checks that students have understood the meanings of the phrases in activity 3a, by requiring them to think up whole sentences.

Point out that the sentences don't need to be long or complicated. Weaker students could be provided with examples to adapt.

> **The nominative and accusative cases (revision)**
>
> This is the subsidiary grammar point linked to Spread 2.9, *Auf Achse*.
> This grammar box offers general revision of cases and can be referred to at any point in the course, although the examples in the activities are specific to the Holidays topic.

4a Choose the correct accusative article in each of the sentences below.

This reading activity requires students to use the gender of each noun, and the information in the *Grammatik* panel, to decide which of the three possibilities given is the correct accusative article.

Remind them to check genders of nouns carefully. Afterwards, you could discuss why the accusative case is needed in each sentence.

Answers:

a den	b ein	c keinen
d eine	e einen	

4b Fill in the gaps with the correct forms of the articles in the nominative and accusative cases.

In this writing activity students must decide which German article is needed, and which accusative ending it should have, to fill the gaps in the sentences given. Genders of nouns are given.

Make sure that weaker students understand the difference in meaning between *den/die/das* and *einen/eine/ein*. Afterwards, elicit English translations of the sentences.

Answers:

a das / das
b der / den
c eine / Die
d Die / keinen

Pages 86–87

Vocabulary
V Holidays

- MP3 files for each vocabulary list

The essential vocabulary used within Topic 2, Context 2 is presented on this vocabulary spread.

Here students can learn the key words for the topic area *Holidays*. You may also want to direct student to the online audio files of these vocabulary lists, so they can hear how the words are pronounced by a native speaker.

Some words are in light grey on the vocabulary spreads in the Student Book. This indicates items that are not included in the GCSE specification vocabulary list, so students do not need to learn these items for Listening and Reading assessment. However, you may wish students to use them in Speaking and Writing Controlled Assessments.

Pages 88–91

Controlled Assessment

Please refer to the section on Controlled Assessment, pages 113–119 in this Teacher's Book.

2 Context summary

- Interactive multiple-choice quiz

The closing page for Context 2, Leisure provides a multiple-choice quiz which tests the key language learnt in the preceding chapter.

A longer version of this quiz is also available online as an interactive, self-marking multiple-choice test.

Answers:

1 hast, habe, haben
2 My sister bought lots (of shopping) in town but I didn't have enough money.
3 sind, ist
4 Wohin bist du letztes Jahr geflogen?
5 *Suggested answer*: … mir meine Eltern genug Geld geben
6 ist, hat, hatte
7 Ich probierte die neue Hose an, aber ich darf sie nicht behalten, weil sie zu teuer ist.
8 *Suggested answer*: Es ist nicht die richtige Größe.
9 Ute fährt nächstes Jahr mit dem Auto nach Italien.
10 als, wenn

3 Home and Environment

Home and local area

Special occasions celebrated in the home

	KS3 Revision: Rooms in the house; Items of furniture; House types and locations; Daily routine; Helping at home.	*Online materials* • Audio files for core reading texts
	3.1 Feier mit uns! ■ Using prepositions taking the accusative case ■ Completing gap-fill exercises	• Audio file for core reading text • Audio file and transcript for listening activity 2 • Reading activity: *Wir feiern!* • Grammar activity: Using prepositions taking the accusative case • Writing worksheet • Extension reading worksheet
	3.2 Bei mir, bei dir ■ Using prepositions with the dative case ■ Using knowledge of social and cultural differences	• Audio file for core reading text • Audio file and transcript for listening activity 2 • Listening activity and transcript: *Mein Haus* • Grammar activity: Using prepositions taking the dative case • Speaking worksheet • Extension listening worksheet • Audio file and transcript for extension listening worksheet • Foundation reading worksheet

Home, town, neighbourhood and region; where it is and what it is like

	3.3 Meine Gegend, deine Gegend ■ Using *in* with the dative or accusative ■ Using grammar to work out meaning	• Audio file for core reading text • Audio file and transcript for listening activity 4 • Reading activity: *Peter wohnt in der Schweiz* • Grammar activity: Using prepositions taking the dative or accusative • Writing worksheet • Extension listening worksheet • Audio file and transcript for extension listening worksheet
	3.4 Kommen Sie nach Baden-Württemberg! ■ Using adjective endings ■ Using knowledge from other topic areas	• Audio file for core reading text • Audio files and transcripts for listening activities 2 and 3 • Reading activity: *Baden-Württemberg ist toll!* • Grammar activity: Using adjective endings • Speaking worksheet • Extension reading worksheet • Foundation listening worksheet • Audio file and transcript for foundation listening worksheet

Reading and listening

	• Audio file for core reading text • Audio files and transcripts for listening activity 2

Grammar

Home and local area

■ Reflexive verbs (revision) ■ Superlative adjectives
■ Comparing things ■ Adjective endings after the indefinite article

Vocabulary

Home and local area	• MP3 files for each vocabulary list

Environment
Current problems facing the planet

3.5 Umweltfreundlich oder umweltfeindlich?
- Using qualifiers
- Making what you say and write more expressive

- Audio file for core reading text
- Audio file and transcript for listening activity 3
- Listening activity and transcript: *Was machen Sie für die Umwelt?*
- Grammar activity: Using qualifiers
- Writing worksheet
- Extension listening worksheet
- Audio file and transcript for extension listening worksheet
- Foundation reading worksheet

Being environmentally friendly within the home and local area

3.6 Unsere Welt, unsere Umwelt
- Using the imperative
- Using German posters for a presentation

- Audio file for core reading text
- Audio file and transcript for listening activity 3
- Reading activity: *Unsere Umwelt*
- Grammar activity: Using the imperative
- Speaking worksheet
- Extension listening worksheet
- Audio file and transcript for extension listening worksheet

3.7 Global denken, lokal handeln
- Using verbs with *zu*
- Dealing with new vocabulary

- Audio file for core reading text
- Video and transcript for video activity 2
- Grammar activity: Using verbs with *zu*
- Writing worksheet
- Extension reading worksheet
- Foundation listening worksheet
- Audio file and transcript for foundation listening worksheet

Reading and listening

- Audio file for core reading text
- Audio files and transcripts for listening activity 2

Grammar

Environment
- Using prepositions with the genitive
- Articles and cases (revision)
- The future tense with *werden* (revision)

Vocabulary

Environment
- MP3 files for each vocabulary list

Summative assessment

Home and environment
- Interactive multiple-choice quiz

The opening page for Context 3, Home and environment, provides a quick-reference overview of how the teaching spreads, grammar and strategies within this Context in the Student Book map to the Topics and Purposes of Context 3 in the GCSE specification. Also included here is an overview of the online resources available for each of these spreads in the Student Book.

Context 3 Home and Environment

Revision
Home and local area

Pages 94–97

Rooms in the house, items of furniture

kerboodle! • Audio files for core reading texts

1a 📖 🎧 Read the descriptions below, then note down the German room being referred to in each case.

A reading or listening activity to revise words for rooms in a house and items of furniture. The descriptions also include examples of *es gibt* and of *in* with the dative. Before doing the activity, you may need to refresh students' memories by displaying or eliciting the words for rooms. After completing the activity, elicit the meanings of the words for items of furniture in the descriptions.

The reading text is also available online as an audio file.

Answers:

- a das Wohnzimmer
- b das Schlafzimmer
- c die Küche
- d das Badezimmer
- e das Arbeitszimmer
- f der Flur
- g das Esszimmer

> **Grammatik**
> This panel reminds students that the accusative is used after *es gibt*. Point out the plural forms of this used in activity 1a. It also explains that when describing where things are, they should use the dative case after *in*. They will need to use both of these constructions in activity 1b – you could try some simple examples to practise them first. The panel also refers students to page 177 to find out more about the dative case after *in*.

1b 🗣 Work in pairs. Take it in turns to talk about different rooms in your house, using the prompts below to help you. Include adjectives if you are confident about adding the endings.

A speaking activity to practise using the words for rooms and items of furniture, using the prompts given. Encourage students to check the genders of the words to be used and to try to use the correct form of the accusative indefinite article. More confident students could try to include adjectives with endings (these will be taught in subtopic 3.4).

The reading text is also available online as an audio file.

Possible answers:

a Mein Haus hat ein großes Badezimmer. Im Badezimmer gibt es eine Toilette und einen kleinen Spiegel.
b In meiner Küche gibt es einen schwarzen Herd und eine weiße Spülmaschine.
c In unserem Wohnzimmer haben wir eine Fernseher und ein bequemes Sofa.
d Mein Haus hat ein helles Esszimmer. Im Esszimmer gibt es einen großen Tisch und vier Stühle.

2a 📖 🎧 Read Lisa's email. What does she have in her room? Note down the items, then draw a plan of the room.

A reading activity involving comprehension of a detailed description of a room. The email includes a range of adjectives (mainly without endings) and prepositions. The reading text is also available online as an audio file.

Answers:

pink walls, colourful curtains, single bed, wardrobe, pictures of favourite group on the walls, bedside table, lamp, radio, books, pillows.

2b ✏️ Using Lisa's email as a model, write a description of your own bedroom.

A writing activity to practise describing a room in German. Weaker students could follow the structure of Lisa's email and simply replace certain words and items with their own. Afterwards, the descriptions could be swapped around and students could read about and try to draw plans of each other's rooms.

House types and locations

kerboodle! • Audio files for core reading texts

1a 📖 🎧 Read Anke's description of her home then read the following statements. For each write T (True) or F (False).

This activity involves comprehension of a longer text about a young person's house and local area. After deciding if each statement given is true or false, students could translate the text into English.

The reading text is also available online as an audio file.

Answers:

a F   b F   c F   d T   e F

1b 🗣 Work in pairs. Practise asking and answering the following questions.

A speaking activity for students to practise asking for and giving information about the type of house they live in and what there is in their local area. For less confident learners, you could provide the sample answers given below as prompts.

Possible answers:

In was für einem Haus wohnst du?
Ich wohne in einer Wohnung / einem Reihenhaus / einem Doppelhaus.
Wo liegt das Haus?
Das Haus liegt am Stadtrand / im Stadtzentrum / in einem Dorf.
Wie ist das Haus?
Das Haus ist schön / zu klein / sehr groß.
Was gibt es in der Nähe?
Es gibt viele Geschäfte / einen Park / nichts in der Nähe.
Wo möchtest du wohnen? Warum?
Ich möchte im Stadtzentrum / auf dem Lande / in London wohnen, weil es interessanter ist / es ruhiger ist / man dort viel unternehmen kann.

2a 📖 🎧 Read Stefan's letter then complete the gaps in the text below, using the words from the box.

A reading activity to further practise comprehension of information about a person's house and local area. You could read Stefan's letter with the class and elicit translations before they proceed with the gap-filling.

The reading text is also available online as an audio file.

Answers:

a Doppelhaus	b Meer	c nicht weit
d findet	e klein	f gefallen
g modern	h größer	i froh
j teilen		

2b ✏️ Write a short piece about where you live, using Anke and Stefan's texts as models.

A writing activity to practise using the language seen in the texts on this page. Encourage use of adjectives to make the accounts more descriptive, and refer to the *Grammatik* panel. Less confident learners could use their answers to the questions in activity 1b as the basis for their writing.

> **Grammatik**
> This panel points out that adjectives do not need an ending if they are not used in front of the noun. This is a useful strategy for avoiding the problem of adjective endings, and could be used in activity 2b. The panel also refers students to page 105 for further information.

Daily routine

kerboodle! • Audio files for core reading texts

1a 📖 🎧 Read the phrases and put them in the correct order from the start to the end of the day.

This reading or listening activity practises comprehension of twenty-four hour clock times in German. You may then wish to revise saying clock times, using a class set of model clocks if possible.

The reading text is also available online as an audio file.

Answers:

d, h, f, k, i, e, b, c, g, j, a

> **Grammatik**
> This panel explains that reflexive verbs in German use a subject pronoun and a reflexive pronoun, and gives examples relating to daily routine. Practise using the *ich* and *du* forms of *sich waschen* and *sich anziehen* in preparation for the questions and answers in activity 1b. The panel also refers students to page 179 for further information.

1b 🗣 Work in pairs. Practise asking and answering questions about your daily routine with a partner. If you need to revise telling the time, see page 188.

A speaking activity to practise asking and talking about daily routine. Using the statements in activity 1a as a basis, you could start by planning with the class the German questions they will ask. As there are reflexive and separable verbs involved, refer to the *Grammatik* panels.

Possible answers:

Wann wachst du auf?
Ich wache um halb acht auf.
Wann stehst du auf?
Ich stehe um Viertel vor acht auf.
Wann frühstückst du?
Ich frühstücke um acht Uhr.
Wann gehst du in die Schule?
Ich gehe um halb neun in die Schule …

> **Grammatik**
> This panel shows students examples of separable verbs, relating to daily routine. The panel also refers students to the *Grammatik* panel on the next page for further information about how separable verbs work.

2a 📖 🎧 Amelia describes what she does at the weekend. Read Amelia's blog, then match the sentence halves.

A reading or listening activity to practise comprehension of information about daily routine. Remind students that they can also use knowledge of grammar to check they have matched the correct sentence halves.

The reading text is also available online as an audio file.

Answers:

a 1	b 3	c 6	d 5
e 4	f 7	g 2	

2b ✏️ Using Amelia's blog as a model, write an account of your daily routine either on a school day or at the weekend.

A writing activity for students to practise producing language about their own daily routine. Encourage them to make use of their answers to the questions in activity 1b, as well as using Amelia's blog as a model. More confident students should vary their word order and include as much detail as possible.

Context 3 Home and Environment 69

Helping at home

kerboodle! • Audio files for core reading texts

1a 📖 🎧 Read what Tina and Jürgen say they do to help at home, then match each picture to the correct name.

A reading or listening activity to revise key phrases for talking about things you do to help at home. Afterwards, you could ask students to pick out these phrases, and write a list of them with English meanings – these will be useful for activity 1b.

The reading text is also available online as an audio file.

Answers:

a Jürgen   b Jürgen   c Jürgen
d Jürgen   e Tina   f Tina

> This panel explains that separable verbs in German have a separable prefix, usually a preposition, and gives an example relating to helping at home: *aufräumen*. It also shows how to use such verbs in the perfect tense. You could practise using the *ich* and *du* forms of separable verbs from the text in activity 1a, in preparation for activity 1b. The panel also refers students to page 70 for further practice in using separable verbs.
>
> *Grammatik*

1b 💬 Work in pairs. Take it in turns to ask each other if you do a particular household job. If you don't do the one your partner picks, mention one which you do do.

A speaking activity to practise using verbs relating to helping at home. As these include separable verbs, refer students to the *Grammatik* panel. With weaker students, you may need to practise the question forms to be used before they start the activity.

Possible answers:

Passt du auf kleine Kinder auf?
Nein, das mache ich nie, aber ich bügle oft. Machst du dein Bett?
Ja, natürlich. Saugst du Staub?...

2a 📖 🎧 Read the magazine extract, then answer the questions, giving the name of the correct person each time.

A reading activity to practise comprehension of additional vocabulary for talking about helping at home. Afterwards, ask students to extract any useful verbs or phrases, which they could add to the list started after activity 1a.

The reading text is also available online as an audio file.

Answers:

a Paul   b Michael   c Andreas   d Anna

2b ✏️ You decide to write in to the magazine to say what you do to help in the home.

A writing activity requiring students to write about what they themselves do to help at home. Remind them to include all the points given, and to take ideas and language from the earlier activities and texts on this page. For the second point, you may wish to elicit from students the most suitable modal verb to use: *sollen/sollten*.

Pages 98–99

3.1 Feier mit uns!

Special occasions celebrated in the home

Subject	Talking about special occasions
G 1	Using prepositions taking the accusative case
G 2	Using reflexive verbs (revision)
🔊	Completing gap-fill exercises

kerboodle!
- Audio file for core reading text
- Audio file and transcript for listening activity 2
- Reading activity: *Wir feiern!*
- Grammar activity: Using prepositions taking the accusative case
- Writing worksheet
- Extension reading worksheet

Starter activity

Introduce students to key words for festivals in Germany, with which they may not be culturally familiar, in preparation for the reading and listening material in this subtopic. Give them pairs of words to try and match, either by guessing, using prior knowledge or logic, or by skim-reading of the text. These could be either German and English words for festivals to pair, or the months of the year in German with festivals (e.g. *Karneval, Rosenmontag, Ostern, Weihnachten, Heiligabend* etc) to assign to them. Discuss their findings afterwards.

Traditionelle Feste

The reading stimulus text describes key festivals through the year around Germany. It includes key vocabulary for these, and examples of prepositions which take the accusative.

The reading text is also available online as an audio file.

> 📖 Advice on completing gap-fill exericises. Look at the examples given for using grammatical knowledge to find the correct answer for a gap, and try them out together. Point out that this technique could be useful in the Reading unit.
>
> *Strategie*

1 📖 🎧 🌐 **Copy the sentences and fill in the gaps with one of the words in the boxes.**

Students find information in the text in order to fill each gap with the correct word from those given. Point out that this will be found in the same order as the questions. Refer to the *Strategie* panel and the *Tipp*. Afterwards, you could read the text in detail with the class, checking that the meanings for all the festivals are clear, and eliciting responses from students about differences in these celebrations between Germany and their country.

Answers:

a Karneval
b Straßen
c draußen
d amüsieren
e nicht
f bekommen
g hört

> **Tipp**
> Point out how useful phrases with *man* are for this sort of topic, for talking about what people in general do. If necessary remind students that *man* is used with the *er/sie/es* verb form, and practise a few examples using familiar verbs.

2 🎧 *Transcript:*

Viele Feste sind voller Traditionen, aber heutzutage wollen nicht alle mitmachen. Diese jungen Leute geben ihre Meinung über typische Feste.

a Wir haben keine Schule am dritten Oktober, denn es ist Nationalfeiertag. Prima!
b Ich finde es sehr langweilig. Ich möchte am Heiligen Abend mit Freunden ausgehen, aber meine Eltern erlauben das nicht.
c Zu Ostern isst man zu viel Schokolade. Das ist total ungesund.
d Die Kostüme und der Umzug am Rosenmontag dieses Jahr waren wunderbar.
e Letztes Jahr hat meine Familie das Oktoberfest in München besucht. Obwohl das Wetter nicht gut war, hat es mir sehr gut gefallen.
f Ich gehe am Wochenende auf die Hochzeit meines Bruders. Ich freue mich schon darauf.
g In 2 Wochen habe ich Geburtstag. Ich bekomme gerne viele Geschenke.

2 🎧 **Listen to the young people (a–g) talking about special occasions. Copy and complete the table, using occasions from the list below. Note down extra details if you can!**

In this audio extract, seven young people each make a brief statement about a festival, and what they think of it. The extract includes key vocabulary for festivals and celebrations, and useful phrases for expressing enjoyment as well as negative opinions.

Students pick the correct English meanings from those given for the celebrations mentioned, and decide whether or not the person speaking enjoys it. Encourage more confident learners to listen again and note down any additional details they can understand. They could then use similar phrases to those heard to say whether they themselves like some of the festivals mentioned.

Answers:

Person	Occasion	Enjoy it (✓) or not (✗)
a	National holiday	✓
b	Christmas Eve	✗
c	Easter	✗
d	Karneval	✓
e	Munich beer festival	✓
f	Wedding	✓
g	Birthday	✓

> **Grammatik**
> This panel on prepositions taking the accusative firstly explains what prepositions are, and that some are always followed by the accusative. It gives a list of these, and points out that the masculine singular form of the article changes in the accusative. Students are referred to p.28 for a reminder about the accusative case if needed. Encourage them to learn this list of useful prepositions and their meanings. Practise using them in simple sentences, and point out the importance of checking the gender of the relevant noun for accuracy.
> This *Grammatik* panel also refers students to p.108 to learn about or revise reflexive verbs.

3a Ⓖ **Copy the sentences and fill in the gaps with the correct form of the definite article – *den*, *die* or *das*.**

This grammar activity requires students to use the correct definite article after prepositions taking the accusative.

Refer to the *Grammatik* panel, and look at the prepositions involved in this activity. Remind students that they will need to be sure of the gender of the noun following the article, in order to use the correct form. Afterwards, elicit translations of the sentences to ensure that new vocabulary has been understood.

Answers:

a das   b die   c den   d den   e die

3b Ⓖ **Now add the correct accusative preposition as well as the correct article.**

This grammar activity requires students to think about the most suitable accusative preposition to use in each sentence, as well as to work out the correct form of the article.

Refer to the list of possible prepositions in the *Grammatik* panel, and remind students to think carefully about gender.

Answers:

a um den   b bis den

Context 3 Home and Environment 71

4 Prepare a presentation on a special occasion of your choice.

Less confident students can prepare brief notes using the language structure grid given. Encourage the more confident to make use of additional language from the reading and listening texts of this subtopic, and to research vocabulary needed for food and drink etc. Remind them to make use of *man* (see *Tipp* above). If homework time can be spent on this preparation, students could find pictures or objects to illustrate their presentation.

Plenary activity

If not already done, ask for volunteers to give their presentation to the whole class, and ask for positive feedback in German from the audience. Alternatively, display a list of anagrams of the festivals discussed in this subtopic for students to solve.

Pages 100–101

3.2 Bei mir, bei dir

Home, town, neighbourhood and region; where it is and what it is like

Subject	Comparing homes
G 1	Using prepositions taking the dative case
G 2	Comparing things
🔧	Using knowledge of social and cultural differences

kerboodle!
- Audio file for core reading text
- Audio file and transcript for listening activity 2
- Listening activity and transcript: *Mein Haus*
- Grammar activity: Using prepositions taking the dative case
- Speaking worksheet
- Extension listening worksheet
- Audio file and transcript for extension listening worksheet
- Foundation reading worksheet

Starter activity

Revise familiar German vocabulary for rooms and furniture in preparation for the activities in this subtopic. Ask half of the class to 'brainstorm' in pairs words for rooms, and the others words for furniture (or let students choose which they do). When discussing, allocate the furniture words to appropriate rooms, or if available, you could display a drawing for which they must try to provide the labels.

Wie sieht die ideale Wohnung aus?

The reading text is a report of what readers say are the most important features in their ideal house or flat. It includes examples of prepositions taking the dative case and key vocabulary for rooms, furniture and features of a home.

The reading text is also available online as an audio file.

1a Read the article and find the German words to match the English ones below.

Students read the text, and find the German for the English phrases given. Quick finishers could research their own list of additional English words or phrases which their partner must find in the text, to develop comprehension further.

Answers:

a Platz für einen Fernseher
b Spülmaschine
c wo man sich sonnen kann
d ein[en] Spielplatz in der Nähe
e Gartenbenutzung
f Farben wie türkis
g ein[en] Dachboden

1b Look at the article again and decide whether these statements are true (T) or false (F).

Students must decide if the German statements about the text are true or false.

Answers:

a F   b T   c F
d F   e F   f T

> **Strategie**
> Advice on using knowledge of cultural and social differences. Point out that flats for families in Germany may have just as many rooms, or be even bigger than, houses here, and that it is far more common to live in a flat, as well as to rent rather than own your home. Ask if any students have visited homes in Germany or other European countries where housing is different from their own area.

2 Transcript:

a *Martin, wie findest du deine Wohnung?*
  Meine Wohnung ist klein aber sehr bequem. Das gefällt mir sehr.
b *Anna, wohnst du gern in deiner Wohnung? Warum?*
  Ich wohne sehr gern in meiner neuen Wohnung. Na ja, sie ist sehr groß.
c *Olivia, wie lange wohnst du schon in diesem Bungalow?*
  Ich wohne seit vier Monaten in diesem Bungalow, aber ich bin gar nicht zufrieden. Es gibt nur ein Schlafzimmer und kein Arbeitszimmer für meinen Vater. Auch haben wir keinen Balkon, wo man sich sonnen kann.
d *Michael, du wohnst in einem Reihenhaus. Gefällt es dir?*
  Meiner Meinung nach ist ein Reihenhaus viel zu klein für unsere große Familie. Bei uns gibt es keinen Abstellraum für unsere Fahrräder und nicht genug Platz in der Küche für eine Spülmaschine.
e *Henrik, du wohnst in einem neuen Haus. Wie findest du das?*
  Unser neues Haus finde ich prima, weil ich endlich mein eigenes Zimmer habe und nicht mehr mit meinem Bruder teilen muss. Obwohl wir in der Stadt wohnen, gibt es einen großen Spielplatz unserem Haus gegenüber, wo meine kleine Schwester spielen kann. Ich kann auch zur Schule laufen, statt mit dem Bus zu fahren. Früher wohnten wir in einer sehr kleinen Wohnung in

Früher wohnten wir in einer sehr kleinen Wohnung in einem Mehrfamilienhaus, und ich bin sehr froh, dass wir umgezogen sind.

f Udo, du bist eben umgezogen. Bist du damit zufrieden? Diese Wohnung ist viel besser als die alte Wohnung. Sie ist geräumiger und es gibt sogar eine Waschküche mit Platz für einen Tiefkühlschrank. Wir haben auch Gartenbenutzung – dass gefällt meinen Eltern.

2 🎧 Listen to the young people talking about their homes. Do they like where they live or not? Give reasons.

The audio extract consists of interviews with six young people, who say what they think of their home. It includes vocabulary for different types of houses, expressions for comparing things, and examples of prepositions taking the dative case.

Less confident students could listen twice, once to decide whether each speaker likes their home, and a second time to try and find reasons why. After discussing the answers, refer to the *Strategie* panel. Ask what sort of houses the speakers in the recording live in, and if necessary listen to it one more time to collect this information and revise vocabulary for types of home.

Answers:

a Martin, ✓, small but comfortable
b Anna, ✓, very big
c Olivia, ✗, only one bedroom and no study for father or balcony for sunbathing
d Michael ✗, too small for big family, nowhere to put bikes, not enough room in the kitchen for a dishwasher
e Henrik, ✓, has own room at last and no longer has to share with brother, large play area opposite house where little sister can play, can walk to school instead of taking the bus, used to live in a small flat and is very glad to have moved
f Udo, ✓, much better than previous flat, more room and has a utility room with room for a freezer, also have use of a garden which parents like

> This panel explains that some prepositions are always followed by the dative, and gives a list of these, together with examples of the shortened versions of *bei, von* and *zu*. It refers students to p.176 if they need a reminder about the dative case. Practise using these prepositions in simple sentences.
> The panel also refers students to p.108 to learn how to compare things.
>
> **Grammatik**

3 Ⓖ Complete the sentences by using *dem, der* or *den*.

This grammar activity requires students to select the correct dative article to fill the gaps in the sentences given.

Refer to the *Grammatik* panel. Point out that students must be sure of the gender of the noun, or whether it is plural, in order to determine the correct form of the article. Elicit translations of the sentences afterwards.

Answers:

a dem   b der   c dem
d der   e dem   f den

4 ✏ You have just got back from a visit to Germany and are writing to your German friend about what your home is like and how it is different from your friend's.

As well as using the language structure grid given, encourage students to include as much detail as possible in their descriptions, and to use ideas from the reading text in activity 1 and the transcript of the recording in activity 2. Refer to the *Tipp* for help with comparing things.

> Use this box to assist students with the writing activity. Suggest that they use the sample comparison sentences in their letter/email, making simple substitutions to adapt them slightly. Point out that phrases like these can increase their marks in the Speaking and Writing units.
>
> **Tipp**

Plenary activity

Ask students to work in pairs to produce a list of five things they have learnt in this subtopic. Afterwards, collate some of these on the board in categories (e.g. cultural info, vocabulary, grammar).

Pages 102–103

3.3 Meine Gegend, deine Gegend

Home, town, neighbourhood and region; where it is and what it is like

Subject	Comparing neighbourhoods
Ⓖ 1	Using *in* with the dative or accusative
Ⓖ 2	Using superlative adjectives
🔍	Using grammar to work out meaning

kerboodle!
- Audio file for core reading text
- Audio file and transcript for listening activity 4
- Reading activity: *Peter wohnt in der Schweiz*
- Grammar activity: Using prepositions taking the dative or accusative
- Writing worksheet
- Extension listening worksheet
- Audio file and transcript for extension listening worksheet

1 Ⓥ Students unscramble the names of six well known cities in Germany, Austria and Switzerland.

They could then look at a map of these countries to locate them. Practise German pronunciation of the six city names – most of which tend to be pronounced very differently when being spoken about in English.

Answers:

a Bern   b Berlin   c Zürich
d Frankfurt   e Leipzig   f Salzburg

Context 3 Home and Environment 73

Core reading text

The reading stimulus text consists of descriptions by three young people of the area where they live. It includes examples of *in* with the dative and accusative, superlative adjectives, and key vocabulary for saying what there is in an area and what you can do there. The reading text is also available online as an audio file.

> **Strategie**
> Stress that the ability to use grammar to work out meaning is one of the major advantages of having some knowledge of German grammar! Elicit ideas of other situations where this strategy could be useful: for example identifying nouns from their capital letter, finding the subject of a sentence by looking for a nominative article, or identifying a past tense by spotting a participle at the end of the sentence.

2 Read what these people are saying about where they live, then read the statements below. For each statement, write T (true), F (false) or ? (Not in the Text).

Students read or listen to the descriptions, and decide whether the statements given in German are true, false, or not in the text. They then correct the statements which are false. Refer to the *Strategie* panel. Students could then be asked to find useful words and phrases in the descriptions for things there are in a place, and things you can do.

Answers:

a T
b F (Nils findet es schwer, in die nächste Stadt zu fahren)
c T
d T
e T
f F (Axel wohnt erst seit drei Monaten in seiner Stadt)
g ?
h T

> **Grammatik**
> This panel explains that *in* is used with the accusative where there is movement involved, and with the dative where there is none, using examples from the reading text to demonstrate this. If necessary, revise with students the accusative and dative changes, then use *in* with both in simple example sentences on the board. The panel also refers students to p.109 to learn about superlative adjectives.

3 Complete the sentences with *in* + accusative or *in* + dative. Remember to decide whether there is movement or not!

This grammar activity requires students to decide if the accusative or dative is needed after *in*, to then choose the correct form of the article, and to decide if a contracted version of the two words is possible.

Refer to the *Grammatik* panel and the *Tipp*. Point out to students that they will need to be sure of the gender of the noun following the gap, and to think carefully about whether there is movement or not. Weaker learners could discuss this decision for each before starting.

Answers:

a in dem (im)   b in die   c ins
d in dem (im)   e in dem (im), in der   f in dem (im)
g in die, in den   h ins

> **Tipp**
> Point out that students have already often used these contracted versions (*ins* and *im*), in phrases such as *ich gehe ins Kino*, without necessarily knowing the grammar behind them.

4a Transcript:

Christa, was kann man in der Stadt machen?

Meine Stadt ist ziemlich klein, aber wir haben ein Kino. Man kann auch sehr gut essen gehen. Leider gibt es zu viel Verkehr und keine Fußgängerzone aber das Hallenbad im Sportzentrum ist toll für sportliche Leute. Ich wohne gerne hier.

In was für eine Stadt wohnst du, Theo?

Ich wohne in einer Touristenstadt. Ein Vorteil ist, dass es viele Restaurants und Cafés gibt. Auch kann man den alten Dom besichtigen und auf den Marktplatz gehen. Das Schwimmbad ist seit zwei Jahren geschlossen, aber meine Freunde und ich gehen jeden Monat ins Kino. Meine Stadt ist toll!

Wohnst du gern in deinem Dorf, Mary?

Mein Dorf ist todlangweilig! Wir haben ein Restaurant, aber dort essen ist sehr teuer. Für Touristen gibt es gar nichts, und für Jugendliche gibt es nur das alte Kino. Wir hätten lieber eine Disko!

Heiko, du wohnst gern in deiner Stadt, oder?

Tja, ich mag meine Stadt. Sie ist viel besser als das Dorf, wo ich früher wohnte. Für junge Leute gibt es das neue Sportzentrum, und Touristen mögen das Museum. Sie können auch das Verkehrsamt in der Fußgängerzone besuchen. Meine Eltern gehen gern ins Theater, aber sie müssen dafür nach Hamburg fahren.

4a Listen to Christa, Theo, Mary and Heiko talking about what there is to do where they each live. Note down the letters of each thing available in their town. Take care – they will also mention things which aren't there!

In this audio extract, four young people talk about the town or village where they live, and say what they think about it. The recording includes examples of *in* with the accusative and dative, and useful vocabulary for places in a town or village, things to do there, and opinions.

Students listen to the extract and identify the correct pictures of places in a town or village for each speaker, from those given.

Answers:

Christa: a, d, g
Theo: a, c, g, i
Mary: a, g
Heiko: b, d, j

4b 🎧 Now decide whether each person likes living in their town or village. Add a tick or cross for each.

Students listen again and note whether each person likes living in their town or village. You could then ask them to try and explain the reasons for the positive or negative opinions.

Answers:

Christa: ✓
Theo: ✓
Mary: ✗
Heiko: ✓

5 💬 Work in pairs. Practise giving information about where you live. One partner asks questions and the other answers. Then swap roles.

Allow preparation time for students to think of things to say in answer to each question, using the language structure grid given and other vocabulary from this subtopic. For weaker students, you might wish to compile lists on the board of things there are in local places (with *es gibt*) and things to do (using *man kann*) to help them and give them more to say. Demonstrate the conversation with a volunteer. If time allows, ask students to speak with several different partners.

Plenary activity

Ask the class to work in groups of three (ideally not including their partner from activity 5), and to each try to give a short mini-presentation about the place where they live, again using the language structure grid for support. The other group members should listen for any mistakes, and give positive and helpful feedback afterwards.

Pages 104–105

3.4 Kommen Sie nach Baden-Württemberg!

Home, town, neighbourhood and region; where it is and what it is like

Subject	Comparing geographical regions
Ⓖ 1	Using adjective endings after the definite article
Ⓖ 2	Using adjective endings after the indefinite article
🌐	Using knowledge from other topic areas
kerboodle!	• Audio file for core reading text • Audio files and transcripts for listening activities 2 and 3 • Reading activity: *Baden-Württemberg ist toll!* • Grammar activity: Using adjective endings • Speaking worksheet • Extension reading worksheet • Foundation listening worksheet • Audio file and transcript for foundation listening worksheet

Starter activity

Show the class the title of this new subtopic, and give them five minutes, working individually, in pairs, or small teams, to collect as many German words as they can which they have already learnt, which they think could be useful for talking about different regions. You might want to allow them to search through previous subtopics in their textbook for ideas. The words could be categorised (nouns, verbs, adjectives etc). You could award a small prize for the longest list, or simply collate and discuss their ideas. The importance of using previous knowledge in this way is stated in the *Strategie* panel.

Entdecken Sie Baden-Württemberg!

The reading stimulus text is a factual article encouraging visitors to come to the region of Baden-Württemberg. It includes examples of adjective endings after the definite article, and useful vocabulary for describing a geographical area.

You might wish to point out Baden-Württemberg on a map before students start this reading and listening activity (and perhaps remind them of the system of *Bundesländer* in Germany). Refer also to the *Strategie* panel. They then have to decide which of the sentences given do not reflect the content of the article. Finally, you could ask more confident learners to tell you in German what they have learnt about Baden-Württemberg, using language from the text for support.

The reading text is also available online as an audio file.

Context 3 Home and Environment 75

> 📖 **Strategie**
> One way of illustrating the strategy of recognising familiar words might be to select a paragraph of the reading text and ask students to say which of the words in it they have never, ever seen before (there should not be many of these). This will demonstrate that at this level, much of the vocabulary they see has arisen previously in their work, and that making sure they know the meanings enables them to achieve more.

1 📖 🎧 🌐 Read the article about Baden-Württemberg. Which of the sentences below are backed up by the article? Write down the letters of the five that are.

Answers:

a, c, e, f, h

2 🎧 *Transcript:*

Hallo Jessica! Wie ist das Wetter in Süddeutschland?
Hier in Ravensburg ist das Wetter viel wärmer als im Norden.
Wie ist deine Stadt, Lana?
Meine Stadt in der Nähe von Wien ist klein aber schön. Ich würde einen Urlaub in Österreich wirklich empfehlen.
Seit wann lebst du hier, Andreas?
Ich lebe schon seit drei Jahren in Südamerika. Wir sind umgezogen, weil mein Vater Manager für eine große Computerfirma ist.
Johannes, du hast schon immer in München gewohnt, nicht wahr?
Nein, vor zwei Jahren bin ich nach München umgezogen. Obwohl ich jetzt ziemlich gern in München wohne, habe ich am Anfang die Stadt viel zu groß und laut gefunden, wahrscheinlich weil ich früher in einem Dorf gewohnt habe.
Hallo Bernd! Sag mal, wie ist das Leben bei dir?
Das Leben hier an der Küste in Norddeutschland ist viel ruhiger als in Stuttgart, wo ich als Kind wohnte.
Wie findest du das Großstadtleben, Christina?
In der Hauptstadt von England wohnen ist toll. Es ist immer was los, aber alles ist leider viel teurer als zum Beispiel in Südwestengland.
Wohnst du gern auf dem Lande, Anna?
Leider sind die öffentlichen Verkehrsmittel auf dem Lande nicht so gut wie in einer Großstadt wie London, aber die Landschaft hier im Osten von England ist wunderschön und das gefällt mir am besten.

2 🎧 Listen to these people responding to questions about their region, country or city. Match each person with the correct place from the box. There are more places than people, so be careful! Try also to note down one extra detail each time.

The audio extract consists of questions to seven young people in different countries about the area where they live, and their responses. It includes key vocabulary for types of area and place.

The listening activity could be done in two stages – firstly identifying the place where each interviewee lives, then finding an extra detail. More confident students should aim to note down further additional information they understand. Elicit the words or phrases for town / city / capital / in the country / on the coast.

Answers:

Jessica – South West Germany (weather warmer than in the north)
Lana – Austria (lives in town near Vienna, would recommend a holiday in Austria)
Andreas – South America (has lived there for three years, moved because father is manager for a large computer company)
Johannes – Munich (moved there two years ago, likes living there now but found it too big and noisy at first, used to live in a village)
Bernd – Northern Germany (on the coast, life there is calmer than in Stuttgart, where he used to live as a child)
Christina – London (living there is great, always something going on, but everything's a lot more expensive than in South West England)
Anna – East of England (lives in the countryside, public transport not as good as in cities like London but the landscape is beautiful and she likes that best)

3 🎧 *Transcript:*

Wohnst du gern in der Schweiz, Peter?
Eigentlich ja. Man sagt immer, dass es teuerer ist, in der Schweiz zu wohnen als in Österreich, Frankreich oder Deutschland, aber das ist nicht mehr der Fall. Überall in Europa sind die Preise sehr angestiegen. Letztes Jahr war ich in London, wo die Unterkunft gar nicht billiger war! Hier ist es auch sehr sauber – das ist sehr wichtig für viele Leute. Die vielen Touristen können sich in der frischen Luft gut entspannen. Für Wintersportler gibt es eine Menge Sportmöglichkeiten. Obwohl ich mich nicht für Sport interessiere, gefällt es mir sehr, in diesem schönen Land zu wohnen.

3 🎧 Peter is talking about life in Switzerland. Listen carefully and answer the questions in English.

In this more detailed and challenging listening extract, the speaker is asked if he likes living in Switzerland and explains why he does. The extract includes examples of adjectives with and without endings.

Suggest that if they find it difficult to immediately translate what they hear into English in order to answer the English questions, students could jot down the relevant German words, and then check their meanings. You may wish to provide key items of vocabulary for less confident learners.

Answers:

a That it's more expensive to live there than in Austria, France or Germany.
b Accommodation in London (just as expensive).
c The country is very clean.

d They can relax in the fresh air; there's lots to do for people who like winter sports.
e He is not that interested in sport.
f He likes living in this beautiful country.

> **Grammatik**
> This panel on using adjective endings explains that when an adjective in German is used in front of the thing it describes, an ending needs to be added. It gives the endings used after the definite article, *dieser* and *jeder* in the nominative, accusative and dative cases. Use simple example sentences to help students to practise deciding if an adjective needs an ending, then adding one.
> The panel also refers students to p.109 to learn how to use adjective endings after the indefinite article.

4 **G** Add the correct adjective endings to this brochure advertising a German town.

This grammar activity requires students to identify the correct case in order to supply the ending for each adjective in the text.

Refer to the *Grammatik* panel. When discussing the answers, ask students to explain the reason for each choice of ending. Also ask them to translate the text into English.

Answers:

a die schönste Stadt
b Das wunderschöne Schloss
c die mittelalterliche Pauluskirche
d mit dem hohen Turm
e die renovierte Altstadt
f den alten Brunnen
g das historische Museum
h das regionale Schützenfest
i die besten Geschäfte
j der ganzen Gegend

5 ✏ Produce a brochure for German-speakers visiting your home region.

Encourage students to include illustrations in their brochure, and to not only use the language structure grid for ideas but to re-use language they have learnt in previous subtopics (for example the structures *es gibt* and *man kann*). They should use adjectives, with endings where necessary, and be creative to entice visitors to their region. Refer to the *Tipp*.

> **Tipp**
> Point out that the marks given for communication and content in the Speaking and Writing units are higher if students can include opinions and explain or justify these. Give examples of ways in which this can be done.

Plenary activity

Display a simple sentence about a local beauty spot known to all, or a particularly unattractive feature of the local area. Tell the class to work in pairs and embellish it with as many adjectives (plus endings) as they can. After hearing their replies, ask the class to vote for the most factual / amusing / accurate ones heard.

Pages 106–107

Reading and listening

Home and local area

kerboodle!
- Audio file for core reading text
- Audio files and transcripts for listening activity 2

Umzug in ein neues Haus in Freiburg

The reading stimulus text consists of tourism-related information about Baden-Württemberg, and an interview with a family who have recently moved to Freiburg. It could be read in two stages – the first part is shorter and more accessible for less confident students. The text includes examples of prepositions taking the dative, prepositions taking the accusative, *in* with both cases, adjective endings after the definite and indefinite article, and cultural differences relating to housing in Germany.

All students should be able to attempt the true/false/not in the text activity 1a. Activity 1b involves a deeper understanding of the text's content to answer comprehension questions in English and is more challenging. They should refer to the Examiner's tip before tackling this. After they have finished, refer students to the *Grammatik* panel.

The reading text is also available online as an audio file.

1a 📖 🎧 Read the article, then read the following sentences. For each sentence write T (true), F (false) or ? (Not in the Text).

Answers:

a F   b ?   c F
d ?   e T   f T

1b 📖 🎧 Read the article again and answer the following questions in English.

Answers:

a The number of overnight stays tourists make each year in Freiburg.
b Herr Biber had a new job in Freiburg.
c Their flat was very small for a family, especially now their children are older.
d Very exhausting (possible reasons: it took a long time to find the right house; they saw lots of houses but these were too expensive or the garden was too small etc.)
e They're tidying up and getting the rooms sorted. They also have to wait four weeks before they get their new kitchen, so they're eating fast food or going to restaurants,
f They weren't as helpful or friendly as in Freiburg (reason: the family hardly ever saw them).

Context 3 Home and Environment

> This panel reminds students of grammatical points used in the article which they have learnt about so far in this Context: adjective endings after the indefinite and definite article and prepositions taking the dative or accusative cases. It refers them to the pages where these grammar points are explained. Elicit and discuss examples of these from the article, taking the opportunity to recap these features with less confident students.

Grammatik

2a 🎧 Transcript:

a Anna wohnt in der Altstadt. Es gefällt ihr gut, weil es sehr ruhig ist.
b Georg wohnt im Stadtzentrum. Er findet das Leben dort zu unfreundlich.
c Monika wohnt im neunten Stock eines Wohnblocks am Stadtrand. Sie findet das nicht praktisch, weil es keinen Lift gibt.
d Erik arbeitet in der Stadt, obwohl er in einem Dorf wohnt. Er braucht jeden Tag eine Stunde, um zur Arbeit zu kommen.
e Andrea wohnt nicht gern auf dem Lande, weil sie ihre Freunde nur selten sehen kann.
f Mark wohnt gern außerhalb der Stadt, weil er jeden Tag im Wald spazieren gehen kann.

2a 🎧 Listen to the descriptions of where each person lives. Copy and complete the table, noting down one advantage or disadvantage of each person's location.

The audio extract consists of six short third person statements, each about a different person, saying what type of location they live in and what they think of it. It includes examples of *in* with the dative, and useful nouns and adjectives relating to locations. It is accessible for less confident students.

After listening to the extract and completing the table in English with the required information, students could listen again and pick out particular language items, for example phrases and adjectives to describe locations.

Answers:

Person	Location	Advantage / Disadvantage
Anna	old part of town	advantage – it's quiet
Georg	town centre	disadvantage – too unfriendly
Monika	9th floor of a block of flats on the edge of town	disadvantage – impractical because there's no lift
Erik	village	disadvantage – he works in town, so it takes him an hour every day to get to work
Andrea	in the countryside	disadvantage – rarely gets to see her friends
Mark	outside of town	advantage – he can go walking in the woods every day

2b 🎧 Transcript:

Hallo, Max hier. Ich wohne sehr gern in Ravensburg in Süddeutschland. Die Stadt ist weder zu klein noch zu groß, und bietet etwas sowohl für Jugendliche als auch für Erwachsene. Jedes Jahr feiern wir das Rutenfest. Es unterscheidet sich von vielen anderen Festen durch seine jahrhundertealte Tradition. Während des Fests kann man den Schützenzug sehen und die berühmten Trommler hören. Genau wie beim Oktoberfest in München kann man natürlich viel Bier trinken! Obwohl das Rutenfest im Juli allgemein nicht so bekannt ist wie Karneval, ist es hier in unserer Gegend trotzdem sehr beliebt.

2b 🎧 Listen to Max talking about where he lives then answer the following questions in English.

This audio extract contains longer and more complex sentences to challenge more confident students. In it, a young person says why he likes his local area, and describes a traditional local festival. The extract includes examples of prepositions taking the accusative, prepositions taking the dative, *in* with the dative, adjective endings after the definite and indefinite articles and cultural information about German festivals.

Point out to students that the information needed will be heard in the same order as the comprehension questions, and refer them to the vocabulary list. Less confident students could work collaboratively with others to answer the questions, and may also need to refer to the transcript for support. Afterwards, more confident students could listen again to find and note useful German words or phrases such as *weder … noch, sowohl … als auch …, jahrhundertealt, berühmt, beliebt*.

Answers:

a One of the following: town is neither too big nor too small, has something to offer for both adults and young people.
b Its centuries-old tradition.
c One of the following: the parade of riflemen; the famous drummers; drinking beer.
d You can drink beer there.
e It's not as well-known as Karneval but is very popular in Max's area.

Pages 108–109

Grammar practice

G Home and local area

Reflexive verbs (revision)

The revision of reflexive verbs is the subsidiary grammar point linked to Spread 3.1, *Feier mit uns!*
Students deal with reflexive verbs when talking about daily routine on Key Stage 3 revision page 96.
This grammar box and activity reinforce this work by introducing different examples to apply, this time linked to the 'Special occasions celebrated in the home' purpose.

1 Complete the following sentences using one of the reflexive verbs given in the box below.

This writing activity requires students to identify the most suitable reflexive verb for each sentence from those given and to fill the gaps, making sure they use the correct verb ending and reflexive pronoun.

You might wish to discuss with weaker students who the subject of each sentence is, and which verb ending and reflexive pronoun will therefore be required, before they start this activity. When discussing the answers afterwards, ask for translations of the sentences.

Answers:

a Ich <u>freue mich</u> auf Weihnachten, weil es so lustig ist.
b Mein Bruder <u>ärgert sich</u>, weil ich seinen Geburtstag vergessen habe.
c <u>Beeil dich</u> / <u>Beeilen Sie sich</u> / <u>Beeilt euch</u>, sonst kommen wir zu spät zur Party!
d Jedes Jahr <u>besäuft sich</u> mein Onkel auf dem Oktoberfest.
e Als ich jünger war, ging ich immer auf den Karneval, aber ich kann <u>mich</u> nicht mehr daran <u>erinnern</u>.
f Wenn ich <u>mich</u> nicht <u>irre</u>, beginnt der Karneval am 11. November.

Comparing things

Comparing things is the subsidiary grammar point linked to Spread 3.2, *Bei mir, bei dir*.
Students are encouraged to make comparisons between their own and a German home in activity 4 on page 101.
This grammar box could be referred to together with the *Tipp* on page 101 before students begin activity 4, to enable them to have as many options as possible for comparisons at their disposal. The grammar box covers both comparative adjectives and making comparisons using *nicht so ... wie ...* .

2a With a partner practise comparing your home/home area using both methods explained on the right. Use the pictures below as prompts. Some adjectives are given in the box below, but try thinking of your own!

This speaking activity requires students to follow the advice given in the *Grammatik* panel to compare the rooms or places shown in the pictures. They should practise using comparative adjectives with *als* and also using *nicht so (Adjektiv) wie...*

If students are not familiar with each other's houses/home areas, encourage creativity (boasting or negativity!) More confident learners should think of as many additional adjectives as possible to use.

Possible answers:

Mein Garten ist nicht so schön wie dein Garten.
Meine Küche ist kleiner als deine Küche.
Mein Badezimmer ist schmutziger als dein Badezimmer.
Mein Schlafzimmer ist nicht so gemütlich wie dein Schlafzimmer.
Meine Stadt ist größer als deine Stadt.
Mein Dorf ist nicht so ruhig wie dein Dorf.

2b Now write up your conversations. Remember to use the correct possessive adjectives (*ihr* = her, *sein* = his). Remember to add an extra *e* to the possessive adjective when the noun is feminine.

Students are now required to accurately write the comparative forms used in the previous activity.
Remind them to check genders of nouns. Afterwards, the class may be interested to hear samples of each other's sentences read out.

Possible answers:

Mein Garten ist nicht so schön wie sein Garten und mein Badezimmer ist schmutziger als sein Badezimmer, aber meine Stadt ist größer als seine Stadt.
Meine Küche ist kleiner als ihre Küche und mein Schlafzimmer ist nicht so gemütlich wie ihr Schlafzimmer. Mein Dorf ist auch nicht so ruhig wie ihr Dorf.

Superlative adjectives

'Superlative adjectives' is the subsidiary grammar point linked to Spread 3.3, *Meine Gegend, deine Gegend*.
There are some examples of superlative forms in the core reading text on page 102 (*das Beste, die schönste Aussicht, am liebsten*). This grammar box also aims to build on the work on comparative adjectives from page 108.
The grammar box could be referred to briefly while going through the core reading text for Spread 3.3, or as a follow-on from the subsidiary grammar activities on Spread 3.2.

Context 3 Home and Environment 79

3 Using comparative and superlative adjectives make sentences comparing the following items. Works in pairs, deciding how the items should compare, then write up your answers.

This speaking and writing activity requires students to use comparative adjectives with *als* and superlative adjectives, following the pattern of the example sentence given. Genders of nouns are provided.

Accept any grammatically correct versions of the answers, and award bonus marks for factually correct versions of **e** and **f**. After writing up their answers, more confident students could think of additional sentences of their own and write them down.

Possible answers:

a Das Schlafzimmer ist größer als das Badezimmer, aber das Wohnzimmer ist das größte Zimmer / am größten.
b Bonn ist schöner als Berlin, aber Wien ist die schönste Stadt / am schönsten.
c Das Doppelhaus ist kleiner als das Einfamilienhaus, aber das Reihenhaus ist das kleinste Haus / am kleinsten.
d Der Dom ist älter als die Kirche, aber das Schloss ist das älteste Gebäude / am ältesten.
e Der Rhein ist länger als die Themse, aber die Donau ist der längste Fluss / am längsten.
f Die Bergstraße ist breiter als die Poststraße, aber die Hauptstraße ist die breiteste Straße / am breitesten.
g Ben Nevis ist höher als der Brocken, aber Mont Blanc ist das höchste Berg / am höchsten.

Adjective endings after the indefinite article

This is the subsidiary grammar point linked to Spread 3.4, *Kommen Sie nach Baden-Württemberg!*
The main spread grammar box and activity on page 105 deal with adjective endings following the definite article. This grammar box gives information on how to use them following the indefinite article.
You may wish to approach this topic as a follow-on from work on definite articles, leading into the productive task at the end of page 105. Alternatively, adjective endings following indefinite articles may be something you wish to refer to briefly then approach separately once students are confident users of one set of endings.

4 Read what Ralf tells you about his family and his friend, Karl, and pick out the indefinite adjective endings, stating what gender and case they are. If you can recognise them, it will also help you to use them correctly!

This reading activity requires students to identify adjective endings after the indefinite article, and the gender and case involved.

When discussing the answers, elicit tips from the class on how they identify the case involved. They could also translate part or all of the text into English.

Answers:

Italics indicate endings from the same group, which students may not be expected to get:

einem kleinen Dorf – neuter, dative
einem schönen Wald – masculine, dative
einen kleinen Bauernhof – masculine, accusative
mein bester Freund – masculine, nominative
eine kleine Schwester – feminine, accusative
mein älterer Bruder – masculine, nominative
einen kurzen Urlaub – masculine, accusative
einem bequemen Hotel – neuter, dative
einer großen Stadt – feminine, dative
seinen letzten Urlaub – masculine, accusative
seine ältere Schwester – feminine, nominative
ihrer neuen Wohnung – feminine, dative
eine alte Kirche – feminine, accusative
keine guten Verkehrsverbindungen – plural, accusative
eine lange Reise – feminine, accusative

Pages 110–111

Vocabulary

V Home and local area

- MP3 files for each vocabulary list.

The essential vocabulary used within Topic 1, Context 3 is presented on this vocabulary spread.

Here students can learn the key words for the topic area *Home and local area*. You may also want to direct students to the online audio files of these vocabulary lists, so they can hear how the words are pronounced by a native speaker.

Some words are in light grey on the vocabulary spreads in the Student Book. This indicates items that are not included in the GCSE specification vocabulary list, so students do not need to learn these items for Listening and Reading assessment. However, you may wish students to use them in Speaking and Writing Controlled Assessments.

Pages 112–113

3.5 Umweltfreundlich oder umweltfeindlich?

Current problems facing the planet

Subject	Discussing environmental problems and solutions
G 1	Using qualifiers
G 2	Using prepositions with the genitive
ⓒ	Making what you say and write more expressive

kerboodle!
- Audio file for core reading text
- Audio file and transcript for listening activity
- Listening activity and transcript: *Was machen Sie für die Umwelt?*
- Grammar activity: Using qualifiers
- Writing worksheet
- Extension listening worksheet
- Audio file and transcript for extension listening worksheet
- Foundation reading worksheet

1 Ⓥ Before students do the vocabulary sorting activity, display halves of compound nouns from the activity, and if you wish a few others relating to this topic (for example, *Windenergie*, *Plastiktüte*). Students must pick a half from each column to build logical nouns relating to the topic of the environment. They then sort the words in activity 1 into two columns, depending on whether they are good or bad for the environment. Check that all meanings are clear (you may need to explain that *FCKW* is the acronym for *Fluorchlorkohlenwasserstoffe* – CFCs in English).

Answers:

Gut für die Umwelt:
Energiesparlampen
recyceln
Solarenergie
Fahrrad
zu Fuß gehen

Schlecht für die Umwelt:
Flugzeug
Abgase
Auto
FCKWs
wegwerfen

Sind wir umweltfreundlich oder umweltfeindlich?

The reading stimulus text consists of the results of a survey of pupils in a German school, to see how environmentally friendly they are. The results are given as percentages. It includes key vocabulary relating to everyday ways of helping or damaging the environment, and examples of the genitive case.

The reading text is also available online as an audio file.

2 📖 🎧 Look at the results of the survey on the environment, and write down the correct percentage for each of the statements.

After reading or listening to the text, students find the correct percentage answer for each of the statements in English. Draw attention to the two key adjectives in the title, *umweltfreundlich* and *umweltfeindlich*. Students could then use the text to 'harvest' useful verbs and phrases, which can later be used for asking and answering questions in the survey for activity 5.

Answers:

a Less than 10%   b 14%   c 21%
d 33%   e 55%   f 62%
g 70%   h 86%   i 75%
j 40%

3 🎧 *Transcript:*

Johannes, fährst du mit dem Auto zur Schule?
Ich fahre immer mit dem Rad zur Schule oder in die Stadt. Das ist viel besser für die Umwelt.

Ingo, was macht deine Familie für die Umwelt?
Wenn meine Mutter zum Supermarkt geht, nimmt sie immer die leeren Weinflaschen mit, um sie in den Container zu stecken.

Anna, wie ist es mit deiner Familie?
Mein Bruder ist nicht besonders umweltfreundlich, da er fast nie die Lichter ausmacht, wenn er ausgeht.

Jürgen, ist deine Familie umweltfreundlich?
Meine Familie benutzt seit einem Jahr öffentliche Verkehrsmittel, zum Beispiel mein Vater, wenn er zur Arbeit fährt und meine Mutter, wenn sie in die Stadt fährt.

Ina, bist du umweltfreundlich?
Ich sollte eigentlich viel mehr für die Umwelt machen, aber ich habe mir neulich ein neues Auto gekauft, weil ich auf dem Lande wohne.

Jens, bist du umweltfreundlich?
Ich bin ziemlich umweltfreundlich, aber ich könnte mehr machen. Meine Frau hasst es, wenn ich die Heizung nicht herunterdrehe, aber ich bin einfach zu faul!

3 🎧 Listen to these people talking about the environment. For each person, find a corresponding picture. Try to add any extra details.

In this audio extract, six young people are asked about their attitude to the environment. The extract includes examples of use of qualifiers, and useful vocabulary relating to the environment.

Encourage more confident students to try to note as many additional details as possible. Afterwards, they could perhaps be asked to paraphrase in German what each speaker said – they may need to listen again to find relevant vocabulary.

Answers:

Johannes, e + better for the environment
Ingo, a + mother takes empty wine bottles to supermarket
Anna, d + brother never turns lights off when he goes out
Jürgen, c + family has been using public transport for a year (dad when goes to work, mum when she goes into town)
Ina, f + should do more but has bought a new car as lives in the countryside
Jens, b + quite environmentally friendly but could do more, wife hates it when he doesn't turn the heating down but he's too lazy

> *Grammatik*
> This panel explains what qualifiers are, and that they can change meanings. It gives a list of the most common. Encourage students to learn this list and their meanings. Practise using them to adapt simple sentences, and point out that they are an easy way to make what you say or write more expressive and precise (see also the *Strategie* panel, below).
> This *Grammatik* panel also refers students to p.120 to learn about prepositions taking the genitive.

4a **G** Find the qualifier(s) in these sentences and write down the meaning of each.

This grammar activity requires students to identify and understand a range of qualifiers.

Refer to the *Grammatik* panel. After discussing the answers to the activity, look at how the qualifiers add to and alter what is said in each sentence.

Answers:

a immer – always
b manchmal – sometimes
c ziemlich – quite
d zu – too
e fast – almost, nie – never
f sehr – very

4b **G** Now translate the sentences into English.

This grammar activity checks comprehension of the sentences used in activity 4a, and of the role played by the qualifier in each.

Refer to the *Grammatik* panel again if necessary. Point out that the phrases in these sentences will be useful for students talking about their own attitude to the environment.

Answers:

a My family always travels by plane on holiday.
b At the weekend I sometimes take bottles to the recycling container.
c For the last month I've been doing quite a lot for the environment.
d My sister is too lazy to walk.
e I almost never leave the TV on standby.
f Sorting the rubbish is very environmentally friendly.

> *Strategie*
> Point out that these are easy methods of making your German more interesting and expressive. A couple of simple phrases using comparatives or superlatives, a few less common adjectives, and a a few favourite qualifiers could all be learnt by heart for regular use.

5 Produce your own survey on how environmentally friendly your class is. You can use the reading survey as a basis for the questions you ask or make up your own. Once you have completed the survey, you can present your results.

Allow time for students to prepare their interview questions. You might want to put some practice questions to the whole class first, using vocabulary from the language structure grid given and additional verbs from the reading text in activity 2, and elicit sample answers. Refer to the *Strategie* panel and the *Tipp* and encourage the use of the suggestions they contain in students' questions and answers. If a fairly extensive survey is conducted, results could be written up and presented in percentages in the style of the reading text or as a bar or pie chart.

> *Tipp*
> Demonstrate use of *seit* with sample questions and answers that might be useful in the surveys.

Plenary activity

Ask students to each pick one interesting / shocking / surprising fact that emerged from their survey, and to read it out to the class for comment or feedback. Discuss their findings. See if the class can reach a consensus in German on whether they are environmentally friendly or not.

3.6 Unsere Welt, unsere Umwelt

Pages 114–115

Being environmentally friendly within the home and local area

Subject	Talking about global environmental issues
G 1	Using the imperative
G 2	Articles and cases (revision)
	Using German posters for a presentation

kerboodle!
- Audio file for core reading text
- Audio file and transcript for listening activity 3
- Reading activity: *Unsere Umwelt*
- Grammar activity: Using the imperative
- Speaking worksheet
- Extension listening worksheet
- Audio file and transcript for extension listening worksheet

1 V Match the problem to the photo.

For this vocabulary-based starter activity, students match key words from the reading text in activity 1 to the correct pictures. Discuss the answers and elicit meanings of useful component parts of the compound words: *sterben, Luft, Verschmutzung*. As further preparation for reading the text, you could ask them to scan what Stefan or Gisela say and find further specific vocab items, work out what they might mean, and be ready to explain how they did this (e.g. similarity to English, guess from context, knowledge of grammar). These might include *retten, bedroht, Lärm, zwitschern* (Stefan) and *Kohlenmonoxid, verpesten, produzieren, Treibhauseffekt* (Gisela).

Answers:

1 c   2 e   3 d   4 b   5 a

Thema Umwelt

The reading stimulus text consists of statements by two people about what they consider to be important global environmental issues. It includes key vocabulary for such issues, much of which will be new to students.

The reading text is also available online as an audio file.

2 📖 🎧 Read Stefan and Gisela's views on environmental issues, then answer the questions in English.

Students read or listen to the text and answer comprehension questions in English. More confident learners could then be asked to make notes in German relating to the key issues Stefan and Gisela raise, by finding the relevant vocabulary in the text, and to answer some questions in German from you about these.

Answers:

a Very important – he wants to do his best to save the environment.
b Animals threatened with extinction.
c Humans make too much noise and there's less living space for animals.
d He would create more nature reserves.
e Gisela lives in the countryside.
f Cars and aerosols.
g These contribute to the greenhouse effect.
h That it's already too late and environmental pollution has already gone too far.

3 🎧 Transcript: _____

Heute sprechen wir mit Jugendlichen, die sich für die Umweltprobleme überall in der Welt interessieren.
1   Bruno wohnt auf dem Lande.
Was mich ärgert ist wie die Bauern die ganze Zeit ihre Felder mit Insektiziden, Pestiziden und Düngemitteln schaden. Sie könnten bestimmt natürliche Produkte verwenden.
2   Jasmin spricht über das Ozonloch.
Jedes Jahr wird das Ozonloch größer und die Ozonschicht dünner. Immer mehr Leute sterben an Hautkrebs, weil ultraviolette Strahlen Sonnenbrand verursachen.
3   Otto war neulich in England.
Mein englischer Brieffreund wohnt auf dem Lande und letzte Woche sind viele Fische im Fluss neben seinem Haus gestorben, wahrscheinlich wegen Wasserverschmutzung oder Biomüll.
4   Thomas spricht über Atomkraft.
Bei mir in der Nähe gibt es ein großes Atomkraftwerk und ich bin sicher, dass es der Umwelt schadet. Das Meer und die Luft werden beide verschmutzt.
5   Carolin wohnt im Schwarzwald.
Ich wohne im Schwarzwald und immer mehr Bäume werden durch sauren Regen beschädigt. In anderen Ländern ist es genau so schlimm.

3 🎧 Listen to these young people talking about environmental problems. Fill in the gaps with the words from the box.

In this listening extract, five young people talk about global environmental issues about which they are concerned. It includes further key vocabulary relating to such issues.

Students listen to the extract, and fill gaps in German sentences relating to the content, selecting from the words given. Afterwards, elicit English translations of the sentences, and use these and the audio transcript to 'harvest' useful words and phrases for students. At this point they could each say which global environmental issues are of concern to them personally, using *Ich ärgere mich über …/ Ich bin sicher, dass …*

Answers:

a ärgert
b Pestizide
c natürliche
d Strahlen
e Biomüll
f Atomkraftwerk
g verschmutzt
h sauren

Context 3 Home and Environment 83

> **Grammatik**
> This panel explains what the imperative is used for, and how to form the *Sie*, *du* and *ihr* versions. Practise forming and using these with some simple examples – perhaps addressing specific students or asking them to play specific roles to make this clearer. You could also use a 'Simon says' game, where students must only respond if they hear the *ihr* form and therefore know that the class is being addressed, or are told individually to respond using the *du* form. Volunteer students could take a turn at the calling.
> The panel also refers students to p.120 to revise articles and cases.

4 Fill in the gaps using the correct imperative form of the verb given in brackets.

This grammar activity requires students to produce the correct imperative form of the verb given themselves, having decided whether the *Sie*, *du* or *ihr* form should be used.

Refer to the *Grammatik* panel and the *Tipp*. With less confident students, you may wish firstly to discuss with them which of the three forms is needed for each, and how they can tell this.

Answers:
 a Fahren Sie
 b bring
 c macht
 d Kaufen Sie
 e Spar
 f Werfen Sie ... weg

> **Tipp**
> Illustrate this with some simple examples (see also the game suggestion in the *Grammatik* panel notes above).

5 Produce a poster on an environmental issue that interests you. The poster should include the problem and some slogans using the imperative with either *du*, *ihr* or *Sie*.

Discuss possible ideas with the class, and allow preparation time for them to decide on their wording and check it carefully. Refer to the *Strategie* panel.

> **Strategie**
> Advice on making posters in German. Point out that short punchy phrases with exclamation marks are effective on a poster, and make sure students have noted the examples of these given for activity 5.

Plenary activity

Students could present their poster to the class or to a small group – either by simply reading out the wording on it while holding it up, or by preparing a slightly longer presentation to summarise the issue it features, and why this issue interests them. You could then discuss in German with the class which were the most popular issues, or which were the most effective / interesting / funny etc. posters and why.

Pages 116–117

3.7 Global denken, lokal handeln

Being environmentally friendly within the home and local area

Subject	Discussing local environmental issues
G 1	Using verbs with *zu*
G 2	Using the future tense with *werden* (revision)
	Dealing with new vocabulary
kerboodle!	• Audio file for core reading text • Video and transcript for video activity 2 • Grammar activity: Using verbs with *zu* • Writing worksheet • Extension reading worksheet • Foundation listening worksheet • Audio file and transcript for foundation listening worksheet

Starter activity

Use a quick vocab quiz to revise five to ten key German words relating to global environmental issues from the previous subtopic, which will come up again in this one (these could include *umweltfreundlich*, *Müll*, *Plastiktüten*, *verpesten*, *Verschmutzung*). You could either simply ask for translations of a list of German or English words, or provide the German words with their vowels missing and ask the class to work out what they are.

UMWELTAKTION: Wie eine Stadt umweltfreundlicher geworden ist!

The reading stimulus text is an article about action taken in a town to improve the environment. It includes familiar and new vocabulary relating to environmental issues, and a range of previously learnt structures such as subordinate clauses, modal verbs and *um ... zu ...* . It also includes use of *zu* with an infinitive, and examples of the present, imperfect, perfect and future tenses.

The reading text is also available online as an audio file.

> **Strategie**
> To demonstrate the strategy for dealing with new vocabulary, ask students to find further examples in the text of compound nouns, or words whose meaning they can guess from the context or from their cultural knowledge. Alternatively, use the transcript for the video in activity 2. Point out that it is important not to panic when faced with new words, and that strategies such as these will give them confidence and could increase their marks in the Reading and Listening units.

1

Find the German for the following words or phrases in the text. Be careful, as you may have to alter things such as the word order.

Students read or listen to the text and work out what the German for the English phrases given will be. Before they start, tell them to look for clues as to what the text is about in the title and illustrations. Refer to the *Strategie* panel. Afterwards, you could ask students to find particular grammatical items in the text: examples of each tense used, modal verbs (in two tenses), and subordinating conjunctions. With more confident students, you could discuss the various uses of *werden* seen in the text – its general meaning (to become), formation of the future tense, and the passive.

Answers:

- a beschlossen
- b die Einwohner das so wollen
- c Vor ein paar Jahren
- d es [gab] nicht genug Parkplätze
- e überhaupt nicht
- f trennten
- g Einwegflaschen
- h total dafür
- i sicherer für [...] Kinder
- j man [sieht] keine Plastikbecher mehr
- k eine Bürgerinitiative

2

Transcript:

Scene 1

Interviewer Hallo liebe Zuschauer! Herzlich willkommen bei „Rund um die Gegend!" Ich bin Stefan Toller und heute geht es um die Umwelt. Also, wie umweltfreundlich ist unsere Gegend? Wir fragen unsere jungen Einwohner! ... Entschuldige! Wie heißt du?
Jens Ich heiße Jens.
Interviewer Hallo Jens! Also, ich habe eine Frage für dich. Wer soll deiner Meinung nach die Verantwortung für die Umwelt übernehmen?
Jens Naja, ich bin der Meinung, dass jede Person etwas für die Umwelt machen muss.
Interviewer Und bei dir, macht man genug?
Jens Ja, ich glaube schon. Zu Hause trennen wir den Müll in verschiedene kleine Container. In meinem Dorf hat man auch angefangen, mehr Sammelcontainer für Glas, Papier, alte Kleidung und Schuhe aufzustellen.
Interviewer Das alles klingt schon gut! Danke, Jens.
Jens Kein Problem.

Scene 2

Interviewer Hallo! Ich bin der Stefan Toller, Reporter für „Rund um die Gegend!". Haben Sie einen kleinen Moment, bitte?
Barbara Ja, natürlich.
Interviewer Wie heißen Sie?
Barbara Ich bin die Barbara. Ich bin Studentin.
Interviewer Barbara, unsere Zuschauer wollen alle wissen, wie umweltfreundlich wir hier in der Gegend sind. Also, was meinen Sie?
Barbara Hmm. Meiner Meinung nach machen wir leider noch nicht genug.
Interviewer Wieso denn?
Barbara Ich finde, dass viele Studenten gar nichts für die Umwelt machen. Einige kaufen umweltfreundliches Papier, aber viele verschwenden Papier! Und wenn man eine Party macht, wollen die meisten Leute etwas trinken, sind aber nicht bereit, die Flaschen zum Recyclingcontainer zu bringen. Das ist eigentlich sehr enttäuschend, oder?
Interviewer Tja, das stimmt. Danke, Barbara.
Barbara Bitte sehr.

Scene 3

Interviewer Wir sind jetzt im Stadtzentrum, um noch mehr von dir zu hören. Und wie heißt du?
Thomas Ich bin der Thomas.
Interviewer Und was machst du jetzt?
Thomas Ich räume den Abfall von der Straße. Glücklicherweise sind die Straßen nicht so schmutzig wie früher.
Interviewer Und ist diese Stadt umweltfreundlich, Thomas? Was meinst du?
Thomas Eigentlich ja. Vor allem jetzt, da es heute die „Greenteams" gibt. Ich bin Mitglied eines „Greenteams" und wir machen viel für die Umwelt. Man pflanzt Bäume, reinigt Straßen und organisiert Aktivitäten für Kinder. Ich finde das eine sehr gute Idee, weil die Kinder viel dabei lernen, und es ist auch gut für die Gesundheit.
Interviewer Gut, dann mache weiter so! Vielen Dank Thomas!
Thomas Bitte sehr. Auf Wiedersehen!

Scene 4

Interviewer Entschuldigung, eine Frage... Hallo! Wie heißt du?
Anke Ich heiße Anke und bin fünfzehn Jahre alt.
Interviewer Anke, gibt es neue Umweltinitiativen in dieser Stadt?
Anke Hmm ... Viele Einwohner hier möchten einen autofreien Tag oder „Car-Sharing" Tage einführen.
Interviewer Und bist du dafür oder dagegen?
Anke Ich bin dafür. Jeder weiß doch, wie die Autos und ihre Abgase die Luft verpesten. Meine Mutter ist aber anderer Meinung, weil sie das Auto fürs Einkaufen braucht.
Interviewer Naja, es gibt immer eine Gegenseite. Vielen Dank, Anke!
Anke Bitte! Tschüss!
Interviewer Und nun, was meinen Sie? Besuchen Sie unser Forum, www.rundumdiegegend.de. Wir freuen uns sehr darauf, bald von Ihnen zu hören! Bis zum nächsten Mal!

2

These people are being interviewed for the local news about the environment in their area. Watch and listen carefully, then answer the questions in English.

The video clip consists of news interviews with four young people from different places within the same area, each giving their opinion about environmental issues in their locality. It includes key vocabulary relating to local environmental action and issues.

Context 3 Home and Environment 85

Students watch the video and answer the comprehension questions in English. Help less confident students to prepare by re-playing and analysing the language of each speaker, identifying and translating key verbs and 'harvesting' useful vocabulary. The advice given in the *Strategie* panel relating to working out meanings from context, will be helpful here.

Answers:

a Everyone should do something.
b His family separate rubbish.
c They've started to have more recycling containers for glass, paper, old clothes and shoes.
d Many of them don't do anything to help and it's very disappointing. Some buy recycled paper but many waste paper.
e Any two of: plant trees, clean streets, organise activities for children.
f Children learn a lot and it's healthy.
g They would like a car-free day or car-sharing days.
h Her mother doesn't like the idea because she needs the car for shopping.

Grammatik

This panel explains that certain verbs in German are used with *zu* and an infinitive. It gives the most common of these, and explains how to construct sentences. Point out that when students think of the meanings of these sentences in English, the word 'to' is always there (decide to, hope to, begin to etc). Practise forming and using this type of sentence with some simple examples.
The panel also refers students to p.121 to revise the future tense with *werden*.

---

3 **G** Decide whether these sentences need *zu* to make them correct and write out the correct version if they do.

This grammar activity requires students to decide whether *zu* should be used with the infinitive in each sentence, and if it should, to insert it in the correct position.
Refer firstly to the *Grammatik* panel. Remind less confident learners that modal verbs will not require *zu* and refer to the *Tipp*.

Answers:

a Yes – Er hat versucht, Energie zu sparen.
b No.
c Yes – Mein Bruder vergisst immer, das Licht auszumachen.
d No.
e Yes – Wir fangen an, umweltfreundlicher zu sein.
f Yes – Ich hoffe, in der Zukunft nach Amerika zu fahren.
g No.

Tipp

After looking at this box with students, if necessary, revise which are the modal verbs.

---

4 Work in pairs: one partner asks the questions about local environmental issues and the other answers. Then swap roles.

Check that meanings of all vocabulary in the language structure grid provided are clear, and support weaker students by demonstrating sample questions and answers. These could also include use of the future tense with *werden* to talk about what they and others will do, with reference to the *Grammatik* panel on page 121. If there are specific environmental projects happening in your school or local area, make sure students have the words they need to describe these. The speaking activity could be followed by a piece of written work.

Plenary activity

Students work in pairs, and each try to talk for 30 seconds (or a minute) in German about the environment, using language from this and previous subtopics. Partners time them and provide constructive help and feedback. Provide some key points to mention or key vocabulary for support.

Pages 118–119

Reading and listening

Environment

kerboodle!
• Audio file for core reading text
• Audio files and transcripts for listening activity 2

Umwelt in Gefahr

The reading stimulus text is an article about man-made threats to the environment. It describes the key problems, future prospects, and possible action we could take. It includes examples of imperative forms, *seit*, prepositions taking the genitive case, and modal verbs.
The reading text is also available online as an audio file.

1a Read the article, then read the following sentences. For each sentence write T (true), F (false) or ? (Not in the Text).

All students should be able to attempt the true/false/not in the text activity 1a.

Answers:

a T b F c T d T e F f F

1b Read the article again and answer the following questions in English.

Activity 1b involves a deeper understanding of the text's content in order to answer comprehension questions in English, and is more challenging. For this, refer students to the Examiner's tip. Afterwards, ask more confident students to pick out useful words and phrases from the text and to note them down for use in their own work.

Answers:

a Three of the following: acid rain, UV rays, organic waste, sulphur dioxide, CFCs.
b It rains more often and the sea level rises.

c On the one hand it's an advantage, but it also means that other plants won't be able to grow due to the heat.
d Carbon dioxide from exhaust fumes.
e We need to do more to save the environment (one example from the following: reuse things; buy calculators run on solar power; only use bottles that can be recycled; wear a jumper instead of turning the heating up).
f Generally negative impression, the environment is in danger and we need to do more etc.

> **Grammatik**
> This panel asks students to find examples of three grammatical features in the listening and reading material: the imperative, comparative adjectives and verbs with *zu*. It also refers them to the pages where these grammar points are explained. Elicit and discuss some of the examples found (it may be easier for students to refer to the transcripts of the listening material while listening). Take the opportunity to recap these features with less confident students.

2a 🎧 *Transcript:*
1 Recyceln Sie Pappe!
2 Benutzen Sie nur Energiesparlampen!
3 Versuchen Sie, eine Alternative zu Spraydosen zu finden!
4 Bringen Sie leere Batterien in die Altbatteriesammlung!
5 Statt mit dem Auto zu fahren, steigen Sie auf öffentliche Verkehsmittel um!
6 Benutzen Sie Sonnenenergie statt Elektrizität!

2a 🎧 Listen to the different pieces of advice. For each, note down the letter of the matching picture.

The audio extract consists of six short pieces of advice, using the imperative form with *Sie*, telling listeners how to help the environment. It includes examples of verbs with *zu* and useful key vocabulary relating to this topic, and is accessible for less confident students.

After listening to the extract and selecting the correct picture for each, students could listen again and pick out particular language items, for example the imperative forms – refer them to the *Grammatik* panel (see above).
Answers:

1 a   2 d   3 c   4 e   5 b   6 g

2b 🎧 *Transcript:*
Um die Umwelt zu schützen, müssen wir vor allem zwei Dinge machen. Erstens müssen wir erneubare Energieformen benutzen, und zweitens müssen wir eine Alternative zum Auto finden. In der Industriestadt Gelsenkirchen gibt es schon jetzt Reihenhäuser, die Solarenergie benutzen. Das ist nicht nur umweltfreundlicher, sondern es senkt auch die Heizungungskosten.
Am wichtigsten für mich aber ist, eine Alternative zum Auto zu finden, weil das Autofahren nicht nur teuer, sondern auch sehr umweltfeindlich ist wegen der Auspuffgase. Ein Leben ohne Autos ist für viele Leute kaum vorstellbar, aber es ist möglich. Man kann zum Beispiel zu Fuß zur Arbeit oder zur Schule gehen, mit dem Fahrrad zum Sportzentrum fahren, das Auto mal in der Garage stehen lassen und den Bus nehmen. So kann jeder dabei mitmachen, die Umwelt zu retten.

2b 🎧 Listen to the radio item on saving the environment and answer the following questions in English.

This audio extract, a radio report, contains longer and more complex sentences to challenge more confident students. In it, more detailed suggestions are made as to how we can protect the environment. The extract includes examples of verbs with *zu*, modal verbs, comparative adjectives and qualifiers.

Less confident students could work collaboratively with others to answer all the comprehension questions between them. They may also need to refer to the transcript for support. Refer students again to the Examiner's tip, and after they have finished, if not already done, to the *Grammatik* panel.
Answers:

a It's more environmentally friendly and reduces heating costs.
b Finding an alternative to cars (expensive, damaging to environment because of exhaust fumes).
c Many people just can't imagine a life without cars.
d Walking to work or school; cycling to the sports centre; leaving the car in the garage and taking the bus.
e Everyone.

Pages 120–121

Grammar practice

G   **Environment**

Using prepositions with the genitive

> **Grammatik**
> Using prepositions with the genitive is the subsidiary grammar point linked to Spread 3.5, *Umweltfreundlich oder umweltfeindlich?*
> Students encounter examples of the genitive passively at various points in the course, including the core reading text on page 112, *Sind wir umweltfreundlich oder umweltfeindlich? (des Schiller-Gymnasiums, sind der Meinung).*
> This grammar box offers a fuller explanation of the uses of the genitive, both to indicate possession and after specific prepositions. It can be referred to at any point in the course, although examples are specific to the environment topic.

1a ✏️ Complete the sentences below, adding the correct genitive preposition.

This reading and writing activity requires students to select the most suitable genitive preposition for the context of each sentence.

Refer firstly to the *Grammatik* panel (see above) and tell students to choose from the list of prepositions it contains for this activity. After discussing the answers, analyse with the class the genitive change made to the definite article after each preposition.
Answers:

a Trotz
b Wegen
c innerhalb
d Außerhalb

Context 3 Home and Environment 87

1b Complete the following texts by adding the correct definite articles in the genitive case.

This reading and writing activity requires students to identify the gender of the noun following each gap, then to work out the correct genitive definite articles to fill the gaps.

After discussing the answers, elicit translations of the texts. Encourage students to learn and try to use the genitive prepositions on the list.

Answers:

a der   b der   c des
d des   e des   f der

> **Articles and cases (revision)** *Grammatik*
>
> The revision of articles and cases is the subsidiary grammar point linked to Spread 3.6, *Unsere Welt, unsere Umwelt*.
> Throughout the Home and environment Context, much grammar work has been based on prepositions and adjective endings. Confidence in recognising and using the correct genders, articles and cases is an essential prerequisite to applying the rules relating to prepositions and adjectives, so these grammar boxes go back over the basics which students should know at this stage.
> These grammar boxes may be referred to at any stage in the course but completion of Context 3 may offer a particularly good point for consolidation.

2a Choose the correct form of the definite article to complete the following sentences. The gender of each noun is supplied in brackets. In each case state which case is being used.

This writing activity requires students to think about which case each definite article should be in, considering all the determining factors they have learnt about and using the *Grammatik* panels for support.

When discussing the answers, ask students to explain the reason for their choice of case. If any problem areas are apparent, this would be a good opportunity to clarify them further.

Answers:

a Der – nominative
b die – accusative
c der – dative
d Die – nominative, der – genitive
e dem – dative
f dem – dative
g die – accusative
h Der – nominative, der – dative

2b Choose the correct form of the indefinite article to complete the following sentences. Again, the gender of each noun is supplied in brackets. In each case state which case is being used.

This writing activity requires students to think about which case each indefinite article should be in, again considering all the determining factors they have learnt about and using the relevant *Grammatik* panels for support.

When discussing the answers, elicit translations of the sentences and once again ask students to explain the reason for their choice of case.

Answers:

a eine – accusative
b einen – accusative
c eines – genitive, einen – accusative
d Ein – nominative
e eine – accusative
f eines – genitive
g ein – accusative, einem – dative

> **The future tense with *werden* (revision)** *Grammatik*
>
> Forming the future tense with *werden* is the subsidiary grammar point linked to Spread 3.7, *Global denken, lokal handeln*.
> This reinforces work on the future tense done in Context 2, Spread 2.7, *Urlaubspläne*.
> In activity 4 on page 117, students are asked to talk about what could still be done to help save the environment. This could be extended to talk about what they and others will do by referring to this grammar box at this stage.

3a With a partner, take it in turns to practise asking and answering these questions using *werden* correctly.

This speaking activity requires students to use the correct form of *werden* with an infinitive in their answers to the future tense questions.

Allow less confident students time to read the questions and prepare their answers, so that they can find suitable vocabulary as well as check the correct form of *werden*. Remind them that they will often be able to take the verb form and other wording from the question itself.

Possible answers:

a Morgen werde ich den Müll trennen.
b Meine Familie wird am Wochenende die Heizung herunterdrehen.
c Nächste Woche wird meine Schule nur Altpapier benutzen.
d In der Zukunft werden meine Freunde nur mit dem Rad fahren.
e Wenn ich das nächste Mal einkaufen gehe, werde ich Energiesparlampen kaufen.

3b You and your family have good intentions about caring for the environment but have yet to put your plans into action! Change the following text from the present tense to the future tense with *werden*.

This writing activity requires students to identify the present tense verbs in the text, and convert them into the future tense, thinking also about word order.

Support weaker students by converting the first two sentences together. You could also elicit translations of both the present tense and future tense versions of the text.

Answers:

> Ich werde umweltfreundlicher als meine Freundin sein. Ich werde alles recyceln. Meine Familie wird keine Einwegflaschen kaufen und wird Flaschen zum Container bringen. Mein Bruder wird mit dem Rad zur Schule fahren und mein Vater wird zu Fuß in die Stadtmitte gehen. Ich werde jeden Tag duschen und ich werde keine Spraydosen kaufen. Die Stadt wird verschiedene Sammelcontainer haben und wird umweltfreundliche Häuser bauen.

Pages 122–123

Vocabulary

V Environment

- MP3 files for each vocabulary list.

The essential vocabulary used within Topic 2, Context 3 is presented on this vocabulary spread.

Here students can learn the key words for the topic area *Environment*. You may also want to direct students to the online audio files of these vocabulary lists, so they can hear how the words are pronounced by a native speaker.

Some words are in light grey on the vocabulary spreads in the Student Book. This indicates items that are not included in the GCSE specification vocabulary list, so students do not need to learn these items for Listening and Reading assessment. However, you may wish students to use them in Speaking and Writing Controlled Assessments.

Pages 124–127

Controlled Assessment

Please refer to the section on Controlled Assessment, pages 113–119 in this Teacher's Book.

Page 128

3 Context summary

- Interactive multiple-choice quiz

The closing page for Context 3, Home and Environment provides a multiple-choice quiz which tests the key language learnt in the preceding chapter.

A longer version of this quiz is also available online as an interactive, self-marking multiple-choice test.

Answers:

1. Any two of e.g. Heiligabend, Weihnachten, Ostern
2. e.g. Reihenhaus, Einfamilienhaus, Doppelhaus
3. größer
4. e.g. Was gibt es in deiner Stadt?
5. mit / in / für
6. Ich mag meinen Garten, obwohl er ziemlich klein ist.
7. Suggested answer: Eine Flasche, die nicht wieder verwendet werden kann und recycelt werden muss.
8. e.g. ich Altpapier kaufe.
9. I do quite a lot for the environment, although I could do more.
10. Ich versuche immer, die Heizung herunterzudrehen.

4 Work and Education

School / college and future plans

What school / college is like

	KS3 Revision: School subjects; Places in school; Jobs and workplaces	*Online materials* • Audio files for core reading texts
	4.1 Wie ist deine Schule? ■ Saying where you do things ■ Giving impressive answers to questions	• Audio file for core reading text • Audio file and transcript for listening activity 2 • Listening activity and transcript: *Wie ist deine Schule?* • Grammar activity: Using subordinate clauses and conjunctions • Writing worksheet • Foundation listening worksheet • Audio file and transcript for foundation listening worksheet • Extension listening worksheet • Audio file and transcript for extension listening worksheet
	4.2 Das Schulwesen anderswo ■ Using the imperfect tense of modals ■ Revising vocabulary	• Audio file for core reading text • Audio file and transcript for listening activity 3 • Listening activity and transcript: *Der Alltag in einer deutschen Schule* • Grammar activity: Using the imperfect tense of modal verbs • Speaking worksheet • Extension reading worksheet

Pressures and problems

	4.3 Schulstress ■ Saying what you could or ought to do ■ Matching people to information	• Audio file for core reading text • Audio file and transcript for listening activity 3 • Listening activity and transcript: *Probleme in der Schule* • Grammar activity: Saying what you could, ought or would like to do • Writing worksheet • Extension listening worksheet • Audio file and transcript for extension listening worksheet
	4.4 Eine bessere Schule ■ Saying what you would do ■ Knowing which tense to use	• Audio file for core reading text • Audio file and transcript for listening activity 2 • Listening activity and transcript: *In meiner neuen Schule möchte ich …* • Grammar activity: Saying what you would do • Writing worksheet • Foundation reading worksheet • Extension reading worksheet

Reading and listening

• Audio file for core reading text
• Audio files and transcripts for listening activity 2

Grammar

School / college and future plans

■ Subordinate clauses
■ Ways of denoting possession
■ The pluperfect tense
■ The conditional forms of *haben*, *sein* and *geben*

Vocabulary

School / college and future plans

• MP3 files for each vocabulary list

Current and future jobs

Looking for and getting a job

Work routine

Advantages and disadvantages of different jobs

Reading and listening

Grammar

Vocabulary

Summative assessment

4.5 Nebenjobs und Arbeitspraktikum
- Remembering when not to use the indefinite article
- Planning a piece of writing

- Audio file for core reading text
- Audio file and transcript for listening activity 3
- Reading activity: *Nebenjobs und Berufe*
- Grammar activity: Remembering when not to use the indefinite article
- Speaking worksheet
- Extension listening worksheet
- Audio file and transcript for extension listening worksheet
- Foundation reading worksheet

4.6 Ich suche einen Job
- Revising how to say 'when'
- Using previously learned material

- Audio file for core reading text
- Video and transcript for video activity 2
- Grammar activity: Revising how to say 'when'
- Speaking worksheet
- Extension listening worksheet
- Audio file and transcript for extension listening worksheet

4.7 Am Arbeitsplatz
- Using dative pronouns
- Taking notes effectively when listening

- Audio file for core reading text
- Audio file and transcript for listening activity 2
- Listening activity and transcript: *Eine Nachricht für Sie!*
- Grammar activity: Using dative pronouns
- Speaking worksheet
- Extension reading worksheet

4.8 Was mache ich nach der Schulzeit?
- Talking about the future
- Varying your language

- Audio file for core reading text
- Audio file and transcript for listening activity 2
- Listening activity and transcript: *Nach der Schule werde ich ...*
- Grammar activity: Talking about the future
- Speaking worksheet
- Extension listening worksheet
- Audio file and transcript for extension listening worksheet

4.9 Jobs und Berufe
- Revising interrogatives
- Finding out information

- Audio file for core reading text
- Audio file and transcript for listening activity 2
- Listening activity and transcript: *Mein Beruf*
- Grammar activity: Revising interrogatives
- Writing worksheet
- Extension reading worksheet
- Foundation listening worksheet
- Audio file and transcript for foundation listening worksheet

---

- Audio file for core reading text
- Audio files and transcripts for listening activity 2

Current and future jobs
- Knowing when not to use the indefinite article
- Using *seit* to say how long you have been doing something
- Talking about the future (revision)
- Conditional sentences (revision)
- Using the correct word for 'you' (revision)

Current and future jobs
- MP3 files for each vocabulary list

Work and education
- Interactive multiple-choice quiz

The opening page for Context 4, Work and Education provides a quick-reference overview of how the teaching spreads, grammar and strategies within this Context in the Student Book map to the Topics and Purposes of Context 4 in the GCSE specification. Also included here is an overview of the online resources available for each of these spreads in the Student Book.

Context 4 Work and Education 91

Page 130

Revision

School / college and future plans

kerboodle! • Audio files for core reading texts

School subjects, places in school

1a 📖 🎧 Read Dieter's description of his school subjects. Make three lists under the following headings.

A reading activity to practise understanding words for school subjects and opinions about them. Students find all the words for subjects, and categorise them according to what Dieter thinks of them. The first *Vokabeln* box is available for support. With less confident students, this could be followed up with further revision of words for subjects, using computer generated word searches or other puzzles, and making a list of all subjects they learn in preparation for activity 1b.

The reading text is also available online as an audio file.

Answers:

Subjects he likes: PE, maths, art
Subjects he finds okay: science, IT
Subjects he doesn't like: German, English, music, geography, history

1b ✏️ Using Dieter's text as a model write about your own school subject likes and dislikes.

A writing activity to practise using words for school subjects and opinions about them. More able learners should be able to extend their writing beyond simply substituting words in Dieter's text.

2a 📖 🎧 Read Dieter's description of his school. Match the following sentences to the locations in the school in the box on the right. One word is left over – why?

A reading activity to revise words for locations in a school. Students match statements to words for locations, based on the content of the text and using the second *Vokabeln* box for support. Afterwards, you could use similar statements about your own school to elicit words for locations in it from the class – more confident learners could prepare statements themselves.

The reading text is also available online as an audio file.

Answers:

a Kantine
b Schulhof
c Lehrerzimmer
d Bibliothek
e Sportplatz

Sporthalle is left over because there is no school sports hall.

2b ✏️ Design a plan of a new school. Label the rooms and open areas in German. Which subjects would be taught in each part of the school?

A writing activity to practise using the words for locations in schools and school subjects.

> This panel reminds students that the verb in a German sentence always needs to be put second, and gives examples relevant to speaking activity 2c. Practise this with some further examples relevant to the activity.

Grammatik

2c 💬 You are showing a German visitor around your new school. Prepare a short speech to describe the school you have designed and say what you do in each area.

A speaking activity to practise talking about school facilities and subjects, using the designs from activity 2b. More confident learners could extend the task beyond simple statements by also giving reasons for their choices. Allow time for preparation, and refer to the *Grammatik* panel.

Possible answers:

Hier ist das Klassenzimmer. Ich lerne Deutsch, Englisch und Geschichte hier. Dort ist die Bibliothek. Hier lese ich und suche Bücher…

Page 131

Revision

Current and future jobs

kerboodle! • Audio files for core reading texts

Jobs and workplaces

1a 📖 🎧 Look at the words in the vocabulary box on the right. Who would work where? Match as many people as you can to the different places on the map.

A reading activity to revise words for jobs and workplaces. Discuss the male/female versions of the job words listed in the first *Vokabeln* box. If needed, you could use a miming game to revise these words further: one student mimes typical actions of a job from the list, others make guesses – *du bist Kaufmann, Metzgerin* etc.

The reading text is also available online as an audio file.

Answers:

a Sekretär/in, Lehrer/in, Koch/Köchin
b Arzt/Ärztin, Koch/Köchin, Krankenpfleger/Krankenschwester, Sekretär/in
c Koch/Köchin, Kellner/in
d Briefträger/in, Polizist/in
e Hausfrau/Hausmann
f LKW-Fahrer/in

1b Design a plan of a new town centre. Label the streets and buildings. Write sentences to describe who works where.

A writing activity to practise using job words and saying where people work. Refer to the *Grammatik* panel, and remind students to check the genders of workplaces carefully when using *in* with the dative. The second *Vokabeln* box is available for support.

Possible answers:

Der Metzger arbeitet in der Metzgerei. Die Mechanikerin arbeitet in der Werkstatt. Der Kellner arbeitet im Café …

> **Grammatik**
> This panel reminds students how to use *in* with the dative case to say when someone works in a particular building. It also refers them to page 102 to find out more about the dative case. Practise using *in der / im* with the words in the second *Vokabeln* box.

1c Work in pairs. Each write down the name of five jobs in German. Take it in turns to try to guess what your partner has chosen.

A speaking activity to practise using male and female versions of job words in German. With less confident learners, you might wish first to practise pronunciation of some of the words from the first *Vokabeln* box, for example focusing on the change when an umlaut is added.

Possible answers:

Hast du "Klempner"?
Nein! Hast du "Mechaniker"?
Ja! Hast du …

1d Work in pairs. Now each write down the name of one job in German. Take it in turns to ask questions to try to guess what your partner has chosen.

A speaking activity to practise words for jobs and using *in* plus the dative with workplaces. Refer again to the *Grammatik* panel, and remind weaker students to make sure they use the correct male or female version of the job word when guessing.

Possible answers:

Arbeitest du in der Stadt?
Ja!
Arbeitest du in einem Geschäft?
Nein …

Pages 132–133

4.1 Wie ist deine Schule?

What school / college is like

Subject	Describing what your school is like
G 1	Saying where you do things (using the relative pronoun *wo*)
G 2	Using subordinate clauses
🔧	Giving impressive answers to questions

kerboodle!
- Audio file for core reading text
- Audio file and transcript for listening activity 2
- Listening activity and transcript: *Wie ist deine Schule?*
- Grammar activity: Using subordinate clauses and conjunctions
- Writing worksheet
- Foundation listening worksheet
- Audio file and transcript for foundation listening worksheet
- Extension listening worksheet
- Audio file and transcript for extension listening worksheet

Starter activity

To develop cultural awareness, discuss students' prior knowledge of differences between school systems in different countries. Ask them to describe the system in their own country, then ask whether they know anything of the German education system (e.g. types of school, ages of pupils, class names, daily routine in German schools), and share your experiences of this with them. Such comparisons will be further developed in subtopic 4.2.

Hermann-Friedrich-Gesamtschule

This reading stimulus text, a website description of a comprehensive school near Hanover by one of its students, includes key vocabulary relating to school subjects, facilities and routine. It contains examples of subordinate clauses and the relative pronoun *wo*.

The reading text is also available online as an audio file.

> **Tipp**
> Students could work collaboratively in pairs to make notes for this suggested activity – deciding for each example they find in the text, why the verb is at the end of the clause. The *Grammatik* panels on pages 133 and 142 examine *wo* as a relative pronoun and subordinate clauses. Point out that knowing where to find the verb will help them with comprehension in the Reading and Listening units, and using such structures themselves will increase their marks in the Speaking and Writing units.

1 Copy and complete each sentence with one of the words below.

Students read or listen to the text, and complete the sentences using the correct word from those given, according to what they have read. Point out to less confident students that there are more words than gaps. Afterwards, look at the text in detail with the class, extracting details about routine at this school and discussing in German how it differs from your own school. Also refer to the *Tipp*.

Answers:

a Hermann-Friedrich ist eine **Gesamtschule**.
b Die Schule ist ganz **modern**.
c In den **Labors** macht man Biologie, Chemie und Physik.
d Die Schule hat ein **Hallenbad**, wo man schwimmen kann.
e Um **sieben** Uhr dreißig beginnt die erste Stunde.
f Das **Essen** in der Schule schmeckt gut.
g Stefan findet es **prima**, dass er am Mittwoch Ganztagsschule hat.

2 🎧 *Transcript:*

a Sport ist mein Lieblingsfach!
b Ich finde Naturwissenschaften gut, auch wenn ich normalerweise keine gute Noten bekomme.
c Ich habe Englisch in der ersten Stunde. Das finde ich in Ordnung. Obwohl ich nicht so gern schreibe, lese ich immer gern.
d Montags lerne ich immer Musik nach der ersten Pause. Ich hasse Musik aber ich mag das neue Sprachlabor, wo wir Fremdsprachen lernen.
e Na gut. Jeden Mittwoch habe ich Geschichte. Das ist ein langweiliges Fach. Mein Zwillingsbruder treibt gern Sport aber ich finde Erdkunde viel interessanter.
f Erdkunde ist nichts für mich. Sport finde ich auch schlecht, besonders weil die Umkleideräume so dreckig sind. Ich mag lieber Kunst, weil ich gern male und zeichne.

---

2 🎧 Which subjects do these pupils do? What do they think of them? Write your answers to a–f in English.

This audio extract consists of six young people speaking about school subjects they do, and what they think of them. It contains useful phrases for giving opinions about school subjects, examples of subordinate clauses, and the relative pronoun *wo*.

Students listen to the extract and note the subjects and opinions heard in English. More confident students should be encouraged to note any extra details they can understand. All could then listen again and note the German opinion phrases used.

Answers:

a PE – favourite subject
b science – likes it even though usually doesn't get good marks
c English – okay, not so good at writing but likes reading
d music – hates it, foreign languages – likes the new language lab (extra details: has music on Monday after first break)
e history – boring, twin brother likes sport but speaker prefers geography (extra details: has history every Wednesday)
f geography – not interested, PE – doesn't like, art – prefers it because good at painting and drawing (extra details: PE changing rooms are dirty)

Grammatik

This panel explains how to use *wo* as a relative pronoun, to make a sentence saying where you do things. It points out that the verb following must then go to the end of the clause. With weaker students, clarify their understanding of what a clause is, and practise with a few simple examples. The reading and listening materials in activities 1 and 2 provide examples of relative clauses with *wo*. You could explain to more confident students that other question words can be used in the same way.
The panel also refers students to p.142 to learn about other words which send verb to the end of the clause.

3 Ⓖ Join these phrases using *wo*.

This grammar activity requires students to form sentences with *wo* as a relative pronoun, from each pair of phrases given.

Refer to the *Grammatik* panel. Afterwards, students could write similar sentences about their own school.

Answers:

a Es gibt einen Sportplatz, wo wir Hockey spielen.
b Ich gehe in die Schulkantine, wo ich zu Mittag esse.
c Die Schule hat viele Labors, wo wir Experimente machen.
d Es gibt auch ein Sprachlabor, wo ich Englisch sprechen kann.
e Neben meinem Klassenzimmer ist die Bibliothek, wo ich meine Hausaufgaben mache.

Strategie

💬 To demonstrate the 'ADORE' memory-jogger on giving impressive answers to questions, discuss examples of details, opinions and reasons for use in students' answers for speaking activity 4. Remind them that using subordinate clauses, e.g. with *weil* to give reasons, combined with this type of content, will increase their marks.

4 💬 🔊 Work with a partner. One partner asks the questions and the other answers. Then swap roles. See if you can think of some other questions to ask.

Ensure that less confident learners understand the questions and model answers provided in the language structure grid. More confident students should spend time thinking of additional questions to ask, and planning detailed answers. Refer them to the *Strategie* panel and suggest that partners give constructive feedback on the content of answers given.

Plenary activity

Divide the class into groups of four students for a memory game to consolidate language from this subtopic. Display a few starter sentences using the items you wish them to practise. For example: *Die Aula ist wo wir Versammlungen haben. Ich mag Mathe nicht, weil es nicht interessant ist.* Student A in each group says the sentence, student B repeats it and adds a different version of their own, student C repeats both and adds another one, and they continue until an error is made, when they move on to the next starter sentence and do the same again.

Pages 134–135

4.2 Das Schulwesen anderswo

What school / college is like

Subject	Comparing schools in different countries
G 1	Using the imperfect tense of modals
G 2	Ways of denoting possession
🔊	Revising vocabulary

kerboodle!
- Audio file for core reading text
- Audio file and transcript for listening activity 3
- Listening activity and transcript: *Der Alltag in einer deutschen Schule*
- Grammar activity: Using the imperfect tense of modal verbs
- Speaking worksheet
- Extension reading worksheet

Starter activity

Display three groups of German words, each of which is the jumbled components of a sentence relating to school, taken from the previous subtopic. Students work in pairs or individually and arrange the words to form a grammatically correct sentence (there may be more than one possible solution). Alternatively, distribute the words on pieces of card for students to arrange.

Der Austausch

In the reading stimulus text, two young people describe their experiences on a recent school exchange visit to Germany. It includes key language relating to school routine, examples of the imperfect tense of modal verbs, and examples of ways of denoting possession.

The reading text is also available online as an audio file.

1a 📖 🎧 Answer the following questions in English.

Students read or listen to the text and firstly answer the English comprehension questions. For activity 1b they re-read the descriptions, and pick out key vocabulary, which they should note with meanings. They then analyse how they worked out the meanings of new words, and make a list of these to revise and use again. Refer to the *Strategie* panel.

Answers:

a Because the first lesson started at 7:55.
b Because she didn't have to concentrate for so long.
c She could chat or play in the school yard.
d She liked being able to go home at midday, as the last lesson ended at 1:15.
e He didn't have to wear a uniform.
f He could eat and drink in the classrooms.
g Because the teachers had to come to the pupils.
h They had to take part in an extra-curricular project or activity (for instance a team sport).

> 📖 **Strategie** Engage students with the suggested strategies for revising vocabulary by asking which of these they think will work well for them personally, how many words they find they can learn at a time, and when or how they find it easiest to learn vocabulary. Practise using the techniques with words from the reading text, and set learning them as a homework task (see also the plenary activity suggestion below).

1b 📖 🎧 🔊 Read Tom and Paula's descriptions again, picking out key words relating to the topic of school life.

Teacher to check and discuss answers.

> **Grammatik** This panel explains how to form and use the imperfect tense of modal verbs. It gives the *ich* form for each verb. With weaker students, clarify their understanding of what the imperfect tense is by translating simple examples using these. The reading text in activity 1 provides examples of imperfect tense modal verb forms.
> The panel also refers students to p.142 to learn different ways of denoting possession.

2 G Rewrite these sentences in the imperfect tense.

This grammar activity requires students to identify the present tense forms of modal verbs in the sentences and change them into the correct imperfect tense forms.

Refer to the *Grammatik* panel. Point out that the imperfect tense of modal verbs is easy to form, and easy to use, working in the same way as the present tense with an infinitive. After discussing the answers, check that less confident students are clear on the meanings of the sentences.

Answers:

a Ich musste um 8 Uhr aufstehen.
b Im Klassenzimmer durfte ich nicht essen.
c In der Pause konnte ich mich mit meinen Freunden treffen.
d In Deutschland mussten die Schüler eine AG machen.
e Wir konnten zu Mittag in der Schulkantine essen.
f In Deutschland durfte man tragen, was man wollte.

3 🎧 *Transcript:*

a *Wann beginnt der Schultag bei dir, Hans?*
  Der Schultag beginnt bei uns um halb 8, also sehr früh.
b *Möchtest du eine Schuluniform tragen, Paul?*
  Nein, gar nicht. Ich finde es toll, dass ich keine Schuluniform tragen muss.
c *Martina, was machst du in der Pause?*
  In der Pause kaufe ich ein Butterbrot vom Hausmeister.
d *Was für eine Schule besuchst du, Bettina?*
  Ich besuche ein Gymnasium, und wir haben jeden Nachmittag frei.
e *Machst du eine AG, Michael?*
  Ich muss jeden Donnerstag eine AG machen. Ich bin in der Theatergruppe.

Context 4 Work and Education 95

3 🎧 These pupils are talking about their school day. Are the following statements true (T) or false (F)? Correct the false ones.

In this audio extract, five young people answer questions about their school day. It includes key language for describing school routine.

Students listen to the questions and answers, and decide if the statements about the speakers are true or false, correcting the false ones. Afterwards, useful vocabulary/expressions could be 'harvested' for learning, by listening again. You may wish to refer once more to the *Strategie* panel.

Answers:

a F – Hans's school day begins early at half past 7.
b T
c T
d F – Bettina goes to a grammar school equivalent and has every afternoon free.
e F – Michael does drama every Thursday.

4 ✏️ Imagine you have just been to a German school on an exchange visit. Write a short report saying what was different. Use Paula and Tom's texts to help you.

Support less confident students by helping them to collate relevant information they could include in their writing before they start, and making sure they understand the words given in the language structure grid. Remind all students that if they don't have experience of German schools themselves, they will find lots of details to use in the reading text for activity 1. Encourage use of the imperfect tense and refer to the *Tipp*.

> **Tipp**
> Point out that sentences with *obwohl* and *während* are useful for making comparisons, and will help raise the level of students' German. Practise with examples relevant for activity 4.

Plenary activity

Refer back to the *Strategie* panel again, and ask students to make a list of ten related words which they think are useful, distilled from those they've met in this subtopic, which they will learn for homework by the next lesson (when they will be tested – see next starter activity suggestion). They could produce a joint list with a partner, or compare lists, and vary the number of words on the list depending on their level of confidence. Alternatively, if lists have already been produced, students can exchange ideas on how best to learn the words (e.g. look, say, cover, write, check – repeating words aloud or silently), and can start to learn them and test each other in pairs.

Pages 136–137

4.3 Schulstress

Pressures and problems

Subject	Talking about pressures and problems at school
Ⓖ 1	Saying what you could or ought to do
Ⓖ 2	The pluperfect tense
🌐	Matching people to information

kerboodle!
- Audio file for core reading text
- Audio file and transcript for listening activity 3
- Listening activity and transcript: *Probleme in der Schule*
- Grammar activity: Saying what you could, ought or would like to do
- Writing worksheet
- Extension listening worksheet
- Audio file and transcript for extension listening worksheet

Starter activity

Recap key language and the communication strategy from the previous subtopic by asking students to spend two minutes testing a partner on the vocabulary learnt for homework, then swapping so that all are tested. Elicit responses as to successful or unsuccessful techniques used to learn the words and how this might work better next time.

Hilfe!

The reading stimulus text consists of three letters from young people to a problem page, about difficulties they are having at school, followed by three responses to their problems. The letters include useful phrases for talking about pressures and problems at school, cultural references to aspects of the German school system, and examples of the pluperfect tense. The responses include examples of *du solltest* and *du könntest*.

The reading text is also available online as an audio file.

1a 📖 🎧 🌐 Read the problem page letters. Which of the teenagers ...

Students firstly read or listen to the letters and decide who each statement is about. Refer to the *Strategie* panel. They then read the responses and match each to the correct letter. Afterwards, you could explain or discuss cultural references in the problem letters – e.g. marks given for work, *sitzenbleiben*, the *Abitur*.

Answers:

a Gabi   b Klaus   c Wilhelm
d Klaus   e Wilhelm   f Gabi

> **Strategie**
> 📖 Point out that tasks requiring candidates to match people to information are common in the Reading and Listening units. Encourage students to use these strategies when tackling activities 1a and 1b.

1b 📖 🎧 🌐 Now read the responses and match each to the correct letter.

Answers:

Letter 1 – Response b
Letter 2 – Response c
Letter 3 – Response a

> **Grammatik**
> This panel explains how to use the imperfect subjunctive of the modal verbs *sollen* and *können* to say what you could or ought to do. It gives the *ich* and *du* forms for each verb. Point out to students that these forms are actually quite easy to use, and a good way of extending the range of their German. With weaker students, clarify their understanding of the use of *sollten* and *könnten* by translating simple examples using these. The reading text in activity 1 provides examples of these imperfect subjunctive forms. The panel also refers students to p.143 to learn about the pluperfect tense.

2 G Complete these sentences with either 'could' or 'should'.

This grammar activity requires students to insert the correct form of the imperfect subjunctive of *können* or *sollen* in each gap.

Refer firstly to the *Grammatik* panel. Remind weaker learners that they must check carefully who is the subject of each sentence and select the correct verb ending. Ask students also to translate the sentences into English to demonstrate their understanding of the difference in meaning between *könnte* and *sollte*.

Answers:

a Ich brauche Geld für meinen Urlaub. Ich **könnte** vielleicht mein Taschengeld sparen.
b Mein Rad ist kaputt. Ich **sollte** ein neues Rad kaufen.
c Wenn es regnet, **könntest** du mit dem Bus zur Schule fahren.
d Wenn du die Schule nicht verlassen willst, **könntest** du nächstes Jahr weiterstudieren.
e Ich **sollte** fleißig sein und hart arbeiten, aber ich habe keine Lust dazu.
f Was **sollten** wir machen, um bessere Noten zu bekommen?

3a 🎧 *Transcript:*

Part 1

Ich verbringe dieses Schuljahr in einem Internat in England. Es ist anders als zu Hause und ich habe Heimweh. Der Schultag hier ist einfach zu lang und ich habe keine Zeit für meine Hobbies.

Part 2

Die Schüler und Schülerinnen sind alle nett, aber ich kann sie nicht verstehen, wenn sie miteinander sprechen. Und die Lehrer sind auch schwer zu verstehen, denn sie sprechen zu schnell. Manchmal kann ich meine Aufgaben nicht machen, weil ich in der Klasse etwas nicht verstanden habe.

3a 🎧 Clara is spending the school year in England. What problems does she have? Listen to the recording and complete the sentences.

This audio extract is a description by a young person, Clara, of difficulties at the school in England where she is spending a year. It includes useful language for describing school-related problems. The recording is in two parts: activity 3a relates to part 1.

Students listen to the relevant part of the recording and fill the gaps in the English sentences about the content. Remind them that the information needed will be heard in the same order as the gapped sentences.

Answers:

a Clara is studying at a **boarding** school.
b She finds the **school day** too long.
c She has little time for her **hobbies**.

3b 🎧 Now listen carefully to the next part and complete the sentences.

This audio extract is a description by a young person, Clara, of difficulties at the school in England where she is spending a year. It includes useful language for describing school-related problems. The recording is in two parts: activity 3b relates to part 2.

Students listen to the relevant part of the recording and fill the gaps in the English sentences about the content. Remind them that the information needed will be heard in the same order as the gapped sentences.

Answers:

a Clara does not understand her fellow pupils when **they talk to each other**.
b She finds the teachers hard to understand because they **speak too fast**.
c She cannot always do her work because **she sometimes doesn't understand something in class**.

4 💭 What problems do you have at school? Work out how to tell your partner about your problems. When you are both ready take it in turns to get things off your chest! Your partner should try to offer some advice.

Allow time for students to prepare how to say what their problems are, and check that less confident students understand the words in the language structure box given. Refer to the *Tipp*. If they don't wish to discuss real problems, fictitious ones could be used instead. Suitably dramatic or frustrated tones of anxiety and soothing tones of advice could be used in the dialogues!

> **Tipp**
> Point out that introducing this sort of variety into their German could increase students' exam marks, but also that it makes them sound more authentic and is satisfying and enjoyable to do.

Plenary activity

Give out slips of paper and allow a few minutes for each student to write down one of the problems they used in activity 4, in the form of a short anonymous problem letter, entitled *Hilfe!* Collect these in and read a selection out for the class to suggest solutions to, using *du könntest* or *du solltest*. Alternatively, redistribute the papers so that each student gets one to write some advice on, collect these back in and read out a selection.

Pages 138–139

4.4 Eine bessere Schule

Pressures and problems

Subject	Describing the ideal school
G 1	Saying what you would do
G 2	The conditional forms of *haben*, *geben* and *sein*
🔧	Knowing which tense to use

kerboodle:
- Audio file for core reading text
- Audio file and transcript for listening activity 2
- Listening activity and transcript: *In meiner neuen Schule möchte ich ...*
- Grammar activity: Saying what you would do
- Writing worksheet
- Foundation reading worksheet
- Extension reading worksheet

Starter activity

Display a selection of possible features or equipment for a school, using familiar vocabulary and phrases, including from the reading text in activity 1, and give students a few minutes to discuss and rank these in order of importance with a partner. If time allows, they could then discuss them in groups of 4 and aim to arrive at a consensus as to the ranking, or discuss them as a whole class.

Als Direktor(in) meiner Traumschule würde ich ...

The reading stimulus text consists of statements by three young people as to what they would do as head teacher of their ideal school. It includes use of *würden* with infinitives to say what they would do, and conditional forms of *müssen* and *haben*.

The reading text is also available online as an audio file.

> **Tipp**
> Encourage students to engage further with the detail of the reading text by deciding which of the three 'dream' head teachers they would most like to have, and explaining why – a useful opportunity to revise subordinate clauses after *weil / obwohl / während* etc. in order to give detailed answers.

1 📖 🎧 **Who would these people most like as a head teacher?**

After reading or listening to the text, students match each wish for a particular improvement to the 'dream' head teacher who would provide it. Elicit the meaning of *ich würde* with an infinitive. Refer to the *Tipp*.

Answers:

a Martha   b Jens   c Thomas
d Martha   e Jens   f Martha

2 🎧 *Transcript:* _____

Michaela:	Was willst du in der neuen Schule haben, Marcus?
Boy 1:	Ich möchte viel Sport treiben. Also ich würde eine große Sporthalle bauen. Ich möchte auch eine Uniform.
Michaela:	Danke. Und du, Matthias, was möchtest du in der neuen Schule haben?
Boy 2:	Das Gebäude sollte nicht altmodisch sein, und ich möchte bequeme Stühle in den Klassenzimmern. Ich würde mindestens zwei Kantinen bauen. Zur Zeit haben wir nur eine, und es gibt nicht genug Platz. Ich würde auch eine größere Auswahl an Speisen anbieten. Man muss früh in der Kantine ankommen. sonst bleibt nur Pizza übrig.
Michaela:	Jutta, was willst du in der neuen Schule haben?
Girl 1:	Für mich ist der Unterricht ganz wichtig. Der Schultag würde um 9 Uhr beginnen, also nicht zu früh. Aber ich würde dann vorschlagen, dass wir bis 5 Uhr in der Schule bleiben würden. Die letzten zwei Stunden wären für Sport und Hausaufgaben, und die Lehrer müssten da sein, um uns bei unseren Aufgaben zu helfen.
Michaela:	Gute Idee. Was willst du in der neuen Schule haben, Maria?
Girl 2:	Also, erstens das Gebäude. Wir brauchen mehr Klassenzimmer, Labors und eine neue Bibliothek. Zweitens, Technik. Jede Schüler soll einen Laptop für sich haben. Dann Sport. Ich würde sowohl ein Freibad als auch ein Hallenbad bauen und ich glaube, wir brauchen sechs Tennisplätze, vier Fußballplätze, zwei Sporthallen und eine Turnhalle. Oh und einen Platz für Leichtathletik.
Michaela:	Vielen Dank. Ich werde eure Meinungen dem Schuldirektor geben. Tschüß.

The audio extract consists of questions to four young people about what they would like to have in their new school, and their replies. It includes use of *würde(n)* with infinitives and *möchte(n)*.

Before students start their note taking for the activity, suggest that they prepare by writing down the different headings, and point out that each speaker may say things relating to more than one heading. Ask more confident learners to write as much detail as possible, listening repeatedly to find this as necessary.

2 🎧 **Michaela is asking her fellow pupils what they would like in their new school. Listen to the recording and write the details in English about each feature mentioned.**

Answers:

Buildings – 1st boy would build new sports hall; 2nd boy says school building shouldn't be old-fashioned; 2nd girl would like more classrooms, labs and a new library.

Equipment – 2nd boy would like comfy seats in the classrooms; 2nd girl thinks every student should have his or her own laptop.

Sport – 1st boy would like to do a lot of sport; 2nd girl would have an open-air as well as a covered swimming pool, six tennis courts, four football fields, two sports halls, a gym and an athletics field.

Lesson times – 1st girl would like lessons to start at 9 and end at 5, with last two lessons for PE and homework.

Uniform – 1st boy would have a uniform.

Food – 2nd boy would build at least two canteens and have a greater choice of food.

Homework – 1st girl says teachers would be there to help with homework.

> **Grammatik**
> This panel explains how to use the conditional mood to say what someone 'would do' in German, using the imperfect subjunctive of *werden*, followed by an infinitive. It gives an example sentence. Point out to students that this form is easy to use, and a good way of extending the range and interest of their German. With weaker students, clarify their understanding by translating simple examples. The reading text in activity 1 and audio recording in activity 2 provide examples of the conditional mood.
> The panel also refers students to p.143 to practise using *hätte*, *wäre* and *es gäbe*.

3 **G** What would these people say? Make up sentences to describe their thoughts using the conditional mood. The box below will help you.

This grammar activity requires students to write sentences using *ich würde* with suitable infinitives, based on the pictures given of thoughts about ideal schools.

Refer to the *Grammatik* panel. With weaker learners, discuss suggestions for infinitives before starting by looking at the language structure grid given. Accept any suitable and grammatically correct answers.

Answers:

a Ich würde einen neuen Tennisplatz bauen.
b Der Schultag würde um halb zehn anfangen.
c Man würde keine Uniform tragen.
d Jeder Schüler würde einen Laptop haben.
e Die Schule würde viele Labors haben und wir würden viele Experimente machen.

> **Strategie**
> Demonstrate this strategy (knowing which tense to use) by asking questions from activity 4 to volunteers, who should answer in the same tense as the question. You could then ask additional related questions in the present tense or conditional mood for further practice.

4 Practise a conversation with a partner about your school and how it could be improved. Include the following questions.

Discuss the content of the language structure grid with less confident students, and allow time for them to plan what they want to say. Refer to the *Strategie* panel. This activity can be differentiated by outcome: more confident learners should extend what they say beyond the four questions and suggested answers given, to include a wide range of issues or possible facilities, and giving reasons for their criticisms and suggestions.

Plenary activity

Give students a categorisation activity to do in a fixed time, referring back to the texts and activities in this subtopic. They could decide on their own categories and collect words or phrases within them, then feed back to the class and explain what their categories are. Alternatively, give them categories and a grid to complete (e.g. verbs in present tense, verbs in conditional mood, infinitives), and reward the pairs of students who find the most examples within the time limit.

Pages 140–141

Reading and listening

School / college and future plans

kerboodle!
- Audio file for core reading text
- Audio files and transcripts for listening activity 2

13 Jahre Schule!

The reading stimulus material is a longer text in which 19 year old Johann Gerber, who has just left school and will be going to university, describes his time at primary and secondary school. It gives information about study in the sixth form, and marks given for subjects (see also the *Vokabeln* box). The text includes examples of the pluperfect tense, subordinating conjunctions and modal verbs in the imperfect.

The reading text is also available online as an audio file.

> **Grammatik**
> This panel asks students to find examples of pluperfect tenses, subordinating conjunctions and modal verbs in the imperfect in the text, and refers them back to pages 143, 133 and 135 where these grammar points were explained. Elicit and discuss some of the examples found, taking the opportunity to recap these features with less confident students. Refer also to the first Examiner's tip panel.

1a Are the following statements true, false or not mentioned in the text. Write T, F or N.

All students should be able to attempt the true/false/not mentioned activity 1a. More able students should be able to explain their answers and correct the false statements. After they have finished, refer students to the *Grammatik* panel. Students could also look for examples of other tenses, and pick out useful words and phrases for use in their own work.

Answers:

a F   b N   c F   d T   e N   f N

Context 4 Work and Education

1b 📖 🎧 Answer the following questions in English.

Activity 1b involves a deeper understanding of the text's content in order to answer English comprehension questions, and is more challenging. After they have finished, refer students to the *Grammatik* panel. Students could also look for examples of other tenses, and pick out useful words and phrases for use in their own work.

Answers:

a He cried when he found himself in the big classroom without his mum.
b He liked being able to learn through play.
c There were different teachers for each subject.
d It smelled bad and you could smell the smoke in the library.
e He had a '1' for English, whereas last time he'd had a 3.

2a 🎧 *Transcript:*

a Ich habe vier Jahre in der Grundschule verbracht.
b Mein Klassenlehrer hat viel Musik unterrichtet.
c In seinem Etui hatte mein Bruder immer ein Lineal.
d Mein Lieblingsfach war Sport.
e In der Pause suchte ich oft ein Buch in der Bibliothek.

The audio extract consists of five short pieces of information about Nicola Gerber's school. It includes examples of the perfect and imperfect tenses, and is accessible for less confident students.

2a 🎧 Nicola Gerber, Johann's sister, is talking about her school. Which pictures best match what she says?

After listening to the extract and selecting the correct illustration from the three choices given for each piece of information heard, students could listen again and pick out particular language items, for example specific nouns, and verbs or tenses.

Answers:

a 1   b 3   c 1   d 3   e 3

2b 🎧 *Transcript:*

Mein Lieblingslehrer war Herr Franz. Ich gebe zu, er war ganz streng aber er konnte auch ganz lustig sein. Er hat mir immer mit der Hausaufgaben geholfen, und konnte alles sehr gut erklären.

Ich habe ihn ganz schlimm gefunden. Der Herr Meier war besser. Ein guter Lehrer muss nicht freundlich sein. Es ist wichtiger, dass man ihn leicht versteht und dass er gut unterrichten kann. Bei Herrn Meier konnte man gut lernen.

Ja, das stimmt – er ist ja ein guter Lehrer – aber er war so langweilig. Ich finde die besten Lehrer verstehen uns und akzeptieren, dass wir keine Kinder mehr sind. In der Oberstufe fand ich es zum Beispiel ganz vernünftig, dass wir unsere Lehrer duzen durften.

This audio extract contains longer and more complex sentences to challenge more confident students. Most should listen to it one section at a time, and answer the corresponding multiple-choice questions, but the most able could listen to the whole extract and then attempt all of the questions. The extract includes examples of the present, perfect and imperfect tenses and of modal verbs in the present and imperfect.

2b 🎧 Nicola and Johann discuss their teachers. Choose the correct answers.

Less confident students could work collaboratively with others and may also need to refer to the transcript for support. The verb *duzen* may be new to the class, and you could discuss the use of *du* and *Sie* between pupils and teachers in German schools. Afterwards, useful vocabulary from the transcript could be noted for students to use to discuss their own teachers.

Answers:

a 3   b 2   c 2   d 2   e 1   f 3

Pages 142–143

Grammar practice

G School / college and future plans

Subordinate clauses

Use of subordinate clauses is the subsidiary grammar point linked to Spread 4.1, *Wie ist deine Schule?* This grammar point builds on work already done on subordinate clauses using *wo* on page 133. This grammar box and activity practises further subordinating conjunctions, such as *nachdem, weil, obwohl* and *dass*. Pupils will have encountered some or all of these earlier, so the activity is primarily reinforcement in a new context.

1a ✏️ Join the phrases below using the conjunctions indicated.

This writing activity practises forming single sentences with a subordinating conjunction.

Translate the new sentences produced to check comprehension, before moving on to activity 1b.

Answers:

a Ich gehe ins Bett, nachdem ich Musik gehört habe.
b Ich mag meine Schule, weil ich viele Freunde hier habe.
c Ich finde Englisch in Ordnung, obwohl der Lehrer streng ist.
d Ich frühstücke, bevor ich in die Schule gehe.
e Ich finde es doof, dass ich jeden Abend Hausaufgaben machen muss.

1b ✏️ Once your teacher has checked your answers, rewrite the sentences from activity 1a, starting each with the subordinate conjunction.

This writing activity practises varying word order in order to change the stress of a sentence, and using sentences with 'verb, verb' in the middle.

Encourage students to reflect on the difference between the two versions of each sentence they have produced. Point out that varying word order in this way increases the range of their German.

Answers:

a Nachdem ich Musik gehört habe, gehe ich ins Bett.
b Weil ich viele Freunde hier habe, mag ich meine Schule.
c Obwohl der Lehrer streng ist, finde ich Englisch in Ordnung.
d Bevor ich in die Schule gehe, frühstücke ich.
e Dass ich jeden Abend Hausaufgaben machen muss, finde ich doof.

> **Ways of denoting possession**
>
> This is the subsidiary grammar point linked to Spread 4.2, *Das Schulwesen anderswo*.
> This grammar box brings together different ways of denoting possession which students have encountered throughout the course.
> Students can practise varying their language using these different structures when comparing their own school with that of someone in a German-speaking country.

2 Read the passage below. Make a list of the things described and who they belong to. How many different ways of showing possession can you find?

This reading activity practises recognition of different ways of denoting possession in German.

After discussing the answers, you could practise actively using the different methods by asking students to translate simple sentences into German, giving more than one version where this is possible.

Answers:

my exchange partner – shown using possessive adjective
exchange partner's classroom – shown using the genitive case
partner's workbook – shown using the genitive case
my jacket – shown using the verb *gehören* plus the dative case
teacher's sandwiches – shown using *dessen* to mean 'whose'
teacher's computer – shown using possessive adjective

> **The pluperfect tense**
>
> The pluperfect is the subsidiary grammar point linked to Spread 4.3, *Schulstress*.
> Students build on earlier verb and tense work at this stage with the pluperfect. The pluperfect could then be incorporated into narrating sequences of events when discussing problems at school.

3a Join the following pairs of sentences with *nachdem*, putting the second phrase into the pluperfect tense (if wished, you could start the sentences with the *nachdem* clause).

This writing activity practises forming the pluperfect tense in subordinate clauses with *nachdem*.

Encourage more confident students to vary the order of the clauses within their sentences. Ensure that weaker students have understood the purpose of the pluperfect tense and can remember *war* and *hatte*. Translate each of their new sentences into English to check comprehension.

Answers:

a Ich bin ins Klassenzimmer gegangen, nachdem ich meine Schulfreunde getroffen hatte.
b Peter hat seine Hausaufgaben gemacht, nachdem er zu Abend gegessen hatte.
c Ich habe mit meiner Freundin geplaudert, nachdem ich in der Schule angekommen war.
d Renate durfte nicht ins Kino gehen, nachdem sie eine schlechte Note in Mathe bekommen hatte.

3b Translate the following sentences into German.

A writing activity to practise making German sentences containing subordinate clauses with *nachdem* or *weil* and the pluperfect tense.

Support weaker students in finding the vocabulary they will need. Point out that use of the pluperfect tense extends the time frame they are able to talk about in German, and is not really any more complicated than using the perfect tense.

Answers:

a Nachdem ich meine Hausaufgaben gemacht hatte, bin ich ins Kino gegangen.
b Ich habe gute Noten in Deutsch bekommen, weil ich in Deutschland gewesen war.
c Gestern bin ich krank gewesen, weil ich in der Kantine gegessen hatte.
d Mein Freund hat schlechte Noten in Englisch bekommen, weil er das Buch nicht gelesen hatte.

> **The conditional forms of *haben*, *sein* and *geben***
>
> This is the subsidiary grammar point linked to Spread 4.4, *Eine bessere Schule ...*
> The main spread grammar box and activity on page 139 deal with using the conditional mood with *würde* plus an infinitive. This grammar box covers the common use of *wäre*, *hätte* und *gäbe* in conditional expressions. *Wäre* and *gäbe* are featured in the productive activity 4 on page 139, so you may wish to explain their use in preparation for this speaking task.

Context 4 Work and Education

4 ✏️ Use the conditional forms of the verbs *sein* and *haben* and/or the phrase *es gäbe* ... to describe an ideal school as indicated by the pictures. The phrases in the box may also help you.

A writing activity to practise using the conditional forms of *sein, haben* and *geben*.

Encourage more confident learners to give additional detail if they can. Make sure weaker students understand which parts of the conditional verbs they will need.

Possible answers:

Meine ideale Schule hätte eine moderne Sporthalle / freundliche Lehrer und Lehrerinnen / ein modernes Labor ...

Es gäbe die neuste Technologie / ein großes Zimmer, wo wir Musik hören und plaudern könnten ...

Die Lehrer und Lehrerinnen wären nicht streng ...

Pages 144–145

Vocabulary
School / college and future plans

- MP3 files for each vocabulary list

The essential vocabulary used within Topic 1, Context 4 is presented on this vocabulary spread.

Here students can learn the key words for the topic area *School / college and future plans*. You may also want to direct students to the online audio files of these vocabulary lists, so they can hear how the words are pronounced by a native speaker.

Some words are in light grey on the vocabulary spreads in the Student Book. This indicates items that are not included in the GCSE specification vocabulary list, so students do not need to learn these items for Listening and Reading assessment. However, you may wish students to use them in Speaking and Writing Controlled Assessments.

Pages 146–147

4.5 Nebenjobs und Arbeitspraktikum

Looking for and getting a job

Subject	Discussing part time jobs and work experience
G 1	Remembering when not to use the indefinite article
G 2	Other occasions not to use the indefinite article
🌐	Planning a piece of writing

- Audio file for core reading text
- Audio file and transcript for listening activity 3
- Reading activity: *Nebenjobs und Berufe*
- Grammar activity: Remembering when not to use the indefinite article
- Speaking worksheet
- Extension listening worksheet
- Audio file and transcript for extension listening worksheet
- Foundation reading worksheet

1 Ⓥ Unjumble the following anagrams to make the names of some job titles in German.

Students unjumble the anagrams of job titles in German given. They could then make up their own anagrams using other job titles, for partners to solve. Refer less confident students back to the list of these on page 131.

Answers:

a Lehrerin b Mechaniker c Arzt
d Koch   e Friseur

Mein Nebenjob

The reading stimulus text consists of accounts by three young people of the part-time jobs they do in their spare time. It includes useful vocabulary for describing the work you do, and examples of sentences where no indefinite article is needed.

The reading text is also available online as an audio file.

> **Tipp**
> Use example job titles to illustrate the male and female versions – or show pictures of workers to elicit the correct title for their gender.

2 📖 🎧 Read the text about part-time jobs. Who does what? Match the pictures to the people.

Students read or listen to the text, and match each picture given to the correct young person. Refer to the *Tipp*. Ask additional comprehension questions about the text (or confident learners could think of their own questions in German to ask each other).

Answers:

a Karin   b Monika   c Karin
d Georg   e Karin   f Karin

3 🎧 Transcript:

Florian

Ich habe mein Arbeitspraktikum in einem Büro gemacht. Der Arbeitstag begann um 9 Uhr. Meine erste Aufgabe war die Post zu sortieren. Dann musste ich Tee oder Kaffee für meine Arbeitskollegen kochen. Am Nachmittag konnte ich die Briefumschläge adressieren, Briefmarken daraufkleben und dann zur Post gehen. Um Viertel nach sechs war Feierabend und ich bin mit der Straßenbahn nach Hause gefahren.

Brigitte

Mein Arbeitspraktikum war in einer Schule. Ich war immer ganz beschäftigt. Am Vormittag war ich im Klassenzimmer und habe vor der ersten Pause den Kindern beim Lesen geholfen. Nach der Pause, also um 11 Uhr, war es immer Sport. Ich habe entweder Tischtennis oder Badminton gespielt. Zu Mittag habe ich mit den Kindern gegessen. Am Nachmittag habe ich mit der Sektretärin gearbeitet. Ich habe das Telefon beantwortet und Dokumente kopiert. Das war langweiliger, als mit den Kindern zu arbeiten.

3 🎧 What did these young people do on work experience? Fill in the gaps in the diaries.

In this audio extract, two young people give detailed descriptions of their time doing work experience. It includes useful vocabulary for talking about work experience tasks in the past, with examples of verbs in the perfect and imperfect tenses.

Students listen to Florian and Brigitte, and make notes in English to show details of the daily routine described. The recording will need to be paused at intervals to allow time for note taking – for weaker learners, this may need to be after each sentence, or even after each activity mentioned.

Answers:

Diary 1:
sorted mail
made tea and coffee
LUNCH
addressed envelopes and stuck on stamps
went to the post office
finished 4:15
took the tram home

Diary 2:
helped children reading before break
PE, played badminton or table tennis at 11am
LUNCH – ate with the children
worked with secretary, answered phone and copied documents – more boring than working with the children

---

> **Grammatik**
>
> This panel explains that in German no indefinite article is used if you want to express what someone's job is. It points out to students that the article is used, however, in sentences about jobs which do not identify a particular person, and gives examples. The reading text in activity 1 and audio extract in activity 3 provide examples of sentences where no indefinite article is used to say what a person's job is.
>
> The panel also refers students to page 158 to note other occasions when the indefinite article is not used in German but would be used in English.

4 G Complete the following sentences. Sometimes you will need an article and sometimes you will not.

This grammar activity requires students to identify situations where no indefinite article is needed in German.

Refer to the *Grammatik* panel. Make sure less confident students are clear on what the pictures given show, so that they can complete the sentences.

Answers:

a Er ist **Mechaniker**.
b Sie ist **Ärztin**.
c In unserer Schule haben wir **eine Sekretärin**.
d Sie ist **Elektrikerin**.
e In meinem Dorf gibt es nur **eine Polizistin**.
f Er ist **Lkw-Fahrer**.

> ✏️ **Strategie**
>
> To demonstrate planning a piece of writing it might be helpful, in discussion with the class, to make a checklist of structures to include in their writing (perhaps two versions for differentiation), and to look together at the ADORE advice referred to on page 133.

5 ✏️ 🌐 Write a report about your work experience (real or imaginary). Include the following information.

Discuss the words and phrases given in the language structure grid before students start the activity. Refer to the *Strategie* panel. Stress the importance of including all the points specified in the instructions for the activity, and encourage students to find useful language in the reading and audio texts of this subtopic which they can use.

Plenary activity

Students work in pairs, and time each other for one minute to speak in German about their work experience placement, real or imaginary (or a part-time job they do). A few prompts on the board, and simple questions or exclamations from partners will help to prolong what is said, but you could shorten the time for less confident learners.

Context 4 Work and Education 103

Pages 148–149

4.6 Ich suche einen Job

Looking for and getting a job

Subject	Understanding job adverts and letters of application
G 1	Revising how to say 'when'
G 2	Using *seit* to say how long you have been doing something
🔊	Using previously learned material

kerboodle!
- Audio file for core reading text
- Video and transcript for video activity 2
- Grammar activity: Revising how to say 'when'
- Speaking worksheet
- Extension listening worksheet
- Audio file and transcript for extension listening worksheet

Starter activity

Display the wording of the job application letter from activity 1 on page 148 without saying what it is, arranged randomly in sections, and ask students to try and arrange it as a text in a logical order, and to work out what it is. With more confident learners, the longer paragraph could be cut into several sections, perhaps with breaks in mid sentence so that they can use their knowledge of grammar to identify the sequence. You might wish then to discuss the characteristics of this formal letter and translate it, or move directly on to activity 1.

Ich will diesen Job

The reading stimulus text consists of three advertisements for available jobs, and a letter of application for one of them – an example of a formal letter in German.

The reading text is also available online as an audio file.

1 📖 🎧 **Complete the sentences in English.**

Students read or listen to the texts and complete each of the English sentences about the content. Afterwards, if not already done, look at the application letter in detail with the class. They will use this as a model for their writing in activity 5.

Answers:

a möller@t-online.de is offering **shift** work.
b bauer@t-online.de is looking for a **secretary**.
c The job is aimed at people with qualifications who are currently **unemployed**.
d adele@gasthauskrone.t-online.de is offering a good **wage**.
e Robert Mann is applying to work as a **butcher**.
f Robert Mann is sending a **CV** attached to his e-mail.

2 🎬 *Transcript:* _____

Herr Beckmann und Frau Rosenfeld:	Guten Tag Fräulein Kassel!
Fräulein Kassel:	Guten Tag! Guten Tag!
Frau Rosenfeld:	Bitte, nehmen Sie Platz. Ich heiße Frau Rosenfeld und bin Systemanalytikerin in unserer Firma.
Herr Beckmann:	Und ich heiße Herr Beckmann und bin IT Projektleiter in dieser Abteilung. Ich hoffe, Sie haben nicht lange warten müssen.
Fräulein Kassel:	Ach nein, gar nicht.
Frau Rosenfeld:	Also Fräulein Kassel, warum haben Sie Interesse daran Ihren bisherigen Job zu wechseln?
Fräulein Kassel:	Ehrlich gesagt ist der Job, den ich jetzt mache, ein bisschen langweilig. Ich möchte mehr Verantwortung haben. Wo ich jetzt bin, gibt es nicht genug Aufstiegsmöglichkeiten. Und …
Herr Beckmann:	Und warum möchten Sie genau diesen Job?
Fräulein Kassel:	Also, ich verbringe viel Zeit mit Computern und möchte gern jeden Tag mit Computern arbeiten. Bei dieser Firma weiß ich, dass ich viel lernen und leisten könnte.
Frau Rosenfeld:	Bei uns ist Lernen bestimmt wichtig, aber ich wüßte gern, was für Arbeit Sie schon gemacht haben?
Fräulein Kassel:	Wie Sie schon wissen, arbeite ich seit sechs Monaten bei der Firma Löwe in der Stadtmitte. Dort habe ich viele Erfahrungen in Büroarbeit sammeln können. Als ich in der Schule war habe ich auch ein IT-Arbeitspraktikum für zwei Wochen gemacht. Das fand ich wirklich interessant.
Herr Beckmann:	Das ist alles schon gut. Aber können Sie jetzt erklären, warum wir ausgerechnet Sie einstellen sollen?
Fräulein Kassel:	Weil ich die richtigen Qualitäten, Qualifikationen und die nötige Erfahrung habe. Außerdem interessiere ich mich sehr für diese Firma. Bekäme ich diese Stelle, dann würde es Vorteile für beide Seiten geben.
Frau Rosenfeld:	Danke, Fräulein Kassel. Und könnten Sie jetzt beschreiben, was für eine Person Sie sind?
Fräulein Kassel	Ich bin freundlich, nett, fleißig, praktisch … habe einen guten Sinn für Humor… Ich bin auch ein Teamplayer. Ich arbeite sehr gern mit anderen.
Herr Beckmann:	Und falls Sie diese Stelle bekommen, wann wäre es Ihnen möglich, bei uns anzufangen?
Fräulein Kassel:	In zwei Wochen. Ich müsste nur zuerst meine jetzige Arbeitsstelle kündigen.
Frau Rosenfeld:	Haben Sie Fragen für uns Fräulein Kassel?

Fräulein Kassel:	Ja … Also, wann beginnt der Arbeitstag?
Frau Rosenfeld:	Jeder muss um halb neun im Büro sein. Der normale Arbeitstag endet um fünf Uhr abends. Ab und zu muss man auch Überstunden machen, aber dafür verdient man auch extra.
Fräulein Kassel:	Und was … was würde ich verdienen?
Herr Beckmann:	€11,50 die Stunde. Also, wenn das alles ist, sollen wir uns verabschieden. Wir bedanken uns für Ihren Besuch. Auf Wiedersehen Fräulein Kassel.
Fräulein Kassel:	Auf Wiedersehen. Auf Wiedersehen. Vielen Dank.
Frau Rosenfeld:	Sie werden bald von uns hören.

2 Fräulein Kassel has applied for a job in IT. Watch the job interview and make notes in English. Use the following headings and include as many details as you can.

The video clip is of a job interview and includes useful vocabulary relating to work experience, personal characteristics and jobs, as well as examples of interview questions. It includes examples of different words for 'when', and the use of *seit*.

Watch the interview all the way through once before tackling the activity, and ask students to say what the scenario is and what they have understood so far. They should then write down the various headings given in preparation for their note-taking, and watch the clip again in sections, several times as necessary, until they have noted as much detail as possible.

Answers:

Geld – 11,50 Euros an hour

Arbeitszeit – 8:30am to 5pm (sometimes have to do overtime but get paid extra)

Erfahrung – has been working for 6 months with the firm „Löwe", has lots of experience

Arbeitspraktikum – did a two-week stint of work experience while still at school

Charakter – friendly, nice, practical, hard-working and has a good sense of humour, team player, likes working with others

Sonstiges – spends a lot of time with computers and wants to work with them, would like more responsibility in her new job, finds her current job a bit boring, has the right qualifications, can start in two weeks after handing notice in, asks questions about hours of work and pay, will hear from them soon.

> This panel explains how to use the different words for 'when' in German. It gives the meanings and usage of *wenn, als,* and *wann* with examples. The video clip and transcript for activity 2 provide examples of using these. The panel also refers students to p.158 to revise sentences with *seit*. *Grammatik*

3 Complete the sentences by using the correct word for 'when'.

This grammar activity requires students to read each sentence and decide from the context the correct word for 'when' to use.

Refer to the *Grammatik* panel. Point out to less confident students that they should look for question marks and tenses as indicators. Refer also to the *Tipp*.

Answers:

a **Wann** können Sie anfangen?
b **Als** ich 15 war, habe ich in einem Restaurant gearbeitet.
c **Wenn** ich arbeite, bin ich immer fleißig.
d **Wenn** ich die Schule verlasse, werde ich einen Job suchen.
e Ich habe oft Tee gemacht, **wenn** ich im Büro gearbeitet habe.
f **Wann** hast du dort gearbeitet?

> The advice in this box about deciding which word for 'when' is needed will be useful for acivities 3 and 4. Point out also that knowing how to do this will help to increase students' marks for speaking and writing, as well as helping them to understand German when reading and listening. *Tipp*

> To help students take on board the importance of using previously learned material, as you discuss each of the interview questions in preparation for activity 4 with the class, elicit ideas of German they already know which could be included in their answers. Write prompts on the board for them to use. *Strategie*

4 Work with a partner. Choose a job you are both interested in and prepare a job interview. One of you is the interviewer and the other is the applicant. Then swap roles.

Discuss each of the interview questions with the class, and check that all students know how to pronounce them and understand them. Then allow time for preparation of possible answers, using language from the video clip in activity 2, and students' own ideas and previous knowledge. Encourage more confident students to give longer answers, including details and opinions. Refer to the *Strategie* panel, and back to the *Tipp*. Creativity and dramatic skills will add to this activity!

5 Write a letter of application for a job. Use the letter on the previous page as a model, changing as many details as you can.

Weaker students can make heavy use of the source letter, simply changing some key details, while the more confident will be able to change more. Encourage them to learn and remember the formal way of starting and finishing a letter in German.

Context 4 Work and Education

Plenary activity

Use a variation of the 'who am I?' game, played in pairs or small groups. Students think of a German job title, and partners must guess what it is by asking open questions in German – aiming to find out after as few questions as possible. These could include questions about where and when they work, what they must do, why they like it, why they are suited to it, and what they previously did.

Pages 150–151

4.7 Am Arbeitsplatz

	Looking for and getting a job
Subject	Communicating in the workplace
G 1	Using dative pronouns
G 2	Using the correct word for 'you' (revision)
	Taking notes effectively when listening

kerboodle
- Audio file for core reading text
- Audio file and transcript for listening activity 2
- Listening activity and transcript: *Eine Nachricht für Sie!*
- Grammar activity: Using dative pronouns
- Speaking worksheet
- Extension reading worksheet

Starter activity

To practise identifying difference in register, display a mixture of German phrases for students to sort into two categories: formal language and informal language. These could include written forms of address such as *sehr geehrte Damen und Herren, Liebe Lena,* and phrases with *Sie* or *du, Ihnen* or *dir, Ihr* or *dein*. When discussing the answers, elicit ideas as to indicators of formality in German.

Nachricht für Herrn Schmidt

The reading stimulus text consists of four different messages left for Herr Schmidt, in a workplace setting. It includes examples of dative pronouns and formal and informal language, with use of *Sie* and *du*.

The reading text is also available online as an audio file.

1 📖 🎧 To which of Herr Schmidt's messages do the following statements refer?

After reading or listening to the messages, students decide to which one each of the statements in German refers. You could then discuss each message, eliciting ideas as to their degree of formality and what each author's relationship to Herr Schmidt might be. Explain the accusative 'n' in *Herrn*. Mention that getting the correct answer will involve understanding tenses.

Answers:

a 2   b 4   c 1   d 2   e 3   f 1

2 🎧 *Transcript:*

a Hallo Dirk. Schade, dass du nicht da bist. Ruf zurück bitte. Telefonnummer 453867.
b Nachricht für Herrn Bauer. Frau Ballack wird Sie morgen um Viertel nach 11 im Büro treffen.
c Hier Frank am Apparat. Ich bin heute krank. Ich gehe später zum Arzt.
d Andrea, ich habe deine E-Mail bekommen. Die Anzeige sieht schön aus. Schicke sie jetzt Herrn Bartel. Er wird die letzte Entscheidung treffen.
e Wo wollen wir uns nächste Woche treffen? Unser Hotel ist nicht so gut und es gibt kein freies Zimmer im Büro. Ich glaube, das Rathaus wäre besser.
f Morgen Herr Müller. Sie wollten wissen, wo unser Büro ist. Vom Bahnhof fahren Sie mit der Straßenbahnen Linie 7, Richtung Stadion. Am Stadion steigen Sie aus, und das Büro ist genau gegenüber der Haltestelle.
g Hallo Julia, hier Stefanie. Ich kann morgen nicht kommen. Wie wäre es mit übermorgen? Schicke mir eine E-Mail.

> 🎧 To encourage students to see how to take notes effectively when listening, ask them to compare the way they made notes for activity 2 with a partner, and to discuss what works well for them. Point out that when answers are needed in English, it may be quickest to note key words as heard in German, then translate them when writing up the answers during pauses. **Strategie**

2 🎧 👁 Listen to the voicemails. Make notes and fill in the missing details.

This audio extract consists of seven short voicemail messages, left for different people and of varying degrees of formality. They include use of *Sie* and *du*.

Students listen to the messages and fill the gaps in the English statements with the required details. Refer to the *Tipp* and *Strategie* panel. Some students could listen again and note any extra details they can understand. Indicate the extra details, e.g. that Herr Bartel will make the final decision.

Answers:

a You need to ring back on telephone number **453867**.
b Frau Ballack will meet Herr Bauer at **11.15** in the **office**.
c Frank is going to the **doctor's** later.
d The **advertisement** looks good. Andrea should now **send it to Herr Bartel**.
e Next week's meeting will be at the **town hall**.
f To get to the office Herr Müller should take the **tram**, **route 7**, in the direction towards the stadium. The office is opposite the **stadium stop**.
g Stefanie would like to see Julia the **day after tomorrow**. Julia needs to contact her by **e-mail**.

> Point out that it is always important to listen out for *nicht* or *kein*. Support weaker students by listening to one of the relevant voicemail messages (a, e or g), and translating the meaning with them. **Tipp**

This panel explains that after some prepositions and some verbs, the dative case is used, and so a dative pronoun may be needed. It lists the dative pronouns, and gives example sentences. Revise with students the prepositions they know which take the dative, show them the most common verbs which do so, and point out that verbs which can be followed by 'to' in English (give, write, say, send etc) will be followed by a dative pronoun. The reading text in activity 1 provides examples of sentences with dative pronouns.

The panel also refers students to page 159 to revise which form of the word for 'you' to use.

3 G Complete the sentences by filling the gap with an appropriate dative pronoun (for the last two, you decide whom the pronoun refers to and then translate what it means!).

This grammar activity requires students to identify the correct dative pronoun for each gap, or choose an appropriate one.

Refer to the *Grammatik* panel.

Answers:

a ihm
b ihr
c mir
d Student's own choice
e Student's own choice

4a Prepare a message to leave on an answerphone.

Allow time for preparation of students' messages, then they should practise saying them in pairs (using notes, but not reading from a script!). The messages could also be recorded. Encourage more confident learners to include a range of language and structures to make their message more authentic and interesting. Encourage students to adopt language they heard in exercise 2 and read in exercise 1.

4b Now make up your own message to record.

Encourage creativity for this activity. Students should decide if their message will be formal or informal, and include as many details as possible. They could also aim to include at least one dative pronoun.

5 Write an e-mail about a forthcoming visit.

The e-mail could relate to a formal visit (work-related) or an informal plan, and should be fairly brief. Encourage students to use ideas from the reading and listening texts from this subtopic, and to include dative pronouns.

Plenary activity

Play a selection of recordings from speaking activity 4b to the class. Ask them to identify if each message is formal or informal, and to give simple constructive and supportive feedback in German.

Pages 152–153

4.8 Was mache ich nach meinem Schulabschluss?

Advantages and disadvantages of different jobs

Subject	Describing your plans
G 1	Talking about the future
G 2	Talking about the future (revision)
	Varying your language

kerboodle!
- Audio file for core reading text
- Audio file and transcript for listening activity 2
- Listening activity and transcript: *Nach der Schule werde ich …*
- Grammar activity: Talking about the future
- Speaking worksheet
- Extension listening worksheet
- Audio file and transcript for extension listening worksheet

Starter activity

Alphabet practice. Students work in pairs, and sit back-to-back, so that only one of them can see the board or screen. Display a short list of vocabulary items relating to this Purpose for one partner to spell out in German to the other, who must listen and write each word down accurately. Then display another list when the partners swap roles and seats. Alternatively, students could select words themselves from the reading text in activity 1 to spell out.

Meine Zukunft

In the reading stimulus text, three young people say what they plan to do after leaving school. The text includes examples of different ways to talk about the future, and key language for describing future educational and career plans.

The reading text is also available online as an audio file.

1 Read about Felix, Lena and Martina's plans and complete the sentences below.

Students read or listen to the text and fill the gaps in the English sentences relating to the content. You could then re-read the text with the class, and ask them to pick out specific grammatical features or vocabulary.

Answers:

a Felix wants to **go to university** providing he gets good marks.
b After that he hopes to **get a well-paid job**.
c Lena wants to be a **mechanic**.
d In the future she wants to have **her own business** (with her dad working for her).
e Martina is not going to university because **she doesn't think she's intelligent enough**.
f Next year she is going to **tour the world**.

2 🎧 *Transcript:*

a Ich werde zuerst gute Qualifikationen bekommen. Dann werde ich einen Job in einer Fabrik oder als Elektriker finden.
b Ich möchte gern Fußballprofi werden, aber ich weiss, das wird unmöglich sein. Ich werde also auf die Uni gehen, um Sport zu studieren. Danach werde ich entweder in einer Schule oder im Sportzentrum arbeiten.
c Ich weiss noch nicht, was ich machen werde, aber ich werde unbedingt die Schule verlassen, und zwar sobald wie möglich. Wenn ich eine gute Stelle finden kann, werde ich glücklich sein, weil ich jeden Monat viel Geld für mein Motorrad ausgebe.
d Ich bin ganz fleißig. Ich möchte auf die Uni gehen, aber es kommt auf meine Prüfungen an. Wenn alles gut geht, werde ich entweder Medizin oder Jura studieren. Dafür braucht man aber besonders gute Noten.

2 🎧 What are each of these young people going to do? Listen to the recording and make notes, including as many details as you can.

The audio extract consists of four young people talking about their future plans. It includes examples of different ways of talking about the future, and useful vocabulary for saying what you will do after leaving school.

Students listen to the recording and make notes about the future plans of each speaker, including as many details as possible. Set pupils a target of x details per extract according to the ability of the class and a stretch target for the more able. Afterwards, listen again and elicit key phrases for referring to the future (e.g. *ich werde / ich möchte gern / ich weiss noch nicht, was ich machen werde*)

Answers:

a get good qualifications, work in a factory or as an electrician
b would like to be professional footballer, knows this will be impossible so will go to university to study sports. Then will work in a school or sports centre.
c doesn't yet know what she wants to do, but will leave school as soon as possible. Would be happy to find a good job as spends money on her motorbike every month.
d works hard, would like to go to university but it depends on exams. If all goes well will study medicine or law, although you need particularly good marks for these.

> This panel reminds students how to form the future tense with *werden* followed by an infinitive, and refers them back to page 77 where this was introduced. It also reminds them that an alternative is to use the present tense with a future time reference, and refers them back to page 37 for further information. The reading text in activity 1 and audio extract in activity 2 provide examples of different ways of talking about the future. The panel also refers students to page 159 to practise more ways to talk about the future. — **Grammatik**

3 **G** Change these sentences into the future tense using the correct part of *werden* and an infinitive.

This grammar activity requires students to produce the future tense with *werden* to replace present tense verbs. Refer to the *Grammatik* panel to revise the future tense. Students could then briefly summarise their own future plans using a future tense sentence (they will do this in more detail in the next activity).

Answers:

a Ich werde auf die Uni gehen.
b Ich werde eine Lehre machen.
c Er wird in einer Fabrik arbeiten.
d Sie wird die Schule verlassen.
e Ralf und Karin werden einen Job suchen.
f Was wirst du machen?

> ✏️ Encourage students to include examples of all the ways of talking about the future mentioned in this and the *Grammatik* panel in their writing for activity 4. Point out that this will make their German sound more natural and interesting. — **Strategie**

4 ✏️ 🌐 Write a short description of your future plans.

Ensure that less confident learners have understood the language provided in the language structure grid, and encourage all to include as much detail as possible in their description, giving reasons for their choices or lack of certainty. Refer to the *Strategie* panel and the *Tipp*.

> Demonstrate with some examples of sentences including the expressions given and a reason. Suggest to students that they learn key phrases like these for saying they are not sure or don't know. — **Tipp**

Plenary activity

Consolidate language for talking about future plans by playing a 'consequences' type game, in groups of three or four. Each student writes the start of a sentence about future plans (*ich werde …, ich möchte …* or *ich will …*) at the top of a blank piece of paper, and folds it over so that the words are hidden, before passing it on to the next player who completes the sentence, finishing with an infinitive. The following player starts a second sentence with one of these options and the word *auch*, then the next player completes it. After that, you could specify sentences beginning with *vielleicht … / wenn ich … / das Problem ist, dass … / ich weiß noch nicht, ob …* etc, depending on time available. Finally, groups unfold the sheets of paper and read out the content.

Pages 154–155

4.9 Jobs und Berufe

Advantages and disadvantages of different jobs

Subject	Discussing what life is like at work
G 1	Revising interrogatives
G 2	Conditional sentences (revision)
🔊	Finding out information

kerboodle!
- Audio file for core reading text
- Audio file and transcript for listening activity 2
- Listening activity and transcript: *Mein Beruf*
- Grammar activity: Revising interrogatives
- Writing worksheet
- Extension reading worksheet
- Foundation listening worksheet
- Audio file and transcript for foundation listening worksheet

Starter activity

To revise familiar interrogatives, play 'fastest finger first'. Display a list of questions using familiar language relating to jobs, each with the wrong interrogative. For example: *Was arbeitest du? Wo willst du später machen?* etc. Students must write out the questions correctly (or write the correct interrogatives next to numbers) on paper or mini whiteboards as quickly as possible, and hold up their answers as soon as they have finished.

Mein Job

The reading stimulus material consists of texts by three young adults about their jobs and working lives. It includes useful language for talking about working routine, and examples of an interrogative and the imperfect subjunctive. It also contains examples of many of the grammatical items covered during this course, such as subordinating and coordinating conjunctions, the present, perfect and imperfect tenses, modal verbs, accusative and dative prepositions.

The reading text is also available online as an audio file.

1 📖 🎧 Read the texts above and complete the table.

Students read or listen to the texts and complete the table in English with the required information about each person's work. You could then ask them to choose their favourite of the three and to explain their choice. Students could also be asked to find examples of specific grammatical items in the texts. Set a target of the number of details to be noted and a stretch target for more able students.

Answers:

	Job	Training	Routine	Opinion
Jasmin	HGV Driver	HGV Licence	gets up early, work begins at 6 then on the road all day	dream job, likes working alone, likes driving
Horst	Hairdresser	apprenticeship (then moved from working for friend to having own business)	8.30–5, work on Sat. but not Mon.	interesting, can chat to customers, working for friend was boring and frustrating
Kai	Office worker	four years at university	sits at computer all day and only has contact with people via e-mail, sometimes works at home	almost always boring, every day's like another

2 🎧 *Transcript:*
a Mein Arbeitstag fängt um Viertel vor neun an.
b Ich arbeite in einer Fabrik.
c Ich kann meinen Job nicht leiden, weil meine Kollegen so unfreundlich sind.
d Ich finde meine Arbeit gut, weil ich gern im Freien arbeite.
e Ich bekomme leider nur €8.50.
f Ich habe viel gearbeitet und habe ein erfolgreiches Arbeitspraktikum gemacht, aber ich habe nur ein Abschlusszeugnis von der Schule.

2 🎧 Listen to the recording. These people are answering questions about their jobs, but what were they asked? Match the questions below with the answers you hear.

The audio extract consists of six answers to questions about working life. The questions are not heard. The answers contain useful vocabulary for giving information about your work, and what you think of it.

Students listen to the recording and match each of the answers heard to one of the questions given on the page, which feature interrogatives. As an extension task, they could also write notes in English to say what the answers to the questions were.

Answers:

a 4 Wann beginnst du morgens?
b 1 Wo arbeitest du?
c 6 Wie findest du deinen Job?
d 5 Warum magst du deine Arbeit?
e 4 Wie viel verdienst du pro Stunde?
f 2 Was für Qualifikationen hast du?

> **Grammatik**
> This panel revises interrogatives: it reminds students of useful words for introducing questions, and lists these. It also gives examples of *wer* in the dative form after prepositions. Practise these with less confident students by using simple examples. You could also tell students to 'interrogate' a partner about what they are doing tonight, using as many different interrogatives as they can – demonstrate with a volunteer first.
> The panel also refers students to page 159 to revise using the imperfect subjunctive.

3 **G** Complete these questions with an appropriate interrogative.

This grammar activity requires students to select an appropriate interrogative to complete each of the questions given.

Point out that there will sometimes be more than one possibility. Refer to the *Grammatik* panel. Afterwards, elicit translations of the questions to support weaker learners. Students could then be asked to make up a question of their own for each interrogative they know.

Answers:

a Wie	b Wie viel	c Wann	d Warum
e Wie	f Wer / Wie	g wem	h wem

> **Strategie**
> Point out that this 'finding out information' strategy is an excellent way of extending their speaking and having a more interesting and natural conversation in German. Encourage students to try and ask impromptu questions when doing speaking activity 4.

4 Work with a partner. You should each imagine you have one of the following jobs. Take it in turns to interview one another about the job. Use the questions suggested, then make up some of your own.

Make sure weaker learners understand the words in the language structure box, and perhaps supply vocabulary relating to the jobs given to support them. You may wish to offer an additional list of jobs, or some supplementary questions. Refer to the *Strategie* panel and the *Tipp*. Encourage more confident learners to extend their conversations as much as possible, and to be creative.

> **Tipp**
> Demonstrate use of *in* and *bei* relating to workplace with some examples of both for the jobs given in speaking activity 4.

Plenary activity

To recap language relating to jobs and working life, ask students to make brief notes in German to describe an imaginary job that they do, and to be ready to speak about it to a partner or small group. They should not mention what the job is, but give information relating to it and give their opinion of it, taking ideas from the activities of this subtopic. Partners then listen and try to guess what the job is as quickly as possible. To finish, volunteers could repeat their information for the whole class to guess.

Pages 156–157

Reading and listening

Current and future jobs

- Audio file for core reading text
- Audio files and transcripts for listening activity 2

Wir arbeiten

The reading stimulus material consists of four texts in which adults describe the work they do, what they think of it, and their future ambitions. The text includes examples of job words used with no indefinite article, the future tense, *seit, wenn, wann* and *als,* dative pronouns and the imperfect subjunctive.

The reading text is also available online as an audio file.

1a Read about each person's job, then fill in the gaps below with the correct names.

All students should be able to attempt the gap-filling activity 1a. After they have finished, refer students to the *Grammatik* panel. Students could also look for examples of other tenses and grammatical features.

Answers:

a Kirsten	b Anika	c Anika
d Kirsten	e Eckhard	f Ralf

1b Read about the jobs again and answer the following questions in English.

Activity 1b involves a deeper understanding of the text's content in order to answer English comprehension questions, and is more challenging. After they have finished, refer students to the *Grammatik* panel. Students could also look for examples of other tenses and grammatical features.

Answers:

a Career-wise, he wants to be independent.
b He needs more money and experience.
c She likes working in the office best.
d There was a strike at the factory.
e She doesn't mind the long working days.
f He wants to learn Spanish or French.

This panel asks students to find examples of avoiding the indefinite article when saying what jobs people do, and the future tense with *werden*, in the reading and listening texts, and refers them back to pages 158 and 159 where these grammar points were explained. Elicit and discuss some of the examples found, taking the opportunity to recap these features with less confident students.

2a 🎧 Transcript:

1 Ich habe furchtbare Zahnschmerzen. Kannst du mir einen Zahnarzt empfehlen?
2 Unser Restaurant ist sehr beschäftigt. Wir brauchen noch einen Tellerwäscher.
3 Ich habe ein Problem im Badezimmer. Das Wasser in der Dusche ist kalt.
4 Die Lampen im Büro sind alle kaputt.
5 Ich möchte in einer Kirche heiraten.
6 Ich sollte den Rasen mähen und die Blumen und Pflanzen bewässern. Ich bin aber zu faul.

2a 🎧 Listen to the recordings. Each speaker needs someone to get a job done. Can you choose the correct picture for each?

The audio extract consists of six short statements by people who need someone specific in order to get a job done. It includes examples of the present tense, and the imperfect subjunctive of modal verbs, and is accessible for less confident students.

Refer to the first Examiner's tip panel, and check that weaker students know the German word for each of the professions shown (though point out that they will not actually hear these words) and some related vocabulary that might be relevant. After listening to the extract and selecting the correct illustration for each statement from those given, students could listen again and pick out particular language items, for example specific nouns, and verbs or tenses.

Answers:

1 d   2 b   3 e   4 c   5 f   6 a

2b 🎧 Transcript:

Ich wollte nur die Details für unsere kommende Konferenz bestätigen. Wir werden am Mittwoch, den 27. März, ankommen und brauchen 7 Doppelzimmer und 5 Einzelzimmer für 3 Nächte. Wir hätten gern nur zwei Konferenzräume, und, wenn möglich, möchten wir 10 PCs oder Laptops mit Druckern. Wir werden von 8 Uhr morgens bis 18 Uhr abends tagen. Wir möchten Kaffee und Kuchen für 19 Personen um 10 Uhr 30 und dann noch um 15 Uhr. Mittagessen soll um 13 Uhr sein. Wenn es Probleme gibt, schicken Sie mir bitte eine E-Mail. Danke. Auf Wiederhören.

2b 🎧 Whilst working in a hotel you receive a message on the answerphone about a forthcoming conference. Your boss wants to know what it is about. Listen to the recording and write down as many details as you can in English.

This audio extract, a recording of an answerphone message for a hotel where a conference will be held, contains longer and more complex sentences to challenge more confident students. The extract includes examples of the future tense and the imperfect subjunctive.

Refer to the second Examiner's tip box before listening, and make a list of possible headings together with less confident students, who could then work collaboratively with others to collect details and may also need to refer to the transcript for support. More confident learners should note as many details as possible, and could even provide a translation of the extract.

Possible answers:

Arrive Wednesday 27 March; need 7 double rooms and 5 single rooms for 3 nights; 2 conference rooms required; need 10 PCs or laptops with printers; will be meeting between 8am and 6pm; coffee and cake required for 19 people at 10:30 and again at 3pm; lunch should be at 1pm; should send an e-mail if there are any problems.

Pages 158–159

Grammar practice

G Current and future jobs

Knowing when not to use the indefinite article

This is the subsidiary grammar point linked to Spread 4.5, *Nebenjobs und Arbeitspraktikum*.
Students encounter examples of not using the indefinite article where it would be used in English when reading about different jobs on the main spread. This grammar box offers further examples of no indefinite article where there is one in English.

1 ✏️ Complete the sentences below to describe each picture.

This writing activity practises describing a person's profession, nationality or an ailment without using an indefinite article.

If necessary, revise words for nationalities before starting the activity.

Answers:

a Ich habe Kopfschmerzen.
b Mein Vater ist Lehrer.
c Heinrich ist Deutscher.
d Meine Mutter ist Ärztin.
e Sarah ist Schottin.

Using *seit* to say how long you have been doing something

This is the subsidiary grammar point linked to Spread 4.6, *Ich suche einen Job*.
This grammar box may be referred to at any stage in the course but it may be particularly useful for students to describe how long they have been doing something for when talking about work and employment.

2a Work in pairs. Using *seit* with the present tense, say how long you have been doing each of the activities pictured (you decide how long in each case). Use the phrases in the box to help you if you need to.

This speaking activity practises using *seit* followed by the dative, with the present tense.

You could firstly elicit possible time phrases in the dative which could be used. Encourage more able learners to do the activity without referring to the phrases in the box. Encourage students to vary their answers by starting with *ich* or *seit*. Explain the difference this will make to the word order.

Possible answers:

a Seit einem Jahr mache ich Babysitten.
b Seit drei Monaten arbeite ich in einem Geschäft.
c Seit vier Jahren spiele ich Klavier.
d Seit gestern trage ich Zeitungen aus.
e Seit fünf Jahren lerne ich Deutsch.

2b Now write up your answers from activity 2a and add two more *seit* sentences of your own.

A writing activity to practise accurate formation of sentences with *seit*.

Students could mark each others' work, using the *Grammatik* panel for reference and correcting any errors they find.

Using the correct word for 'you' (revision)

Du / ihr / Sie usage is the subsidiary grammar point linked to Spread 4.7, *Am Arbeitsplatz*.
This reinforces work on the words for 'you' in Context 1 (see activities 1a–1b on page 46).
Here, the theme of workplace communication can be used to reinforce the importance of using the correct form of address in German.

3a Write down which word for 'you' you would use in each of the following scenarios.

A writing activity to practise thinking about when to use *du*, *ihr* and *Sie*.

After discussing the answers, students could think up further scenarios for a partner or the class to consider.

Answers:

a du   b Sie   c ihr   d du   e Sie   f Sie

3b Prepare a series of questions to ask in the following situations. Remember to decide first which word for 'you' to use.

A writing activity to practise forming questions using the *du*, *ihr* and *Sie* forms of verbs.

Remind students to think carefully about which form of 'you' to use, and that asking questions is a good way of keeping conversations going. Weaker students may need to revise the verb agreements for the three words for 'you'.

Talking about the future (revision)

Talking about the future is the subsidiary grammar point linked to Spread 4.8, *Was mache ich nach dem Schulabschluss?*
This reinforces work on talking about the future in the main content spread.

4 How many different references to the future can you find in the text below? Make a list.

A reading activity to practise identifying references to the future in German. These may be the future tense with *werden*, the present tense with a time indicator, or *möchte*, or a verb that clearly indicates the future.

Point out that being able to identify when the future is being referred to aids comprehension, and being able to understand and use these methods could lead to higher marks in all units of the exams.

Answers:

conditional forms – möchte

present tense with future indicator – Nächste Woche läuft …, Bis dann muss ich …, Nächstes Jahr gehe ich …

using verb 'to plan' – ich habe vor, …

future tense with werden – … werde ich nur einen oder zwei Filme in einem Jahr machen, … wo ich Medienwissenschaft studieren werde.

Conditional sentences (revision)

The revision of conditional sentences is is the subsidiary grammar point linked to Spread 4.9, *Jobs und Berufe*. This grammar box builds on and reinforces work on conditional forms throughout Context 4.
The grammar box and activity may be referred to at any point after Topic 1 is completed.

5 Write five (or more) sentences describing what your ideal workplace would be like, using different conditional forms. If wished, use the phrases below as prompts, but try to include your own ideas.

A writing activity to practise using different conditional forms, as shown in the *Grammatik* panel.

Encourage more confident students to use their own ideas and be creative as well as accurate.

Possible answers:

Wir hätten wenig Arbeit.
Wir würden um elf Uhr anfangen.
Ich würde viel Geld verdienen.
Die Kollegen wären immer freundlich. Es gäbe immer freundliche Kollegen.
Ich würde früh nach Hause gehen.

Pages 160–161

Vocabulary

Ⓥ Current and future jobs

kerboodle! • MP3 files for each vocabulary list

The essential vocabulary used within Topic 2, Context 4 is presented on this vocabulary spread.

Here students can learn the key words for the topic area *Current and future jobs*. You may also want to direct students to the online audio files of these vocabulary lists, so they can hear how the words are pronounced by a native speaker.

Some words are in light grey on the vocabulary spreads in the Student Book. This indicates items that are not included in the GCSE specification vocabulary list, so students do not need to learn these items for Listening and Reading assessment. However, you may wish students to use them in Speaking and Writing Controlled Assessments.

Pages 162–165

Controlled Assessment

Please refer to the section on Controlled Assessment, pages 113–119 in this Teacher's Book.

Page 166

④ *Context summary*

kerboodle! • Interactive multiple-choice quiz

The closing page for Context 4, *Work and education* provides a multiple-choice quiz which tests the key language learnt in the preceding chapter.

Revision quiz

Answers:

1. die Grundschule
2. das Lehrerzimmer
3. weil
4. imperfect tense
5. In my dream school the first lesson would start at half past ten.
6. Mechaniker
7. your CV
8. Wann beginnt dein Arbeitstag?
9. Student's own choice
10. (die / eine) Klempnerin

Controlled Assessment

Controlled assessment is probably the most convenient way of assessing students' progress. Teachers control when it is done, where and under what conditions. Students are not under immediate pressure to complete it and some of the research can be done at home.

Controlled assessment allows centres to have more control over the content of the assessment. Teachers can choose between tasks provided by AQA or devise their own.

Centres who devise their own tasks create the opportunity for students to talk / write about topics of interest to them. The tasks are designed to be open-ended and can encompass a wide range of topics, including students' own learning experience in and out of the German classroom. Making the assessment more individualised is more motivating for students.

In the Student Book we have provided examples of typical tasks for Speaking and Writing Controlled Assessment. They can be used in the classroom as practice for the Controlled Assessment part of the examination.

■ How to use the tasks

When students are ready to practise their Speaking and Writing skills within the Context they have studied, show them the tasks for that Context in the Student Book, and encourage discussion on how to approach them.

For Speaking Controlled Assessment, the specification requires that each of the points that make up the tasks must be developed. For Writing Controlled Assessment, it is the task only that needs to be addressed for the purpose of the assessment. The points listed below Controlled Assessment Writing tasks in the Student Book are for guidance only therefore, but could be followed for constructing a suitable response.

As our Controlled Assessment tasks are designed to provide practice opportunity and guidance for students on how to construct suitable responses, we suggest that you go through each of the seven points listed for both Speaking and Writing, but highlight the distinction between Speaking and Writing regarding how these points should be used in the real Controlled Assessment scenario.

To access the highest marks in Controlled Assessment, students need to:

- use a good range of vocabulary
- give opinions
- use a range of time frames and / or tenses
- be accurate
- extend responses by developing ideas
- use a variety of structures
- use complex sentences
- use long sentences
- show initiative.

Ask students to study how the tasks are addressed in the Student Book and discuss how the ideas presented there are developed. Focus on just one of the seven points from the task under discussion as a starting point. Then ask students for four different ideas which they can incorporate in their response for this point. For example, the Controlled Assessment Writing task from Context 2, point 1 is: 'location and weather'. The following ideas are suggested in the Student Book:

- say which country and / or town you are in at the moment
- give details on where the country and / or city is
- mention why you chose this destination
- say what the weather is like at the moment.

Students should also be pointed to the Examiner's Tip, which will help them to formulate their response.

Invite students to offer further ideas and expand on those listed in the Student Book. For example, the third idea 'mention why you chose this destination' could be expanded by adding the following details: Who else is with you? Did they discuss the choice with you? Have you found what you hoped for in your destination?

Encourage students to:

- develop their ideas
- use connectives in order to have longer sentences
- give their opinion, using a variety of vocabulary and structures
- check accuracy – in this case, by looking at the use of the perfect tense in the grammar section of the Student Book.

Repeat the process for each idea and each point that make up the tasks. Have a group / class discussion exploring different ways of addressing the tasks.

■ Topic coverage of our tasks

Context 1 Speaking	Relationships and choices
Context 1 Writing	Health
Context 2 Speaking	Free time and the media
Context 2 Writing	Holidays
Context 3 Speaking	The environment
Context 3 Writing	Home and local area
Context 4 Speaking	Current and future jobs
Context 4 Writing	School, college and future plans

There are also two Cross-Context tasks, one for Speaking and one for Writing.

Our controlled assessment tasks

Context 1: Speaking	Meine Familie: heute und in der Zukunft
Context 1: Writing	Ich will gesund leben
Context 2: Speaking	Einkaufen ist toll!
Context 2: Writing	Meine Ferien
Context 3: Speaking	Umweltumfrage
Context 3: Writing	Mein Wohnort
Context 4: Speaking	Geld verdienen
Context 4: Writing	Das britische Schulwesen
Cross-Context: Speaking	Mein Geburtstag
Cross-Context: Writing	Kommen Sie nach!

Please note that the Controlled Assessment tasks in the Student Book are designed as a teaching resource and not as an assessment tool. They include levels of support and guidance which are not permissible in tasks used for assessment purposes.

These tasks cannot, therefore, be submitted to AQA. For any tasks which you adapt from the tasks in the Student Book or which you devise for your students, the level of guidance and support must comply with the guidelines in the specification and in AQA's Controlled Assessment Handbook.

■ Online sample

Online you will find a sample answer for each of the tasks. They are not intended to be 'model' answers, but good answers, accompanied by a commentary that highlights what is good about them and also what could be improved upon.

The comments directly link to the assessment criteria and show students how to score well in the different criteria.

There are also further Examiner's Tips to help students tackle the tasks.

Speaking controlled assessment

Task setting – Limited Control

Although only one task will be submitted to AQA, students have to complete two Speaking tasks. The tasks should be untiered, in the form of dialogues, and different from the tasks covered for Writing Controlled Assessment.

Each Speaking task should have an unpredictable element (presented as an exclamation mark). Students, however, can (and should be) trained to predict the unpredictable! Given the context of the task, students should ask themselves: 'What can I realistically be asked at this point?' and come up with, say, four possibilities, one of which is likely to be the one that will actually be asked.

It is important to get students to practise the skill of working out what those possibilities might be.

Answers to those questions should then be prepared and incorporated in the 'plan'.

As the 'plan' cannot exceed 40 words, it may be difficult to incorporate all four possible answers in it. Students may want to consider the use of visuals / pictures to account for the unpredictable element.

You can choose to use tasks devised by AQA or devise your own. Devising suitable tasks is not easy. In order to give students the chance to show what they can do, questions have to be open-ended so that they generate the sort of response that will get the best possible mark using the GCSE assessment criteria.

As tasks are untiered, they must be 'elastic' and therefore suitable for students of all abilities. A short and simple answer can be offered by Foundation Tier candidates and be appropriate. Similarly, a well developed answer has to be achievable by Higher Tier candidates.

Assessment in general should be an integral part of teaching and thus be interesting and motivating. You have to be aware of students' interests, lifestyles, personal experiences both at school and at home and build into the task the possibility of bringing those elements into the dialogue. Involving students personally in the dialogue will make the task taking experience more satisfying for students and probably increase their motivation to communicate and speak German.

When devising tasks, you should also remember that students will not access certain marks in Range and Accuracy unless they can demonstrate the ability to refer to past, present and future events using a variety of tenses. Questions within the task should lead students to talk about their past experiences e.g. holidays, work experience, what they did last weekend, etc, as well as their intentions / hopes for the future (for example: work; holidays; what they will do next weekend, etc).

Finally, students should be able to give their opinion on different matters and the wording of the task should lead them to do that. If the task is designed in such a way that it elicits a lot of personal information, students will have many opportunities to give their point of view.

Teachers are reminded that they can use the same tasks for two consecutive years only (but that minor changes may be made to extend the task's 'shelf life').

Task taking – Medium Control

All three stages below must be completed under informal supervision. This means that supervision must be sufficient to ensure that plagiarism does not take place.

The experience of task taking should replicate real life situations. In real life, if you wanted to communicate a message to someone, you would prepare by having access to dictionaries, books and Internet resources. You could also discuss with other people what you intend to say and use their advice to formulate your own message.

In practical terms, this means that class / group discussion should be encouraged in preparation for task taking but you should check that the students' responses to the task are individual. Moreover, if they think it necessary to do so, you should cross reference the work done by students who prepared for the task as a small group.

During the preparation, access to resources should not be limited.

Stage one: This is the teaching / learning stage. Students have not been given the task. Your involvement is not limited at this stage. Teachers are free to point students in the direction of suitable resources for the task and incorporate those resources in their teaching if they so wish.

Stage two: Stage two begins when students are given the task.

You should discuss the task with the students. The task needs 'unpacking'. Typically, there will be four to eight bullet points with questions in English. As students have to speak for four to six minutes, they are likely to be concerned about running out of things to say. The approach we have taken in the AQA GCSE German course is to take one bullet point at a time and divide its content into four different ideas for developing and expanding the answer. The tasks, points and ideas presented in the Student Book are designed for students to practise this approach themselves, to implement when they are given their Controlled Assessment tasks. The working out of those four ideas for each point is a skill worth developing in the classroom as it equips students with enough material for them to carry out the task.

For example, in Context 1 Speaking:

What are your family members like?:

- Say what your parents or brothers / sisters are like
- Give examples of their behaviour
- Mention something you did together
- Say what you thought about it. Give a reason.

Each of the four points is open ended enough to allow students the opportunity to give a well developed answer. For example:

- Say what your parents or brothers / sisters are like. They could give physical characteristics but also some description of their personality.
- Give examples of their behaviour. They could say what is typical and give an example, making it clear whether they view this behaviour positively or negatively.
- Mention something you did together. They could refer to a family event, an outing or a leisure activity, which they did together with one or more of the other members of the family.
- Say what you thought about it. Give a reason. They could say whether it went well or badly; if badly, what went wrong; if well, what was good about it.

Having broken down the task into manageable questions, you can then discuss with students the kind of language they might need to use. That is not to say that you should give students ready made phrases or structures as it would result in all students producing similar work and it would not be the students' individual responses to the task. What you should point out to students is the kind of vocabulary needed to cover a particular point. For example, helping round the house includes cooking, washing up, tidying your room, etc. You could also point out that in vocabulary lists, verbs are always given in the infinitive and that verb formation has to be considered. You could refer students to reference materials, for example: look in the grammar section for advice on how to form the perfect tense.

Having guided students through each bullet point that makes up the task, you can offer no more support.

It is then up to the students to prepare themselves for the task. They continue to have access to reference materials in and out of the classroom and can also continue to work with others for the rest of stage two. They write their 'plan' and submit it to their teacher for comment.

Stage three: The student produces the final task which is recorded and then marked by the teacher.

A task will last between four and six minutes. You should use your professional judgement in deciding whether to stop the dialogue with a particular student after four minutes or continue with it up to the maximum of six minutes.

Task marking – Medium Control

The mark scheme applies to each task. The criteria for assessment are: Communication (10 marks); Range and Accuracy of Language (10 marks); Pronunciation and Intonation (5 marks); Interaction and Fluency (5 marks). The total for a task is 30 marks.

Communication

This criterion focuses on the ability of students to:

- communicate a good amount of information
- develop answers
- express opinions and points of view.

You will have to interpret terms such as a 'good amount' and a 'reasonable amount' of information, 'regularly' and sometimes 'developed' answers. The marks awarded in the other three criteria cannot be more than one band higher than the mark awarded for Communication. The mark awarded for Communication can therefore affect the marks awarded in the other criteria. For instance, a candidate saying little but in complex German delivered accurately and fluently would not score a very high mark. It is worth pointing out to candidates that it is essential to give a lot of information to gain a high mark.

Marked exemplar work is available from AQA to assist teachers in this work.

Range and Accuracy of Language

Range of Language:

Candidates producing

- isolated words will score 1 or 2 marks
- short, simple sentences will score 3 or 4 marks
- generally simple sentences will score 5 or 6 marks
- complex structures and a variety of tenses will score 7 to 10 marks.

Accuracy:

Candidates

- who make errors that often impede communication will score 1 or 2 marks
- who make frequent errors (many of which do not impede communication) will score 3 or 4 marks
- whose German is more accurate than inaccurate will score 5 or 6 marks
- who make occasional errors will score 7 or 8 marks
- whose errors usually appear only in more complex structures will score 9 or 10 marks.

Both Range and Accuracy have to be taken into account to award a mark in this criterion.

Pronunciation and Intonation

What candidates have to do to score in this criterion is fairly explicit. However, what is understandable to a

Modern Languages teacher is not necessarily what a German native speaker who does not speak English would understand. It is the latter that matters!

Interaction and Fluency

The key ideas in this criterion are: Interaction; Initiative; Hesitancy.

A candidate who has scored well in Communication because he/she has developed answers and therefore given a good amount of information is likely to score well in this criterion too (as long as he/she is not hesitant in his/her delivery).

Initiative can be demonstrated by moving the conversation on to another area that is still relevant to the original question asked. For example: *Kannst du bitte deine Familie beschreiben? In meiner Familie gibt es 4 Personen: meinen Stiefvater Klaus, meine Mutter, meine Stiefschwester und mich* (direct answer); *meine Stiefschwester ist 5 Jahre älter als ich.* (development). If the candidate then adds for instance: *Mein Vater hat wieder geheiratet und jetzt wohnt er in Hamburg*, that is showing initiative. The candidate was not asked about that but chose to include it in his/her answer. It is linked to the development and relevant to the original question.

Internal standardisation of marking

Schools must standardise their marking to make sure that all candidates have been marked to the same standard. Note that AQA will also hold annual meetings for teachers to provide support in developing tasks and applying the marking criteria.

■ Writing controlled assessment

Task setting – Limited Control

What is required of the student are two different types of task. These two tasks will ensure that students demonstrate the ability to use language for different purposes. They will be untiered and different from the tasks covered for the Speaking Controlled Assessment.

You can choose to use tasks devised by AQA or devise your own.

There is no unpredictable element in Writing.

For advice and comments on how to devise an appropriate task, see Speaking Controlled Assessment – Task setting.

Task taking – High Control

Stage 1: See Speaking Controlled Assessment: Task taking – Stage one.

Stage 2: See Speaking Controlled Assessment: Task taking – Stage two.

It is the task itself which is important. If a student does not address all the bullet points, this will not automatically be reflected in their mark.

Teachers can offer students feedback on their 'plan', but this feedback can only relate to the extent to which they are meeting the requirements of the task.

Stage 3: Students produce the final version of the task and are allowed up to 60 minutes to complete each task.

Students aiming at grades G–D should produce 200 to 350 words across the two tasks.

Students aiming at grades C–A* should produce 400 to 600 words across the two tasks.

Students will be in the direct sight of the supervisor (exam conditions) at all times when writing up the final version.

Task marking

AQA (the Awarding Body) marks the Writing part of the Controlled Assessment.

Frequently asked questions (FAQs) by candidates: Speaking

1 How many tasks do I have to complete for the speaking part of my GCSE German?

There are two tasks, both of a similar kind. Your teacher will ask you the questions and listen to your answers. One of your tasks will be recorded as it may have to be submitted to the AQA Examination Board. Each task lasts between four and six minutes. The Speaking test counts for 30% of the whole GCSE German – so, each of the two speaking tasks is worth 15%.

2 At which points do the tasks have to be done?

There is no specified time for the completion of the tasks. When your teacher thinks that you have been taught the language you need to complete a particular task and feels that you are ready for it, you will be given the task to prepare. It could be a task designed by the AQA Examination Board or a task designed by German teachers in your school. Your teacher will decide how long you are allowed to prepare for the task (but it cannot be more than six hours).

3 Who will mark my work?

Your teacher will mark your work. A Moderator (i.e. an examiner) will sample the work of your school and check that it has been marked correctly. A Team Leader will check the work of the Moderator. The Principal Moderator will check the work of the Team Leader. The Chief Examiner will check the work of the Principal Moderator – a complicated but secure system to ensure that candidates are given the correct mark for their work.

4 What am I allowed to write on my plan?

You are allowed to write a maximum of 40 words on your plan. These words can be in German or in English. Choose them carefully so that your plan works well as an aide-mémoire. Remember that you are not allowed to use conjugated verbs (i.e. verbs with an ending other than the infinitive or the past participle) on your plan. Codes, letters or initialled words e.g. *i ... b ... gf ...* as being *ich bin gefahren* are not allowed. There is no limit to the number of visuals you can use, and you can mix visuals and words if you wish.

5 What help is allowed from the moment I am given the task to prepare?

Your teacher is allowed to discuss the task in English with you, including the kind of language you may need and how to use your preparatory work. You can have access to a dictionary, your German books and Internet resources. This is the stage when you will prepare your plan using the Task Planning Form. You will then give this form to your teacher who will give you feedback on how you have met the requirements of the task. When you actually perform the task, you will only have access to your plan and your teacher's comments (i.e. the Task Planning Form).

6 How can I prepare for the unpredictable element (the exclamation mark)?

Ask yourself: What question would logically follow the questions I have already answered? Practise guessing what the unpredictable bullet point might be about. You are likely to come up with two or three possibilities. Prepare answers to cover those possibilities so that you do not have to completely improvise. Practise your possible responses. When you are asked the question, focus on the meaning of the question itself to make sure you understand it and then give it your full answer.

7 How best can I practise for the test?

Treat each bullet point as a mini task. Practise your answer to one bullet point at a time. With the use of your plan, say your answer aloud for what is illustrated by one word on your plan. Repeat the process for each word on your plan. Next, try to account for two words, then for three words, etc ... Time your answer for one whole bullet point. Repeat the process for each bullet point. Always practise saying things aloud. Record yourself if possible.

8 Does it matter that my verbs are wrong as long as I can get myself understood?

Communication can break down because of poor grammatical accuracy. If that happens, you will lose marks in Communication and also in Accuracy. If you give the correct message but grammatical accuracy is poor, you will only lose marks in Accuracy. Communication is of primary importance, of course, but the quality of that communication matters too and is enhanced by grammatical accuracy.

9 How do I make sure I get the best possible marks for my answers?

You will score well in the Speaking test if:
- you say a lot that is relevant to the question
- you have a good range of vocabulary
- you can include complex structures
- you can refer to present, past and future events
- your German accent is good
- you can speak fluently
- you can show initiative
- you can speak with grammatical accuracy.

10 How will my mark be affected if my German accent is not very good?

You will receive a mark for Pronunciation. However, as long as your spoken German is understandable, your Communication mark will not suffer.

11 What will I gain by giving long answers?

Consider the task as an opportunity for you to show off what you can do in German. Offer long answers whenever possible, develop the points you are trying to make, give your opinion and justify that opinion as appropriate, etc. As a general rule, the more German you speak, the more credit you will be given (provided that what you say is relevant and understandable).

12 What does speaking with fluency mean?

Fluency is your ability to speak without hesitation. Try and speak with fluency but not too fast. If you are likely to be nervous when performing the task, practise it and practise it again. Time your whole response. Make a point of slowing down if you feel that you are speaking too fast. Practise with your plan in front of you so that you know what you are going to say next and therefore do not hesitate when delivering your contribution to the dialogue.

13 What does showing initiative mean?

Showing initiative does not mean that you suddenly ask your teacher 'What about you, where did you go on holiday?' (although you could do that, but then you will lose your own speaking time!). You are generally expected to answer questions. For instance, a question like *Machst du gern Fußball?* you would first answer directly then try to develop your answer e.g. *Nein, ich interessiere mich nicht für Fußball, ich spiele lieber Tischtennis.*

Showing initiative means that you take the conversation elsewhere in a way that is connected to your answer and still relevant to the original question e.g. *Meine Schwester und ich spielen oft Tischtennis, weil es Spaß macht.* You were not asked about table tennis. You decided to add it to your response. It is relevant, linked to what you were asked and follows your developed answer quite naturally. That is showing initiative. Use it to extend your answers and therefore show off extra knowledge of German.

14 Why is it important to refer to present, past and future events?

If you are aiming at a grade C, you will need to use a variety of structures, and you may include different time frames and reference to past and future events in your spoken language. To achieve grade A, you will be expected to use a variety of verb tenses.

15 How many bullet points are there in each task?

There are typically between five and eight bullet points. One of the bullet points will be the unpredictable element and will appear on your task as an exclamation mark. All bullet points will be written in English.

16 Will I be asked questions which are not written in the task?

That is possible. Although you will have prepared the task thoroughly and will have a lot to say, your teacher may want you to expand or give further details on particular points you have made. You must listen to your teacher's questions attentively as you will have to understand his/her questions in the first place.

17 What will happen if I run out of things to say?

If you are well prepared, you will use up all of the time with your answers to the questions on the task card, including the unpredictable question. However, if you run out of things to say, your teacher will ask you further questions, linked to the ones written on your card and will make the task last four minutes i.e. the minimum amount of time.

18 What will happen if I speak for longer than the maximum time allowed?

Whatever you say after the six minutes have elapsed will not be taken into account when your work is marked. You will not be penalised in any way but equally you won't get any credit for it.

19 When preparing for the task, should I allow the same amount of time for each question?

There may be questions that you consider easier to deal with than others and on which you will have more to say. Give yourself an answering time to specific questions. Consider each question to be a task in itself. The whole task will probably seem to be more manageable if you do that.

20 What is the point of a plan?

It is the only support you will have in front of you when you perform the task. It is something that allows you not to have to rely on your memory in order to know what you should be saying next.

21 What happens to my Task Planning Form after the test?

Your German teacher will look after it until the end of October after which it can be destroyed.

22 How do I prepare developed answers?

You will mostly be asked open-ended questions e.g. *Was machst du, wann du Freizeit hast?* As you are rewarded for using a lot of German, develop all your answers if at all possible. In this case, you would say what you do after school, what you do in the evenings, at the week-end. Add extra details such as your opinion, then you could justify that opinion, give examples of your activities in the past and explain what you would like to do in the future. The list of possible extensions to a basic answer can be very long. Give a full answer to the question but, as a general rule, don't take longer than one minute to do so.

23 Is referring to the three time frames the same as using the present, past and future tenses?

You can certainly use the tenses to refer to the three time frames. However, there are other ways which you may find easier to handle, particularly with reference to the future. Instead of using the future tense, you could use *ich würde, ich möchte* – both are followed by a verb in the infinitive.

24 How can I show a good range of vocabulary?

Vary your vocabulary as much as possible. For instance, don't repeat the same phrases to express or justify your opinion e.g. use *sich interessieren* as well as *machen gern*. Don't overuse *es gibt* or *es ist*. Show off the German you have learnt. In your preparatory work, use all the resources at your disposal.

25 Should I keep to simple German in order to ensure accuracy?

If you are not sure what range of language you may be able to cope with, start by preparing a fairly simple answer, and when you are confident that you can remember that, see what additions you can make which might increase your grade.

26 How do I know that I am using complex language?

At a fairly simple level, you can link sentences using *und, aber, weil*, etc. You can also show that you can manage structures that are different from the English equivalent e.g. *Ich fahre jedes Jahr mit meinen Eltern nach Schottland* shows that you are aware of rules about 'time' – 'manner' – 'place' which mean that word order in German is different from English.

Another example of complexity: *Ich fahre nach Frankreich, um Französisch zu lernen*. This shows that you know how to use *um ... zu ...* and the word order that must be followed, which differs from English.

There are countless examples of complexity you could include in your responses. Select those you can cope with and use them appropriately and accurately.

27 Why should I take great care when using a dictionary?

a) Words often have more than one meaning, for example: 'the landing'. It could be a place in your house but it could also be the landing of a plane. Choose well!

b) Verbs are only given in the infinitive form in the dictionary. They have to be given their correct form depending on what you want to say. For example: 'I saw' is not *Ich sehen* but *Ich habe gesehen*. Generally, use the infinitive form when you mean to say 'to do' / 'to work' / 'to say' etc., e.g. *Ich will arbeiten* = 'I want to work'.

c) Adjectives have to agree with the nouns that they describe. In the dictionary, you will find the masculine singular part e.g. *blau* = blue, but if you want to put the adjective in front of a feminine noun, you need to change this e.g. *Meine blaue Tasche* (the feminine form of *blau*).

28 Should I frequently give my opinion and justify it?

Give your opinion frequently but phrase it in different ways. Using *Ich ... gern, weil ...* is very repetitive and does not show that you know a lot of German. Offering an opinion is a way of developing your answer to a question. There are other ways of expanding on your answer, e.g. by adding extra details, by describing, by explaining, by comparing, etc. Use as many strategies as possible to show that your knowledge of German is not limited.

Frequently asked questions (FAQs) by candidates: Writing

1 How many writing tasks do I have to complete and what proportion of my German GCSE is the writing test?

You have to complete two writing tasks. The tasks can be those provided by AQA, although your German teachers have the option of devising their own tasks if they wish. As in the speaking, the two tasks count for 30% of your grade (15% for each writing task).

2 How much time do I have to complete the final version of a task?

You will be given 60 minutes in one session to complete the final version of a task. It will be done under the direct supervision of your teacher. You will not be allowed to interact with others.

3 What resources will I be able to use on the day?

You can have access to a dictionary. You will also have the task itself, your plan and your teacher's feedback on your plan. These will be on the AQA Task Planning Form. That is all. You cannot use your exercise book or textbook or any drafts you may have written to help you practise.

4 What am I allowed to write on my plan?

Much the same as you are allowed in your plan for Speaking, i.e. a maximum of 40 words, no conjugated verbs, or codes. You also have the option of using visuals instead of, or as well as words, in your Task Planning Form. Your teacher will comment on your plan, using the AQA Task Planning Form. Make sure you take that information on board before you write the final version.

5 How many words am I expected to write for each task?

Students aiming at grades G–D should produce 200–350 words across the two tasks, i.e. 100–175 words per task.

Students aiming at grades C–A* should produce 400–600 words across the two tasks, i.e. 200–300 words per task.

6 Can I write a draft?

You may produce a draft (for either Speaking or Writing), but this must be done in the classroom, under the supervision of your teacher. Please note that your teacher cannot comment on it, and you cannot have access to any draft when you write the final version.

7 What do I have to do to gain the best possible mark?

You will score well if:

- you communicate a lot of relevant information clearly
- you can explain ideas and points of view
- you have a good range of vocabulary
- you can include complex structures
- you can write long sentences
- you can refer to past, present and future events
- you can write with grammatical accuracy
- you organise your ideas well.

You will have noticed that there are similarities between the ways Writing and Speaking are assessed. As most of the points above are discussed in the FAQs for Speaking, you are advised to read the answers again, before you embark on your first task.

8 When will I do the tasks?

When your teacher has taught you the necessary language for you to complete a task, you will be given the task to prepare. You may be asked to do a plan using the Task Planning Form. You will get some feedback on your plan from your teacher at that point on how you have met the requirements of the task. The final version will be done after that under the direct supervision of your teacher.

9 How many bullet points are there in each task?

Typically between five and eight. Make sure you prepare for and write about each one.

10 Who will mark my work?

Your teacher will not mark the writing part of your GCSE German. Your work will be sent to an examiner from the AQA Examination Board and he/she will award you a mark for your two tasks. In order to ensure fairness, that examiner will be monitored by a Team Leader whose marking, in turn, will be monitored by the Principal Examiner who will himself/herself be monitored by the Chief Examiner. As you will have realised by now, the same measures are taken for all the components of your GCSE German exam to make sure that you are given the correct mark for your work.

11 How can I act upon the advice given to me by my teacher on the AQA Task Planning Sheet?

From the general advice given on the Task Planning Sheet, you should take another look at your work and try to improve it. When you are satisfied that you have done as much as you can about your teacher's comments, you may have to amend your plan accordingly. If there is a part of the task that you think might be difficult to deal with on the day of the final version, you may want to learn the German for that part.

12 My handwriting is poor. Is that a problem?

Examiners can only credit what they can actually read. If your handwriting is so poor that there is a risk of you losing marks because of it, you may want to consider the possibility of word processing your work. Discuss that possibility with your German teacher before the day of the final version. If you word process the final version, you will not have access to an online spell check, translator or foreign language grammar aid.

13 Are there marks given for spelling and punctuation?

There are no marks for punctuation. Although spelling is not assessed as an individual element, it is part of Accuracy, which is assessed. Moreover, if spelling is so poor that it prevents communication from taking place, it might also affect your mark for Content.

14 What if I forget my plan on the day of the final version?

Unfortunately, you will have to do without it!